German Popular Cinema and the Rialto Krimi Phenomenon

German Popular Cinema and the Rialto Krimi Phenomenon

Dark Eyes of London

Nicholas G. Schlegel

LEXINGTON BOOKS
Lanham • Boulder • New York • London

Published by Lexington Books
An imprint of The Rowman & Littlefield Publishing Group, Inc.
4501 Forbes Boulevard, Suite 200, Lanham, Maryland 20706
www.rowman.com

86-90 Paul Street, London EC2A 4NE, United Kingdom

Copyright © 2022 by The Rowman & Littlefield Publishing Group, Inc.

All rights reserved. No part of this book may be reproduced in any form or by any electronic or mechanical means, including information storage and retrieval systems, without written permission from the publisher, except by a reviewer who may quote passages in a review.

British Library Cataloguing in Publication Information Available

Library of Congress Cataloging-in-Publication Data

Names: Schlegel, Nicholas G., 1970- author.
Title: German popular cinema and the Rialto Krimi phenomenon: dark eyes of London / Nicholas G. Schlegel.
Description: Lanham : Lexington Books, [2022] | Includes bibliographical references and index. | Summary: "This book examines the significance of the thirty-two Krimi films produced by Rialto Film from 1959 to 1972, canonizing their role in the era of German popular cinema during Krimi's rise to popularity and inevitable decline and evolution"—Provided by publisher.
Identifiers: LCCN 2021049076 (print) | LCCN 2021049077 (ebook) | ISBN 9781498570725 (cloth) | ISBN 9781498570749 (paperback) | ISBN 9781498570732 (epub)
Subjects: LCSH: Horror films—Germany—History and criticism. | Motion Pictures—Germany (West)—History—20th century. | Wallace, Edgar, 1875-1932—Film adaptations. | Rialto Film (Firm : Germany)
Classification: LCC PN1995.9.H6 S275 2022 (print) | LCC PN1995.9.H6 (ebook) | DDC 791.43/61640943—dc23/eng/20211014
LC record available at https://lccn.loc.gov/2021049076
LC ebook record available at https://lccn.loc.gov/2021049077

For the *Krimi* queen, Karin Dor, 1938–2017

May she rest in peace.

Contents

Acknowledgments	ix
Introduction	1
PART I: HISTORY	**13**
1 The Allied Occupation and the Federal Republic 1946–1959	15
PART II: THE FILMS	**55**
2 Krime in Chiaroscuro: 1959–1966	57
3 Krime in Single-Strip Color: 1966–1972	133
PART III: CONCLUSION	**181**
4 Krime Scene: The *Krimi* Autopsy	183
Selected Filmography	191
Bibliography	195
Index	199
About the Author	211

Acknowledgments

The support and kindness of many friends and colleagues made *German Popular Cinema and the Rialto Krimi Phenomenon: Dark Eyes of London* possible. I want to first thank my institution, Alfred University, for funding my research abroad. Nicolette Amstutz and Jessica Tepper, my editors at Lexington, deserve many thanks for their encouragement and patience. Thanks also to my dear friends and colleagues for keeping my spirits high during the long writing process: Carlos Aguilar, Irene Belyakov, Hope Childers, Sarah Cote, Tim Cox, Patricia Fitzpatrick, Dani Gagne, Kevin Gagne, Robyn Goodman, Anita Haas, Meghen Jones, Rob Reginio, Pamela Schultz, Sandra Singer, Jeff Sluyter-Beltrao, Mallory Szymanski, Colleen Wahl, and Emrys Westacott. Finally, I want to thank my late advisor, Dr. Jackie Byars, without whom none of this would have been possible.

While conducting research in Frankfurt and Berlin, I had the good fortune of consulting archivists at the Deutsches Filmmuseum, the Artur Brunner Archive, and the Deutsches Kinemathek. The observations, recollections, and advice from these professionals greatly enhanced the scope and quality of my work. I wish to extend gratitude, in particular, to Jens Kaufmann and Christof Schoebel at the Deutsche Filmmuseum, Julia Riedel, Cordula Döhrer, and Tarek Strauch at the Deutsches Kinemathek, and to my new friends in Frankfurt, Ursula, Grünenwald, and Holger Mütz.

The Anglophone pioneer on this topic was Tim Bergfelder. Tim was a generous and helpful colleague when I began my research; my heartfelt thanks go out to him. His book, *International Adventures: German Popular Cinema and European Co-Productions in the 1960s*, remains the most comprehensive single-authored volume on the subject, and I highly recommended it.

I am indebted to Tim Lucas who, in the United States, led the charge on this (and so many other) paracinema topics. I also extend my gratitude to

Kim Newman whose Krimi "Pocket Guide" published in the pages of Lucas' *Video Watchdog* provided a lot of fuel for thought.

As always, thanks go to my Millercon pals in Columbus, Ohio. These treasured friends also happen to be the most knowledgeable cinema historians that I know: Anthony Ambrogio, Margaret, and Ron Borst, Mark Clark, David Harnack, David Hogan, Leonard Kohl, Teresa Miller, Ted Okuda, Bryan Senn, Steven Thornton, David Walker, and the late Mark Miller and Lynn Naron.

My friend Bryan Senn deserves special thanks for the peerless copyediting of this manuscript and for his many eleventh-hour pep talks. His enthusiasm and dedication to this project helped see me through to the end.

I would also like to thank Quentin Tarantino, whose release of *Once Upon a Time in Hollywood* (2019) coincided with the writing of a crucial portion of this book. His passion and dedication to the craft and to the art of filmmaking served as inspiration during a challenging period. I was heartened to learn that Mr. Tarantino is, unsurprisingly, a big fan of director Alfred Vohrer, who directed fourteen of the thirty-two films examined in this book.

I love and thank my family, those who are here and those who sadly are not—Elizabeth Schlegel, Frederick William Schlegel, Frederick William Schlegel Jr.; Nicholas and Mary Gray; John and Alice Schlegel; and Robert, Thomas, and Johnny Schlegel.

Finally, to the fascinating and generally overlooked body of German postwar popular cinema which I consider to be a trove of discursive treasure—I thank the distributors, studios, producers, writers, directors, actors, cinematographers, technicians, and so on.

It's been said that an author's sophomore effort is more challenging and demanding than their first. I found this to be true with *Dark Eyes of London*. As is often the case, the lesson learned was to not surrender but rather persevere and simply continue to fight the good fight.

Introduction

"*I do not write good books, I write bestsellers.*"—Edgar Wallace

"*Nobody really seems to have liked this cinema other than the public.*"—Olaf Möller

When taken together, these two rather blunt statements tidily summarize the major themes explored in this book. The legendary, self-effacing Edgar Wallace quote—famously recounted by his daughter Penelope for the *BBC*—was given while visiting the United States when an American reporter asked, "Do you write good books?"[1] Wallace's reply reveals not only an acute self-awareness of his own strengths (and weaknesses) as a prose stylist, but more importantly signals a thorough understanding of the tastes and desires of his fan base. The second quote, from film scholar Olaf Möller, wittily yet astutely confirms what Wallace knew all along.[2]

German Popular Cinema and the Rialto Krimi Phenomenon: Dark Eyes of London examines how a specific group of films produced, distributed, and exhibited during Germany's post–World War II era not only nurtured a convalescing film industry but also provided unequaled national entertainment.[3] This spectrum of postwar popular entertainment was rounded out with many other successful series including the "schnitzel" westerns of German author Karl May (set in the "American Frontier" of the United States but made in Germany and the former Yugoslavia), the *Heimatfilme* (escapist films with lighthearted themes and idyllic mountain settings), the Eurospy films (epitomized by the *Kommissar X* series), the Bavarian/German sex comedy (later dubbed *Lederhosenfilme*), and the exculpatory *Landser* films ("common soldier's" film). Yet it was the West German crime thriller (known as *Kriminalfilme* or *Krimis*), specifically those based on English author Edgar

Wallace's novels and those produced by Preben Philipson's Rialto Film that saw unprecedented popularity and are the focus of this book.

Originally based in Denmark, Rialto Film produced a well-defined film cycle informed by West German perceptions of Wallace's work and fictitious representations of England. This book surveys the thirty-two productions and coproductions produced by Rialto between 1959 and 1972. The mid-century era of the Edgar Wallace *Krimi* inaugurates with the back-to-back releases of *Der Frosch mit der Maske* (*Face of the Frog*, 1959) and *Der Rote Kreis* (*The Crimson Circle*, 1960). As Sascha Gerhards notes,

> Although both films were made in Denmark, they targeted the German film market and were enormous box-office successes. The production was subsequently relocated to Germany, and the German Rialto was founded as a subdivision of

Figure I.1 Darkwood Castle's Sentinel Strikes a Baleful Pose—You've Been Warned. *Der unheimliche Mönch* (*The Sinister Monk,* 1965). *Source:* Stifung Deutsche Kinematek Berlin.

Constantin-Film, which then exclusively distributed the Edgar Wallace films. What followed in the next fifteen years was Germany's longest feature-film series, with thirty-two films produced by Rialto.⁴

This book focuses solely on the Rialto productions from 1959 to 1972. The remaining features listed in the appendix of this book (adapted from the virtually identical novels of Edgar's son, Bryan Edgar Wallace) begin with *Das Geheimnis der schwarzen Koffer* (*The Secret of the Black Trunk*, 1961) and were made by Rialto's chief competitor Artur Brauner's industrious Central Cinema Company (CCC).

Neglected for decades in both mainstream and academic circles, post–World War II German popular cinema (GPC) has been the subject of recent scholarly interventions. Foremost among them are Tim Bergfelder's *International Adventures: German Popular Cinema and European Co-Productions in the 1960s* and *Beloved and Rejected: Cinema in the Young Federal Republic of Germany from 1949 to 1963*. The former devotes a chapter to the Edgar Wallace *Krimis* as well as other chapters on commercially popular genres such as the abovementioned Karl May westerns, while the latter provides, through an impressive collection of essays, historical and cultural context that commences with the immediate postwar years and culminates with 1962's famous Oberhausen Manifesto. Bergfelder argues,

> In part, the deliberate neglect in critical writings on New German Cinema of the preceding era of film-making can be explained by a partisanship of those critics for the auteurs of the 1970s, who never tired of articulating their antagonism towards the West German films and filmmakers of the 1950s and 1960s.⁵

To be sure, the critics of France's *Cahiers du Cinema* and their polemical *auteur* theory set in motion a critical reappraisal of the bodies of work from significant directors. In the ensuing years and decades, to some cognoscenti, this lent a sense of legitimacy among certain sectors of populist entertainment. Yet I believe a fundamental and reoccurring misapplication of *auteur* theory gave rise to another set of reception concerns, particularly among the gatekeepers of so-called "sanctioned" tastes.⁶ Bergfelder, even more acutely, takes aim at this apprehension when he continues, "Moreover, the rhetoric of the New German Cinema was often instinctually informed by an elitist disdain for lowbrow forms of mass entertainment per se, a disdain that originated in the cultural hierarchies of the German *Bildungsbürgertum*."⁷ This often pejorative critical stance toward the popular cinema of Germany's recent past coupled with a declarative rejection of these forms of entertainment from Germany's new class of filmmakers essentially consigned these genres and their films to the ash heap of history.

Along these lines, my ongoing work has been committed to eroding such hierarchies and their deleterious effects. Indeed, I have attempted through my own critical agenda to bring to light specific eras, movements, cycles, films, and their directors, and, in the process, hopefully elevate the discourse surrounding them.

The term German "popular cinema" characterizes an already well-defined collection of commercially *en vogue* genres, such as the abovementioned homeland films, comedies, thrillers, and westerns, among others, but the imperative questions of who Edgar Wallace is and what exactly is a *Krimi* clearly require elaboration. These answers are forthcoming, but simply put, Edgar Wallace was a *Krimi* writer—a writer who wrote crime fiction—and cinematically speaking, *Krimis* are a species of crime film under the larger genus of thrillers. Additionally, as film historian Ken Hanke notes, *Krimis* are "one of the most under-explored areas of the horror genre, and quite possibly the ultimate in the realm of 'international horror cinema.'"[8] This book proposes redressing some of the Anglophone silence surrounding the Wallace *Krimi*, its enormous popularity, and its place in world cinema.

THE EDGAR WALLACE *KRIMI*

To the best of my recollection, I first became aware of the Wallace *Krimis* in the pages of *Filmfax* magazine in the early 1990s, advertised under the title "Edgar Wallace & Co." through home video distributor *Sinister Cinema's* customary and generously illustrated double-page spread. The header caught my eye, and from what I could initially surmise, the cinematic pedigree looked quite impressive. The titles were sufficiently lurid, and series regulars Karin Dor and Klaus Kinski were an inducement. But in those pre-Internet (and pre-DVD) days, finding anything (in any language) about a *niche* subject like Wallace *Krimis* was a daunting task. This was my initial, rather ephemeral and appropriately mysterious introduction to the series; little existed in print on the subject and the absence of an authorized North American distributor only served to maintain the *Krimi*'s obscurity. Perhaps my desire to see a book-length study of the Wallace *Krimi* began on that day.[9]

This was not the case in Europe, however, where the *Krimi* was more widely known. Indeed, within the Germanic concert of arts, the rise and popularity of the Edgar Wallace *Krimi* signify a very important movement. It is also one of the most successful series in Germany's history. Germanic history, particularly cinematic history, is densely layered with preoccupations with and predilections toward darkness and madness. As cinema scholar Steffen Hantke observes,

Histories of the horror film often pinpoint the cinema of this period as an inventory of tropes and styles from which horror films have been drawing in all their national and thematic variations. This is the heritage of German cinema from the silent film era—films associated with the glory days of the *Ufa* and the Decla, with the stylistic influence of Expressionism, and with a thematic preoccupation with the darker aspects of the human psyche.[10]

For a brief period, Germany nourished Europe's cinematic womb of dark and disturbing things. Germany was the home of the insane carnival hypnotist Caligari and his somnambulist assassin Cesare in Robert Wiene's *Das Cabinet des Dr. Caligari* (*The Cabinet of Dr. Caligari*, 1920); of vampire Graf Orlok in F. W. Murnau's *Nosferatu* (1922); of Jack the Ripper and the unfortunate Lulu in G. W. Pabst's *Die Büchse der Pandora* (*Pandora's Box*, 1929); of the brilliant Rotwang and his Maschinenmensch Maria in Fritz Lang's *Metropolis* (1927); and of the criminal mastermind Dr. Mabuse in Lang's *Dr. Mabuse, der Spieler* (*Dr. Mabuse: The Gambler*, 1922) and *Das Testament des Dr. Mabuse* (*The Testament of Dr. Mabuse*, 1933). Lang's Mabuse movies, along with his brilliant proto-serial killer film *M* (1931), are especially important to note. They, more than any other examples of early German cinema, laid the groundwork for the *Krimi* wave of the 1950s and 1960s.[11]

The origin of the *Krimi*, however, is literary, not filmic. *Der Krimi*, "the crime novel" in the German-speaking world, is used as shorthand to describe all varieties of crime literature, from the psychological thriller to the police procedural.[12] And while German-language *Krimis* were popular in the pre and post–World War II eras, it was the collective works of the prolific English crime and mystery author Edgar Wallace that broadly and fervently captured the imagination of German audiences, giving rise to one of the most successful literary series in German history.

While it is true that GPC has been the subject of recent inquiries, the Edgar Wallace *Krimis*, however, languished in relative obscurity outside of their country of origin (particularly in the United States of America where they lacked a distributor) despite their characterization as "one of Germany's most popular cultural artifacts of the postwar era."[13] This disregard for the Wallace *Krimi* can also be viewed as largely symptomatic of the horror film's and other "lesser" genre's early marginalization in cinema studies. And indeed these pictures, while not strictly horror films per se, unequivocally shared similar DNA. The Edgar Wallace *Krimis*

> are often seen as proto-horror films. Based on the novels of British writer Edgar Wallace and christened "*krimis*," the increasing violence and emphasis on murder scenes in these films throughout the 1960s certainly place them within a broad definition of the horror film.[14]

The agenda of late twentieth and early twenty-first-century global cinema studies, however, has fortunately expanded to accommodate previously overlooked and potentially obfuscated areas of investigation. What was once consigned to the province of populist magazines and fanzines is now fertile soil for academics to sow. When I began work on my first book in the late 2000s, *Sex, Sadism, Spain, and Cinema: The Spanish Horror Film*,[15] it was in this spirit that I guided my methodological hand—to shed some needed light on neglected or forgotten eras, movements, or niches in the arena of the global horror film. In that particular case, it was Spain. And to be sure, remarkable similarities exist between Spain and Germany's efforts to craft films devoted to a particular mainstream genre.

Primary late twentieth-century critical work on the horror film focused on German (principally the Weimar expressionist texts), American, English, Italian, and eventually Japanese horror films—with all of these nations ultimately receiving generous ink. As the millennium drew to a close, collected volumes dedicated to international offerings emerged. At the forefront of this investigative charge were several valuable books donning transnational titles such as *Immoral Tales: European Sex & Horror Movies 1956–1984* (Tohill and Tombs, 1994), *Mondo Macabro* (Tombs, 1997), *Fear Without Frontiers: Horror Cinema Across the Globe* (Schneider, 2003), and *Horror International* (Schneider and Williams, 2005). It was in these important volumes that I first encountered critical analyses of the *Krimi* phenomenon.

It was inevitable that book-length studies centered on additional cinema-producing cultures with standing traditions in horror (Mexico, Spain, Hong Kong, Thailand, South Korea, etc.) ultimately drew authors, found outlets, and quenched the thirst of readers searching for something new. Comparatively lost in this publishing milieu, however, were the German *Krimis*. This is a staggering fact considering the immense popularity and enduring love these films engender in their native Germany as well as their potential appeal to global cinephiles. Producing around fifty films in a mere thirteen years,[16] Germany's *Krimi* cycle set a frenetic pace which easily eclipsed the global phenomenon of the immensely popular and lucrative James Bond franchise (which at the time of this writing stands at fifty-nine years and twenty-five films, also adapted from an English author's series).[17]

As noted, although the Edgar Wallace *Krimi* has not received an abundance of Anglophone scholarship, pioneering work on the genre was done in English in the late 1980s and early 1990s, most notably by film historian and *Video Watchdog* editor Tim Lucas, and film scholar David Sanjek.[18] Lamentably, I did not discover their *Krimi* writings until the 2010s while gathering research for this book. Of Wallace's prodigious output, Lucas notes:

> Born in 1875, he [Wallace] didn't discover his true calling until his thirties, when he decided to write fiction suitable to his times. "I am going to give [my

readers] crime and blood and three murders to the chapter," he decided, adding, "such is the insanity of the age that I do not doubt for one moment the success of my venture." Within a period of 25 years (1905–1930) Wallace wrote 175 novels, 17 plays, and hundreds of short stories on the subject of bloody murder.[19]

Likewise, in his important and insightful essay "Foreign Detection: The West German *Krimi* and the Italian *giallo*," Sanjek provides valuable historical context for situating the *Krimi* within a larger, intercontinental framework of generic composition and expectations. He writes:

> The West German crime narratives draw their name from the line of paperbacks known as *Taschenkrimi*, the paperback form of the *Kriminalroman*, that the society read in prodigious numbers, and of which quite a few were written by British crime specialists Edgar Wallace and his son, Bryan Edgar.[20]

Of the cinematic adaptations, Sanjek continues, "The resulting films are, in effect, self-conscious acts of bricolage. Each ransacks established visual and narrative codes and interpolates elements from them, giving each work a distinct intertextual dimension." While intertextual tropes are unquestionably present in the *Krimi* canon, it is also true that a distinctly German expressionist bloodline flows through the aesthetics of the Wallace *Krimis*: These works deliberately reanimated visual and narrative tropes of the German expressionist heyday:

> That eerie mood [of nightmare and terror] furthermore illustrates the degree to which the *Krimis* carried over from the German Expressionism, particularly from the works of the silent period, the practice of Stimmung or mood. In the hands of such prominent *Krimi* directors as Alfred Vohrer or Harald Reinl [the best practitioners of the genre], standardized generic tropes help to conjure up a bleak and uncertain universe.[21]

It is also important to note that while English language explorations remain sparse, there are a handful of German monographs dedicated to the *Krimi* including Joachim Kramp's comprehensive *Hallo—Hier spricht Edgar Wallace! Die Geschichte der deutschen Kriminalfilmserie 1959–1972*. Kramp's entry is a handsomely bound, lavishly illustrated, and historically detailed account of the Wallace *Krimi* that essentially covers the same years and films as *German Popular Cinema and the Rialto Krimi Phenomenon: Dark Eyes of London*. The remaining scholarship is rounded out by Florian Pauer's early monograph on the history of Wallace adaptations *Die Edgar-Wallace-Filme* (1982), Christos Tses' *Der Hexer, der Zinker und andere Mörder* (2002), and Tobias Hohmann's coffee table-sized *Edgar & Bryan Edgar Wallace* (2011).

While this innovative work on the *Krimi* is certainly helpful in situating the genre to German-language readers, the question for English-speaking audiences remains: what exactly *is* a *Krimi*? Moving forward, a bolder definition should now be risked, however, this is no easy task. As noted earlier, *Krimis* are indeed a species of crime film under the larger genus of thrillers and are considered proto-horror films. But further winnowing of the genre becomes complicated. As former *Fangoria* magazine Editor-in-Chief, Phil Nobile Jr., explains, "For such a specific cinematic moment in time, what fascinates about krimi [sic] is all the ways they defy categorization." He continues that although *Krimis* are not horror movies, they were historically marketed as such. Nor are *Krimis* traditional murder mysteries (in the Agatha Christie vein), as they feature—indeed boast—excessive prurient elements ("burlesque-style skin, ugly violence, and then-modern, jazzy scores"). Nobile then pinpoints perhaps the series' most salient characteristic, namely that although *Krimis* "are exclusively German, they are equally—and curiously—Anglophilic." He concludes that

> [the *Krimi*] sits at a very particular cinematic intersection, connecting one era with another, and discovering the krimi [sic] film is like finding a missing puzzle

Figure I.2 Rialto's Frequent Leading Lady Karin Dor Enjoys Her *Goldmann Taschen Krimi* (Goldmann Pocket Krimi) in This Promotional Still and Book Tie-in for *Der grüne Bogenschütze* (*The Green Archer*, 1961). Source: Stifung Deutsche Kinematek Berlin.

piece under the table, with all the satisfaction that comes from finally clicking that piece into place.²²

Like other historically hard-to-define genres, eras, and movements, the project of establishing a classification schema for them becomes all the more attractive and I fully embrace this undertaking in chapter 1.

Given its long-standing popularity, it is unfortunate that the *Krimi* has been so neglected, especially in Anglophone academic scholarship. As Hanke notes, Krimis "are insufficiently known and appreciated, even by fans of the stronger *gialli*, and, as a result, have never really gained a foothold in the history of the development of the horror film."²³ Happily, in recent years, scholars have begun to give the *Krimi* the attention it deserves. One of the first to address the academic neglect of the Wallace cycle was the abovementioned Tim Bergfelder. Bergfelder provides first-rate economic and industrial analyses of the Wallace *Krimi* cycle, ultimately characterizing their thematic and aesthetic elements as a "form of progressive nostalgia" that transcends—in fact, deliberately avoids—questions of German national identity. As he puts it:

> For German audiences in the 1960s, I would suggest the Wallace series articulated a very particular fantasy about England and London, a fantasy grounded both in established generic expectations (which in some cases reach back to . . . as early as the 1910s), and in the interrelationship with other forms of cultural consumption.²⁴

In other words, the Wallace Krimis were, more or less, stateless comforts (not bound to any particular dominant or residual ideologies) that allowed audiences to safely obsess over the past but simultaneously look forward to postwar peace and prosperity. Bergfelder asserts that this, perhaps more than any other factor, explains the "phenomenal success of these cultural forms."²⁵ On the other hand, film historian Sascha Gerhards sees the Wallace *Krimi* cycle as germane to German national character and interests, just not manifestly so. In his essay "Ironizing Identity: The German Crime Genre and the Edgar Wallace Production Trend of the 1960s," he suggests that while "Bergfelder's argument concerning escapism through another (imagined) culture is very persuasive, it does not . . . take what scholars have termed the generic life cycle of the Wallace cycle into adequate account."²⁶ Gerhards ultimately asserts that throughout the 1960s, German identity was articulated in the Wallace films through a pervasive sense of irony and self-reflexivity.

My intent with *Dark Eyes of London* is not to moderate, intervene in, or attempt to settle this discussion. In fact, I am in total agreement with both scholars' larger claims. In my judgment, although they take somewhat different positions regarding the *Krimi*—Bergfelder emphasizes its overt transnationalism, while Gerhards stresses its latent nationalism—both are amply supported by the genre. I believe the best way to contextualize the broader *Krimi* cycle is through a book-length, broad-based cultural studies approach that considers these and other points of intervention. In this manner, I cover the range of cultural, political, social, and industrial factors that shaped this era and genre of filmmaking. In the pages that follow then, *Dark Eyes of London* unfolds as part cultural history and part critical filmography.

In an effort to grant the Wallace Krimis of Rialto the historical context and specificity they require, chapter 1 examines the immediate post–World War II era. The policies and causal factors of the Allied occupation of Germany shape and form the context and conditions under which these films were later made. Comprehensive analysis of the cultural, political, social, and industrial is neither attempted nor possible within the space limitations of this undertaking. What is possible, however, is an examination of these apparatuses in relation to their effects on the newly formed West German motion picture industry and, in particular, its popular cinema.

Chapter 2 presents the first collection of Wallace *Krimis*. The films have been separated into two chronological canons: black and white, and color. Chapter 2 is devoted solely to the former, which presents the Rialto offerings from the inaugural *Der Frosch mit der Maske* (*Face of the Frog*, 1959) to *Der Unheimliche Mönch* (*The Sinister Monk*, 1965), the last of the black and white *Krimis*.

Chapter 3 shifts the focus away from the black and white era to the color years of 1966–1972. Beginning with 1966's *Der Bucklige von Soho* (*The Hunchback of Soho*) and culminating with the *Krimi-giallo* hybrid coproduction *Rätsel des silbernen Halbmonds* (*Sette orchidee macchiate di rosso*, *Seven Blood-Stained Orchids*, 1972). The mid-series shift to color signified not only an aesthetic change but one of tone as well. By the late-1960s, films that shied away from issues of generational conflict embodied by the polemics of the political, musical, sexual, and drug cultures (and other hot-button topic issues) perilously risked their livelihood. Moreover, by the end of the decade, the Rialto (and CCC) Wallace films had simply burned themselves out. The Oberhausen Manifesto's objectives had gathered momentum during the 1960s and the dawn of the *Neuer Deutscher Film* or New German Cinema (NGC) loomed.

Chapter 4, my conclusion, looks at the *Krimi*'s enduring legacy, calculable global influence, inevitable decline, and eventual migration to television, where it has thrived but ultimately took on a more somber tone. Other contributing factors led to the series waning popularity and chapter 4 presents these findings. In the final analysis, *German Popular Cinema and the Rialto Krimi Phenomenon: Dark Eyes of London* offers an account of the *Krimi* that, I argue, inevitably exposes manifestations of an evolving German national identity while simultaneously granting access to safe, escapist entertainment where heroes prevail, and villains are thwarted. No ambiguity exists between evil and the greater good—and for traumatized post–World War II audiences anxious to put the atrocities of war behind them—this was wish-fulfillment.

Dark Eyes of London appends with a general filmography of the relevant films discussed in the chapters that follow. All of the films covered herein have multiple titles based upon their respective language markets. The films are listed under their original German titles first and then by coproduction partnership, and finally by United States or North American release. There are also discrepancies with years of release according to different sources. The years of release for each title in this volume are based exclusively on Joachim Kramp's exhaustively researched *Hallo—Hier spricht Edgar Wallace! Die Geschichte der deutschen Kriminalfilmserie 1959–1972*.

NOTES

1. BBC Radio 4 Extra. Archive.org. March 27, 2021. https://archive.org/details/BBC_Radio_4_Extra_20210327_180000?start=0

2. Olaf Möller, "Adenauer Country," in *Beloved and Rejected: Cinema in the Young Federal Republic of Germany from 1949 to 1963*, eds. Claudia Dillman and Olaf Möller (Frankfurt, Germany: Deutsches Filminstitut - DIF e.V., 2016), 16.

3. Portions of this chapter were originally published in Nicholas G. Schlegel "'Hallo, hier spricht Jess Franco': How Franco Recoded the *Krimi*," in *The Films of Jess Franco*, ed. Antonio Lázaro-Reboll and Ian Olney. (Detroit, MI: Wayne State University Press, 2018), reprinted with the permission of Wayne State University Press.

4. Sascha Gerhards, "Ironizing Identity: The German Crime Genre and the Edgar Wallace Production Trend of the 1960s," in *Generic Histories of German Cinema: Genre and Its Deviations*, ed. Fisher Jaimey (Rochester, NY; Woodbridge, Suffolk: Boydell & Brewer, 2013), 133–56.

5. Tim Bergfelder, *International Adventures: German Popular Cinema and European Co-Productions in the 1960s* (New York: Berghahn Books, 2006), 315–16.

6. Directors working in so-called low culture genres (such as horror)—who were dependent on formulaic narratives, low budgets, repetitive casting, and limited distribution—were especially subjected to critical disdain.

7. The term *Bildungsbürgertum* refers to a mid-eighteenth century bourgeoisie social class. Bergfelder, *International Adventures*, 2.

8. Ken Hanke, "The Lost Horror Film Series: The Edgar Wallace Krimis," in *Fear Without Frontiers: Horror Cinema Across the Globe*, ed. Steven J. Schneider (Godalming, UK: FAB Press, 2003), 111–23.

9. Film historian and former *Filmfax* magazine editor Ted Okuda notes: "Sinister Cinema did a brisk business selling VHS tapes (both direct sales and through 'Filmfax Products'), and their selection was remarkable (even if the quality was often hit-or-miss). Their Edgar Wallace selection was particularly intriguing--and mysterious because there was virtually no in-print information available, not in English, anyway. In fact, the Sinister Cinema catalogue listing was the closest thing to a filmography I had seen up to that point. And I didn't mind that the films were the English-dubbed versions (culled mostly from 16mm TV syndication packages). For me, there's a strong element of nostalgia seeing English-dubbed editions because that's how I was

first exposed to foreign films, via television and, later, videotapes (often bootlegs or releases of questionable origin)." Personal correspondence, May 17, 2018.

10. Steffen Hantke, "Postwar German Cinema and the Horror Film Thoughts on Historical Continuity and Genre Consolidation," in *Caligari's Heirs: The German Cinema of Fear after 1945*, ed. Steffen Hantke (Lanham, MD: Rowman and Littlefield, 2006), vii–xxiv.

11. Artur Brauner's CCC resurrected the Dr. Mabuse character in a series of stylish films intended to capitalize and compete with Rialto's *Krimis*.

12. For more on the Krimi's literary origin, please see Katharina Hall's edited volume, *Crime Fiction in German: Der Krimi* (Cardiff, UK: University of Wales Press, 2016).

13. Gerhards, "Ironizing Identity," 133.

14. European Nightmares: Horror Cinema in Europe since 1945 edited by Patricia Allmer, Emily Brick, David Huxley, 182. Print. *European Nightmares: Horror Cinema in Europe since 1945* (London: Wallflower Press, 2012).

15. Nicholas G. Schlegel, *Sex, Sadism, and Spain: The Spanish Horror Film* (Lanham, MD: Rowman and Littlefield, 2015).

16. From 1959 to 1972, approximately fifty Edgar Wallace (and Bryan Edgar Wallace) adaptations were produced by Rialto and CCC.

17. Perhaps another reason why the Wallace Krimis have remained a largely unclaimed topic by Anglo historians and scholars is simply that the Wallace novels adapted into motion pictures and telefilm productions span multiple decades, multiple countries, multiple studios, multiple distributors, and so on. Sorting out this data and compiling a cinematic flow chart are challenging. This is one of the primary rationales for limiting the scope of this book to the thirty-two *Rialto* productions.

18. For additional in-depth coverage of the Edgar Wallace Krimi in English please see Tim Lucas' "Dial W for Wallace: The West German Krimis," Fangoria, November-December 1989. Reprinted in Lucas' compendium The Video Watchdog Book.

19. "Horrotica! The Sex Scream of Jess Franco," *The Video Watchdog Book* (January 1989): 138.

20. See Sanjek, "Foreign Detection: The West German *Krimi* and the Italian *Giallo*," The filmed *giallo*—or Italian murder-mystery—was inspired in part by the Wallace *Krimi* cycle and made popular in the 1960s and 1970s by Mario Bava, Dario Argento, Lucio Fulci, and others. Many in print books and essays exist for the enthusiast seeking more on the subject.

21. Ibid.

22. Phil Nobile Jr., "A Genre between Genres: The Shadow World of German Krimi Films," *Birth. Movies. Death.*, October 11, 2015. https://birthmoviesdeath.com/2015/10/11/a-genre-between-genres-the-shadow-world-of-german-krimi-films (accessed May 20, 2019).

23. Hanke, "The Lost Horror Film Series," 123.

24. Bergfelder, *International Adventures*, 166.

25. Ibid., 167.

26. Gerhards, "Ironizing Identity," 134.

Part I

HISTORY

Chapter 1

The Allied Occupation and the Federal Republic 1946–1959

Few nations in the world have had as rich a cinematic history as Germany. In particular, the Weimar-era motion pictures of the 1920s, such as *Das Cabinet des Dr. Caligari* (*The Cabinet of Dr. Caligari*, 1920), *Der Golem* (*The Golem,* 1920), *Dr. Mabuse, der Spieler* (*Dr. Mabuse: The Gambler*, 1922), *Nosferatu* (1922), *Der Letzte Mann* (*The Last Laugh,* 1924), *Die Nibelungen* (1924), *Faust* (1926), *Der Student von Prag* (*The Student of Prague*, 1926), *Metropolis* (1927), *Die Büchse der Pandora* (*Pandora's Box*, 1929), have become a mainstay in film studies curricula, influenced generations of filmmakers, and are routinely included in prestigious canonical lists assembled by historians, scholars, and filmmakers. Indeed, 100 years later, as a testament to their enduring legacy, these films appear to cast even larger shadows.

Paradoxically, few nations were as embroiled with twentieth-century global conflict as Germany. World War II's cumulative toll still remains unequaled. The mass destruction, suffering, and death imposed upon tens of millions stand as a testament to previously unmeasured levels of human barbarism. Brought to devastation and ruin twice in the first half of the century, Germany's disastrous attempts at *Neuordnung* (New Order) plunged the world into abject misery.[1] Simply stated, the monumental task of the vital Allied occupation of Germany was to ensure that conflict of this magnitude would never happen again.

For the many who lived through both World Wars, the twofold project of rebuilding an entire nation in the span of two generations seemed insurmountable. It is easy to destroy, particularly under the influence of *nebel des krieges* or "the fog of war," but to survive, to rebuild, to reform, and to modernize require massive levels of capital, political will, cooperative labor, multilateralism, coordination, and precise communication. To be sure, the immediate aftermath of V-E Day hurled unprecedented obstacles at the Allied forces.[2] As Heide Fehrenbach notes,

> On 9 May 1945, the day of unconditional surrender, few in Germany were preoccupied with thoughts of Cinema. By all accounts, most Germans were intent on one thing, *das Überleben*, or mere survival, and Allied armies were grappling to impose a victor's order on the wartime chaos. Over a dozen major cities had been badly damaged: the former Reich capital . . . had 75% of its buildings destroyed, Düsseldorf was more than 90% uninhabitable, and a British observer was trying to ascertain just how many "catacomb people" were living in the underground labyrinths below the rubble of what had been Cologne. The allies needed to establish order, locate and arrest Nazi officials, contain the spread of disease, insure public hygiene, and organize the basic requirements of life for the conquered population and its newly liberated victims. There were serious shortages of housing, clothing, food, and soap; cities were without water, gas, or electricity; transportation and communication lines were damaged or destroyed; roads were impassable; and mountains of rubble had to be cleared. Moreover, the Allies were faced with the historically unprecedented dislocation and migration of millions.[3]

This grim reality was true for not only Germany but many other severely damaged countries, including Japan, Austria, Italy, the Netherlands, Belgium, France, and England. Yet even in the wake of such calamitous failures of enlightenment, the indomitable human spirit endures, and the insurmountable project of rebuilding Germany and Europe seemed somehow achievable.

But what role would cinema—a thriving empire of commerce, art, and ideology in both the Weimar and Third Reich eras—play in the aftermath of World War II? It was said that "Hitler's Fourth army after the Army, Navy, and Air Force was Propaganda, of which the psychological 'atom bomb' was the film."[4] Accordingly, by 1936, filmmaking in Germany was part of a new nationalized industry responsible for the creation and dissemination of news media, literature, theater, music, and broadcasting. As Stephen Brockmann notes,

> The Nazis rapidly moved to take control of the entire system of film production and distribution. Hitler appointed one of his most trusted lieutenants, Joseph Goebbels, as head of the newly created Reich Ministry of Popular Enlightenment and Propaganda, and Goebbels established a large bureaucracy that exerted control over all of the arts, from painting and music to literature and film.[5]

By 1941, the *entirety* of the German film industry was "transformed into a monolithic and monopolistic state enterprise" known under the acronym

UFI or UFA-Film GmbH.⁶ Given that sections of this infrastructure still existed, would a comparable model endure in postwar Germany? This seemed unlikely. Moreover, would cinema remain, as Minister of Propaganda Joseph Goebbels vowed, a powerful force for galvanizing, cultivating, and reinforcing hegemony? And if so, around what and for whom? Complicating matters, in 1949 Germany was divided into two vastly different republics: the Western Federal Republic of Germany (FRG) and the Eastern German Democratic Republic (GDR). This East-West fracture additionally damaged an already fragile framework of German national identity, which was central—via geography, history, ancestry, and demography—to Hitler's pledge of a *Tausendjähriges* (Thousand-Year Reich) and his rapid ascendency.

This chapter offers context to, and a practical timeline of, the events that led to the creation of a German *commercial* film industry that not only catered to (and cultivated) popular tastes but prospered domestically during the *Wirtschaftswunder* (economic miracle) of the 1950s and 1960s. The subsequent *Krimi* boom of the late 1950s and 1960s is and must be seen as a product of this commercial endeavor.

There are five rather distinct periods of German cinema after World War II: the postwar *Trümmerfilm* (1946–1949), the commercially oriented, genre-driven "popular" cinema era of this book's title (the Konrad Adenauer era of the 1950s and 1960s), the artistic Young German Cinema era (inaugurated with the Oberhausen Manifesto in 1962), the French Nouvelle Vague inspired New German Cinema (1970s and 1980s), and the post-wall, post-reunification era (1990–forward). This chapter focuses on the first two periods: the *Trümmerfilme* and the commercial wave of motion pictures that followed.

Central to this historical timeline is the reformation of German production, distribution, and exhibition models and practices. Enormous changes faced the German people at every conceivable turn in their new military-occupied reality. For film production, this meant a prolonged period of Allied governance, inspection, and cinematic inactivity. Piercing through this postwar idleness, however, was the first film from occupied Germany, the much-admired *Die Mörder sind unter uns* (*The Murderers Are Among Us*, 1946). The film's success and reception established the transitional phase of the *Trümmerfilm*, which anchored and rekindled the German industry over the next few years.

As German motion picture production segued away from the dreary historicism of the *Trümmerfilm* toward new dawn in the 1950s, I too move away from the rubble film to focus on the incremental steps taken by the four-power Allied occupation that inevitably led to the popular cinema of the next two decades. After which I briefly pause to examine the writer of these hugely popular novels, English author Edgar Wallace. Prodigious and hugely popular (with over 300 million books sold), Wallace's lurid cheapies were read en masse and provided the dark engine of combustible criminal elements for new studios like West German Rialto and CCC. Finally, this chapter analyzes the complex and rather slippery genre of the *Krimi* and then recommends a useful theoretical lens through which, I argue, the *Krimi* can and should be viewed. By doing so, we access layers of meaning that both amplify their significance while also revealing something about the culture and people that created them.

THE *TRÜMMERFILME*

The German Popular Cinema (GPC) boom of the 1950s and 1960s (thus the *Krimis*) is crucially linchpinned to the era of the *Trümmerfilm* and the Allied occupation. The subject of the *Trümmerfilm* and the history of the immediate postwar years in Germany and Berlin is multifaceted and has raised many questions. Books and articles devoted to the topic offer more discursive depth than what is possible within the space limitations of this chapter and the larger goals of this book. But a brief overview will help guide the reader through the rubble of post–World War II Germany.

The interstice between Germany's surrender in May 1945 and its eventual bifurcation into two states in 1949 produced a fascinating and powerful but also manifestly depressing body of German films known as *Trümmerfilme* (rubble films). Much like the powerful neorealism movement that shadowed post–World War II Italy, Germany also experienced a direct period of filmmaking that captured, indeed mummified, the broken Berlin (and other cities) in perpetuity. German history scholar Eric Rentschler offers the following description of the *Trümmerfilm*:

> Strictly speaking not a genre, *Trümmerfilme* are a series of feature films produced in Germany between 1946 and 1949 that confront postwar realities. Using various narrative formulas and styles, these films share a historical situation, a production context, and a political mission. With Germany's film industry out of commission, its studios demolished or seized, and many of its key figures compromised by their Nazi-era activities, the first movies after a year's hiatus (the so-called *Filmpause*) bore the mark of material shortages and artistic uncertainty. Shot largely on location with restricted amounts of film stock, these productions were closely controlled by the Allied occupiers, with different approaches at work in each of the four military zones. *Trümmerfilme* took stock of a shattered nation and registered a state of physical and psychological ruin.[7]

Yet, the *Trümmerfilm* was slow to emerge; the arduous process of filmmaking in occupied Germany became, albeit for different motives and goals, politicized to nearly commensurate levels of the former Nazi era. The assessment of the occupying forces (formerly the Allied Supreme Command) called for a decartelization (and gradual democratization) of the German filmmaking apparatus. And indeed, all four powers in their respective zones (the United States, the United Kingdom, France, and the Soviet Union) "embarked on a process of denazifying media personnel and reorganizing the media industries." By 1948, however, "it was clear ideological differences between the Western Allies and the Soviets would result in the creation of two separate German states, each marked by the dominant victor's vision of the political, economic, and cultural organization."[8] Equally important to the Allied dismantling of the state-controlled media industry was the desire to immediately increase exhibition; theaters were to be operational and busy (even if the films were projected on a wall or bed sheet). As early as July 1945, Hollywood films were screened regularly in the US zone.[9]

Crucial to the viability of German cinema in the US zone was the creation of the Information Control Division (ICD), formerly known during the war as the Psychological Warfare Division (PWD). The ICD's task was to transform itself from a blunt wartime propaganda machine into a finely tuned instrument of civil reform. Officially, the ICD's mission was to

> provide the Germans with information, which will influence [changed on April 16, 1947, to "enable"] them to understand and accept the United States program of occupation, and to establish for themselves a stable, peaceful, and acceptable government. Such information will impress upon the Germans the totality of their military defeat, the impossibility of rearmament, the responsibility of the individual German for war and atrocities, the disastrous effects of the structure and system of National Socialism on Germany and the world, and the possibility that through work and cooperation Germany may again be accepted into the family of nations.[10]

Among the strategies to create a "stable, peaceful, and acceptable government" was the indoctrination of "thousands of publications readied by the Americans for use in reeducating Germans," including the "political writings of the American founding fathers and American literature deemed representative of the ideals they [the U.S.] wished to instill in the Germans, such as the writings of Benjamin Franklin and James Fenimore Cooper."[11] In soldierly lockstep, the US military government "considered film an instrument not only for confronting Germans with the atrocities they committed, but also for providing Germans relief from the horrible conditions in postwar Germany. Film was thus to serve an educational, democratizing, and escapist purpose."[12] An influential power (and powerful influencer) during the war, Hollywood sent dozens of American films to fill the vacuum left by the removal of German films from circulation. Only unlike the publishing industry, whose products were often given away, Hollywood intended to make money in a market that had, for many years, been closed to American films.[13]

The results, however, were disappointing for all concerned. The German public came to resent the heavy-handed attempts at reeducation through the cultural imperialism of Hollywood artifice (although, over time, some preferred the Hollywood films compared to the grim reality of the steady stream of *Trümmerfilme*),[14] and Hollywood quickly learned that "while Germans still possessed currency, it was not convertible in any way that would be of value to the Americans."[15] Consequently, Hollywood decreased the overall number of films slated for theatrical distribution in Germany. The ICD proposed (much to Hollywood's irritation) to compensate by increasing the number of "French, English, Italian, Scandinavian, and even acceptable old German films to offset the decrease in available American films."[16]

More importantly, however, in the summer of 1945, it was decided that films made by the eight largest film production companies would now pass through the hands of a newly formed "kind of cartel" prior to international distribution.[17] Created under the auspice of the Motion Picture Association of America (MPAA), the Motion Picture Export Association of America (MPEA) was a trade association that represented the interests of the eight major studios.[18] Its objective was to globally combat motion picture monopolies and to essentially reduce overall competition. As Wolfgang Schivelbusch sums up,

> Hollywood's attitude at the end of World War II can be summarized in one sentence: war had been waged to win back the European film market. The Motion Picture Export Association (MPEA) was supposed to coordinate exports and, in particular, prevent the thousands of American films that had amassed during the years of exclusion from the European market from ruining the industry in a wild competition with one another and leading to the collapse of the market only just regained.[19]

Thus, the MPEA was frequently at loggerheads with the ICD and, in particular, the chief of its MPB (Motion Picture Branch), German-born Erich Pommer. A former head of production with Germany's DECLA Film, later a colossal figure at *Ufa*, and finally a US producer for both Paramount and MGM, Pommer was perfectly suited to act as a liaison between the German and American interests. When Pommer arrived in Berlin in July of 1946, like Eisenhower, he was granted supreme powers (non-military, but vitally important) to carry out countless duties encompassing virtually every conceivable aspect of the German motion picture industry.[20] The MPEA, however, fueled by the belief that the "German film industry had been Hollywood's most prominent and dangerous competitor in the prewar international market," consistently lobbied to win back its old share of the market and, eventually, the construction of American studios in Berlin. The notion that under Pommer's protection the Germans would cinematically re-arm themselves was met with increasing resistance.

To this point, one of the ICD's many responsibilities was, in fact, the granting and issuing of production licenses to producers wishing to make German movies. It did so reluctantly. At the behest of both Hollywood and the MPEA, the ICD was initially more inclined to let American motion pictures sell the American message of "democracy, individualism, and free enterprise" to the German public.[21] This was not to be the case, however, for the local German population who increasingly resented their strict diet of Hollywood film consumption. The actions (as well as the inactions) of the ICD—coupled with the MPEA's ongoing attempts to kneecap the ICD's directives—had a slow but cumulative effect on the German public. An intelligence report submitted to the MPB communicated that

> Germans are more or less homesick to hear their own language in films rather than have a language they don't understand dinned into their ears. Secondly, they want backgrounds and themes as well as . . . actors, which are familiar to them and somehow indigenous, rather than foreign backgrounds with which they have no associations. Thirdly, the carefree and superficial escapism of many pre-war American films irritates the Germans who are now faced with biter realities.[22]

Faced with increasing scorn and resentment from German audiences, the ICD was finally forced to shift their efforts to a "positive program of . . . native film production" in 1946.[23] Eager to be operational again, German filmmakers pursued these licenses—yearning to fill the German motion picture vacuum left by the war and, they hoped, to compete favorably in the European film market.

The first film to emerge from the rubble was Wolfgang Staudte's *Die Mörder sind unter uns* (*The Murderers Are among Us*, 1946). Considering the ICD's initial reluctance to issue these licenses, it is not at all surprising that *Die Mörder* did not, in fact, originate in the US zone, but rather the Soviet district. This proved to be a serious misstep for the MPEA, the ICD, and thus American interests; the production of *Die Mörder* helped to cement the establishment of the Soviet-controlled German film monopoly, Deutsche Filmaktiengesellschaft (DEFA). Moreover, had it not been for Staudte's fervent persistence, *Die Mörder* would likely not have been made at all. Sebastian Heiduschke recounts how in 1946, German film director Wolfgang Staudte knocked on the doors of the commanders in charge of occupied Berlin to receive a license for a film entitled *Der Mann den ich töten werde* (*The Man I Am Going to Kill*). His idea was rejected in the three Western sectors; in the Soviet sector, however, he was granted the license to shoot what became the first German feature film made after World War II. When it premiered under the title *Die Mörder sind unter uns* (*The Murderers Are among Us*) on October 15, 1946, it represented the first feature film by the newly founded Deutsche Filmaktiengesellschaft (DEFA). *Die Mörder* became an instant success—and a timeless classic of German cinema, as its selection as sixth-most important film of German cinema attests to.[24]

In *Die Mörder*'s opening frames, hollowed-out, skeletal structures, stripped of their façades and former identities surround the muddy and debris-strewn streets of Berlin. From this opening shot emerges a man, Hans Mertens (Ernst Wilhelm Borchert), a German surgeon during the war who now spends his days drinking, frequenting cabarets, and squatting in an abandoned and dilapidated apartment. The apartment's former owner, Susanne Wallner (Hildegard Knef), has returned to Berlin having survived a concentration camp internment (due to her father's political affiliation). After squabbling over who has the valid claim to the space, the two eventually strike an arrangement whereby they will share the flat. A romantic relationship slowly develops between the two damaged survivors, but tormented by the war, Mertens is unable to love properly. The situation worsens dramatically when Mertens discovers his former superior officer, Ferdinand Brückner (Arno Paulsen), the root of much of his trauma, is alive and prospering in "peacetime" Berlin (profiting from the sale of German military steel helmets as pots). Under Brückner's command, Mertens witnessed the slaughter of innocent Polish civilians for which Brückner gave the order of execution. Later, Mertens decides that he must pronounce judgment on Brückner's war crimes, but at the film's climax on Christmas eve, Susanne intervenes and staves off Merten's lust for justice. The film's title is invoked as a cautionary warning to the German public.

The stark postwar urbanism on display in *Die Mörder* aesthetically links the film to the expressionist roots of Germany's past but simultaneously places the diegesis firmly in the contemporaneous realism movements experienced in other traumatized nations' works (e.g., Italy's *Roma, città aperta* [*Rome, Open City*, 1945]). Above all, *Die Mörder* was the first of its kind for Germany; it established a four-year trend that generated a bulge in production that focused on life amid the rubble and should be sought out for its unique blend of artistry and social excavation. Some other notable *Trümmerfilme* include *Irgendwo in Berlin* (*Somewhere in Berlin*, 1946), *und über uns der Himmel* (*And the Heaven Above Us*, 1947), *Ehe im Schatten* (*Marriage in the Shadows*, 1947), *Berliner Ballade* (*The Berliner*, 1948), and *Lang ist der Weg* (1949). *Trümmerfilme* produced by non-German competitors, but shot in Germany, were also popular, for example, Roberto Rossellini's third entry in his unofficial World War II trilogy, *Germania anno zero* (*Germany, Year Zero*, 1948), Paramount Picture's *A Foreign Affair* (1948), RKO's *Berlin Express* (1948), and Carol Reed's *The Man Between* (1953).

For Germany, the aftermath of World War I produced numerous masterpieces in the realm of the visual arts. In like manner, the immediate aftershock of World War II produced films that registered and measured the psychological state of the nation. In them, some attempts to answer sobering questions about Germany's past, current reality, and new destiny were probed and dramatized. As a new decade drew near, however, filmmakers and audiences had predictably tired of the rear-view mirror perspective offered by the *Trümmerfilme*. By then, the trauma and guilt with which the nation wrestled in the immediate postwar-era environment were pervasive and increasingly unwelcome. Viewers were simply inclined to be entertained differently. Transitionally, the *Trümmerfilm* offered a natural springboard to vault motion picture production into the genre-driven popular cinema of the *Wirtschaftswunder* era (economic miracle of the 1950s and 1960s). Over time, West Germany's long period of postwar growth and prosperity, both international and domestic, became the envy of Europe—which begs the question: what did this portend for their filmmakers and their audiences?

BABY STEPS: TOWARD ALLIED CONSENSUS

How exactly did the tightly controlled rubble-strewn cinema of postwar occupied Germany mobilize to become this genre-fabricating juggernaut of the 1950s and 1960s? To be sure, it did not happen overnight. Glacially slow, methodical, and often contentious steps were taken by the occupying powers, in concert with the German public, toward emancipation. Reaching cinematic solvency was merely a function of this lengthy process.

A crucial part of this massive mobilization can best be understood via the wider context of the US film industry. As Thomas Elsaesser rightly observed, "this is true of every Western European country since 1945, and it could be argued that the Hollywood hegemony dates back not to the end of the Second but to the first World War."[25] With Germany's cinema apparatus splintered, largely depleted of resources, and seized by the Allied powers, the United States began to take a more active role in shaping its eventual form. Hollywood product was not, as hoped, promoting American values and ways of life with German audiences. This realization prompted the ICD to reconsider its policy. Adding to this unease, a submitted report indicated that the Soviet zone was becoming a hotbed of production.²⁶ Arriving at the intersection of failed expectations and competitive encroachment, the ICD gradually developed an alternative agenda—with the constant vocal objections of the MPEA.

"From the beginning of the occupation, film policy had been organized on a zonal basis, with each occupation authority exercising sovereignty within its zonal boundaries."²⁷ Beginning with the creation of Bizonia (the merging of the American and British zones in January 1947), a series of policy debates began concerning the decartelization of the German film industry. The British favored state sponsorship, allowing for the future German government to control and regulate its own industry, while the Americans insisted that free-market policies were the best path forward. From these early, relatively unproductive debates, however, a crucial first step was taken, namely, the operational licensing of German film distributors and the approval to export "German films in order to raise money to import rawstock and equipment needed by the German film industry—a move that drew the wrath of Hollywood."²⁸ The ICD believed these baby steps toward a competitive, open, and free market would ultimately align with American economic and political interests. The French, British, Soviets, and Hollywood strongly disagreed.

Over time, these contentious disagreements subsided and common ground was tentatively reached. One sticking point, however, continually reasserted itself: censorship. The Americans proposed to "repeal all censorship legislation of the German Reich and explore the possibility of substituting self-censorship by the German film industry for censorship by the state."²⁹ Essentially, the Americans were arguing the case for implementing a German version of the Motion Picture Production Code, famously headed by Wil Hays and ruthlessly enforced by Joseph Breen. Predictably, the French, Soviets, and British all opposed a self-censoring industry.

Positions eventually changed and the consensus was reached when, under the economic umbrella of the Marshall Plan and the imminent formation of the North Atlantic Treaty Organization (NATO), the British joined the Americans in a united front. The French eventually acquiesced, leaving the Soviets alone in their economic and ideological dissent. More importantly—and especially true after the Truman doctrine's anticommunist stance—a common enemy emerged as a collective focal point in the Soviet zone: the communist. The impending split of Berlin and the Cold War loomed ominously.

CINEMATIC REFORM AND RECONSTITUTION

Germany has dealt several massive blows by the Cold War. Perhaps the ultimate confirmation of this occurred on May 23, 1949, when the FRG was established, with Bonn as its capital, bifurcating Germany into East (Soviet Allied) and West states for the next forty years. The occupying troops of the Western Allies, however, remained in the newly formed West Germany. Gradually, more authority and sovereignty were accorded to the German public, which led to the formation of the first federal government in September of 1949 with Konrad Adenauer as chancellor.

Meanwhile, in the more rural and Catholic areas of Germany, censorship was unexpectedly on the rise. The ICD was surprised to learn that German teens were being increasingly banned from attending local cinemas. Reports from Bavaria stating that clergy and school teachers had "corporeally punished children for watching American films" were disconcerting and reinforced the pressing need for some sort of film advisory mechanism.[30] The sentiment was not rooted in any specific denunciation of American films per se, but rather the broader idea that "Nazi defeat was expected to herald the end of encroaching secular materialism in the outlying villages and initiate a period of 'normalization'—in the sense of a return to earlier religious practice and cultural traditions—for Christian believers throughout Bavaria."[31] The ICD was perplexed as, indeed, they had censored films, at times heavily, before they saw the exhibition. However, these edits were primarily politically informed, not culturally informed. Subsequently, this inability to acutely read audiences more broadly revealed severe misunderstandings and fissures over what concerned and troubled rural elders and their local governments. The misinterpretation gap only widened in the coming months, adding more weight to an already overburdened Allied control. The Americans were learning that to occupy a culture does not mean you necessarily will understand it.

As the debate continued, a proposal eventually surfaced which led to a compromise. As described several times in this chapter, Allied negotiations between multiple governments, particularly in Germany, were often slow and complicated. In May 1948, however, after long and laborious negotiations (and three failed attempts at ratification), the Freiwillige Selbstkontrolle der Filmwirtschaft (FSK) emerged. Fundamentally an advisory board (not unlike the MPAA, the present-day American rating association formed in 1968), this establishment committee consisted of fifteen members. Eight seats represented the film industry, with the seven remaining seats split between delegates from the state ministry of culture, the church, and the youth offices.[32] The majority of votes were ultimately awarded to the film industry, ensuring a voluntarily self-regulating board and wiping away the fascistic blot of the prior era of Nazi state control. Under American, French, and British supervision, additional restructuring of the FSK template occurred until it became fully operational on July 15, 1949. In 1951, the FSK would be granted more responsibility with their issuing of appropriate age ratings and holiday restrictions vis-à-vis the *Jugendschutzgesetz* or JuSchG (Protection of Young Persons Act). The FSK's timing proved perfect for the tidal wave of popular cinema (particularly the upcoming *Krimis* with their conflation of sex and violence) that would wash over Germany's cinemas over the next two decades.

Joining the regulatory FSK body were the two major and secular film journals: the Catholic *Filmdienst der Jugend* (*Film Service for the Youth*, 1947) and the Protestant *Evangelischer Filmbeobachter* (*Evangelical Film Observer*, 1948). German scholarly contributions to film studies are vast and difficult to measure. The writings of Siegfried Kracauer and the Frankfurt School of critical theorists (Theodor Adorno, Walter Benjamin, Max Horkeimer, Herbert Marcuse, etc.) are foundational, canonical, and, in many cases, remarkably prescient works. The Frankfurt School was considered a home for much of the twentieth century's leading critical theory. Threatened by the rise of Hitler, the Frankfurt theorists fled to New York where they continued their major works—many dealing with the failures of modernity—in absentia. "After 1945 the Catholic and Protestant churches became prominent players in film criticism in their attempt to reclaim the social and cultural power denied them under Hitler and National Socialism."[33] The journals provided topical articles about cinema and reviews of German-made motion pictures as well as imported films. The capsules tended toward three or four hundred-word summaries and critiques, and also included technical data (e.g., studio, cast, crew, running time, and the FSK rating).

1950S–1960S: THE ADENAUER ERA AND RISE OF GERMAN POPULAR CINEMA

With emerging distribution channels, operational studios, an industry-focused self-censoring rating commission, new film journals, and, most of all, a public thirsty for new pictures, all that remained was for fresh production companies to employ writers and directors possessing the commercial vision and an ability to tap the vein of West Germany's cinematic fancy. But what did German audiences desire? And would their desires export well into other important markets? What genres and subjects would constitute the GPC's *éclosion* of the postwar era?

Perhaps no other genre in the postwar era came to define the pleasures of escapism more than the *Heimatfilm*. Moreover, set in a nostalgic era freed from the psychological stresses, anxieties, and traumas of the war, *Heimatfilme* offered spectators a sedate, almost meditative space where representations of a bygone age could provide comfort for the German public. As a result, they were made in enormous numbers. The *Schlagerfilm* or "chart-hit" film—essentially musical revues often targeting teen culture—gyrated into cinemas in huge numbers as well (over one hundred films by the end of the 1960s). Similarly, from 1959 to 1972, approximately forty West German films were adapted from the works of Edgar Wallace and his son, Bryan Edgar Wallace, the majority of which were "either produced by Rialto film, a production company run by Horst Wendlandt and Preben Philipsen, or by the Central Cinema Comp. (CCC) headed by the better known Artur Brauner."[34] During the 1960s,

> The Karl May westerns, produced like the Edgar Wallace films by Horst Wendlandt's Rialto, were among the most popular films in the domestic market and were among the few West German genres in the 1960s that exported well to other countries.[35]

Likewise, inspired by the international success of the James Bond series, the German Eurospy film—fueled by the seven *Kommissar X* films starring Tony Kendall and Brad Harris—rocketed into widespread popularity. What's more, the Weimar master criminal *Dr. Mabuse* was resurrected for six films; the *Jerry Cotton* G-Man film franchise (starring George Nader) accepted missions for eight films; the popular *Fu Manchu* series tallied five; the *Frau Wirtin* (*Sexy Susan*) collection titillated for a total of six (along with numerous other soft-core sex comedies); and the prurient "pseudo-documentary" series *Schulmädchen-Report* (*Schoolgirl Report*) churned out thirteen "official" titles. More to the point, all were professionally produced, efficiently completed, garnered excellent domestic box-office, and offered reasonable export potential. Above all, however, they were *popular* with audiences.

These were the freshly formed West Germany's *new* films; they were seen, enjoyed, and eventually beloved by the masses. One can only marvel at the more than three hundred *Heimatfilme* made during this period as incontrovertible proof of this. Moreover, there seemed to be some form of the cinematic lane for moviegoers of every generation. Within their lifespan, however, German popular films were also the target of derision, particularly from rebellious, progressive, young comers and artists. The famous declaration "*Papas Kino ist tot*" (Papa's cinema is dead) became the motto for the famed Oberhausen Manifesto of 1962. Its twenty-six signatories proclaimed death to a stale cinema and an entrenched mindset—calling instead for the establishment of a New German Cinema. In retrospect, is it possible that the broad condemnation against these motion pictures was too narrow and harsh? Do these accusations suggest that meaningful work was not possible, or indeed made? In 2015, Eric Rentschler commented on the dialectical exchange between generations and also on "Papas" collective legacy:

It has been forty years since the Oberhausen Manifesto proclaimed the death of the old German film. Oberhausen's auteurist initiative, the antiauthoritarian impetus of 1968, and the programmatic resolve of the New German Cinema have played a predominant role in how commentators have approached the films of the Adenauer era. In fact, "Papas Kino" and its proponents had much more energy left than the Oberhausen activists imagined; and, indeed, West German features of the fifties, for all their detractors, have had a remarkable staying power . . . Late night weekend television is unthinkable without Edgar Wallace movies, and screenings of the Sissi-trilogy with Romy Schneider are an integral part of the holiday season. During the mid-nineties, Bernd Eichinger remade a number of fifties classics with contemporary stars. Even today, some German filmmakers wonder how they might create a popular cinema and, as they do so, look back with envy at the Adenauer era. Others remain far less eager to let this sector of film history serve as a role model. Indeed, it comes to us today as a contested and controversial cinema. No matter what reservations we might have and what conclusions we might reach about these productions, if we want to comprehend the shape and substance of West German dreams during the early postwar years, we surely have no better resource.[36]

Here, Rentschler accurately targets the often-used dream-factory metaphor as a means to measure particular zeitgeist fantasies, fears, and so on. The reciprocity between genre, text, and reader suggests that German audiences were consumed by, and desired more of, these types of films. Indeed, postwar box-office soared to inconceivable heights, reaching a peak in 1956 with 817 million tickets sold in West German cinemas (compared to, for example, 140 million tickets sold in a unified Germany in 2015).[37] For some, mainstream "pop culture" filmmaking triggers an immediate conflation with pejorative signifiers: unrefined, tasteless, vulgar, and so on. Simply stated, cultural elitism is problematic to the project of history. Peter Ellenbruch has written about the films of this era, particularly the crime films, and he rightfully and unequivocally states,

[The] situation should be confronted in order to consider the crime thrillers of the period without the reservations of the Oberhausen Manifesto and the "cinema crisis" so that they are taken seriously as a cinematic form and in doing so to classify them historically for what they were at the time: highly popular genre films which took up the tradition of German cinematic crime thrillers in times when there was a concern for democratisation.[38]

I am in complete agreement with Ellenbruch; the films need no more strident defense other than to simply assert that they exist and exist in great numbers over the span of many years. This sizable canon of films—spanning more than two decades—is an enormous and integral part of the German cinematic jigsaw puzzle; without them the portrait is unfocussed and incomplete. Likewise, the *Krimis* are a crucial piece (as well as a connector and bridge) to the byzantine jigsaw puzzle of the horror film.

It remains an important question, however, by what production and distribution means were these film series and cycles fabricated and released? The American distribution sector, though crucial during the initial postwar years, was not as successful in placing Hollywood products into West Germany in the late 1950s and 1960s. Hollywood's

> aim to dominate the West German market through quantity [oversupply] and quality [production values] met . . . a far more selective response from West German exhibitors and audiences than is normally acknowledged. Throughout the 1960s, no single American company managed to gain overall dominance in the West German distribution sector.[39]

Instead, several German distributors enjoyed respectable business during the postwar years, but over time many more closed, liquidated, and sold off their assets, among them "Union, Atlantik, Neuer Filmverleih, Stella, Loewen, Europa, and Prisma."[40] This downturn in the free market unexpectedly (and ironically) led to consolidations and the staking of cinematic territories (as the next sections will underscore).

CONSTANTIN FILM

The two principal survivors of the distribution wars were Gloria and Constantin. Of the two, Constantin merits our attention as the primary distributor of virtually all of the *Krimis* (and other popular genres) discussed in this book. "Compared with Gloria, which represented continuity from the 1950s to the 1960s and cautious, reluctant changes, Constantin was the West German distributor that most quintessentially represented the changed film culture and social climate of the 1960s."[41] Founded in 1949 by Waldfried Barthel and Preben Philipsen, the West German Constantin initially served as a distributor for United Artists and Columbia but eventually began to distribute original films for the West German market. Barthel was crucial to Constantin's success. Commonly referred to as "der Konsul" in the industry, he was "responsible for the company's profile and public image."[42] In 1955, Philipsen departed Constantin to manage Rialto full time while Barthel's wife Ingebord assumed the position of managing director from 1955 to 1960.

Constantin's model and subsequent success are reminiscent of American International Productions' (AIP) ascension to a position of status in the Los

Angeles of the 1950s and 1960s. A production and distribution company formed in 1954, AIP became the home to producer-director whiz kid Roger Corman who cultivated a Petri dish of talent so formidable that his film cultures would go on to conquer and dominate Hollywood for decades to come. AIP clobbered the major Hollywood studios by targeting the energetic and vital youth market of the boomers and by developing ambitious young talent. In like manner, Constantin had established a similar ethos by preferring not to hire "established production companies and personnel, but younger [albeit resolutely commercial] talent and emerging production outlets. Rather than spending money on stars of previous decades, it built up its own stable of new stars, very often recruited from television."[43] Similarly, AIP and Constantin both knew the value of sensational marketing and ballyhoo. Once a steady stream of colorful genre-driven pictures began distribution through their channels, Constantin invested in exploitation ephemera that boasted

> glossy and garishly colourful posters and press books with lurid headlines, titillating illustrations, and hyperbolic slogans. Compared with Gloria's conservative approach to marketing, emphasizing middle-class-respectability and wholesome family values, Constantin's market thrived on sensationalism and on its promise of action-packed entertainment, notoriety, and scandal.[44]

A hospitable supporter of the experimental, avant-garde, and director-driven works of the art house era, Constantin focused on helping aspiring filmmakers get their projects exhibited. This proved to be a winning strategy and subsequently encouraged loyalty from upcoming talent. Sponsoring country-specific film festivals (a Czech film week in Munich, for example), distributing works that embodied "high and low" planes of culture (i.e., seminal films from Fellini, Buñuel, Polanski, and Resnais in addition to populist peplums from Italy), and fostering a cinema culture that happily received outside product while creating and cultivating indigenous voices, Constantin flourished and continues to do so today as an even larger independent communications corporation. For our purposes, however, it must be stressed that "nearly all of the successful genre series in the West German market of the 1960s were distributed and co-financed by Constantin," including especially "through its exclusive contract with Preben Philipsen and Horst Wendlandt's Rialto" a monopoly on the Edgar Wallace cycle.

RIALTO FILM

While Constantin was the distributor most responsible for the genre eruption in West Germany, the production house inextricably linked to the

Edgar Wallace *Krimi* was Rialto Film. Despite domestic competition from Artur Brauner and others, Rialto became the *Krimi* factory par excellence. Constantin Philipsen founded Rialto Film in 1897 but eventually handed over the reins of the company to his son, Preben (also cofounder of Constantin). Tim Bergfelder explains that "while Rialto's early films were made for the Danish market, by mid-decade the emphasis shifted towards a strategy to produce films mainly for the West German market and more specifically for the West German Constantin."[45] At that time (the early 1950s), the more than thirty Edgar Wallace *Krimis* that Rialto would produce and trademark were still some years away. Bergfelder continues, "The lack of indigenous crime films in the 1950s is surprising in view of the fact that foreign crime films were regularly shown on West German screens, and with great success."[46] But as Peter Ellenbruch rightly points out,

> Broadly speaking, crime thrillers as a popular cultural phenomenon are always an expression of democratization processes and liberal tendencies since for the benefit of comprehensive crime culture a society must concede that not everything in its own populace proceeds without problems, that there is a spectrum of crime, and that state power cannot prevent everything.[47]

Given this, it is not surprising that a shortage of domestic crime films characterizes the early 1950s—a period when civil reform was a national priority. This is not to say, however, that they did not exist. Artur Brauner's productive and prescient CCC was responsible for many of the decade's earliest offerings. In fact, a postwar flirtation with the crime thriller began as early as 1950.

From 1950 to 1952 there was a "crime thriller movement" which can be understood as the first recurrence of the German crime thriller.[48] Tentative at first, the earliest efforts lacked the real power the genre affords those who choose to harness it. For example, Kurt Hoffmann's *Fünf unter Verdacht* (*City in the Fog*, 1950) is, as Ellenbruch points out, an "unremarkable start and also one which hardly reflects contemporary conditions in West Germany since it is set in a small town in Denmark."[49] Hoffmann's next effort, however, *Der Fall Rabanser* (*The Rabanser Case*, 1950), proved to be a much more significant entry, both as an analog to Germany's Weimar Republic past and as a progenitor to the later Rialto Wallace adaptations. Ellenbruch agrees:

> This work, produced by the Junge Film-Union, lays out a typical city crime thriller in Hamburg and revives motifs and sentiments from films of the Weimar Republic while at the same time working in additional influence of the American film noir trend.[50]

Among these early efforts a few classics emerged, perhaps the most famous of which is CCC's *Die Spur führt nach Berlin* (*Adventure in Berlin*, 1952).

> The film depicts an American lawyer who becomes involved with a counterfeiter gang in Berlin led by a Nazi as well as involuntarily finding himself caught between the front lines of the Cold War in East Berlin. This all culminates in an action-packed shootout in the ruins of the Reichstag.[51]

Unlike its contemporaries, which shot around the evidence of war to project a sense of urban normality, *Die Spur führt nach Berlin* embraces and photographs the ruins of Berlin in an almost *cinéma vérité* fashion. Ellenbruch stresses the movie's importance by stating that *Die Spur führt nach Berlin* "is perhaps the most complex and most spectacular film of the crime thriller movement in the early 1950s."[52]

These and other titles from the short-lived but significant experiment with the crime thriller genre, however wobbly at first, swiftly found surer footing. The films rapidly absorbed the strong bloodline that flowed through Germany's historical love affair with dark and disturbing things. In the end, their inability to promote a larger trend was simply a function of "bad timing." The impulse to embrace these films existed but was not entirely socially sanctioned in the nascent Adenauer era. Ellenbruch ultimately categorizes these initial postwar efforts as simultaneously contemporary and sensationalist. He concludes, "From 1952 to 1957 the West German cinematic crime thriller was largely displaced by the popularity of other genres, firstly with the *Heimatfilm*, and then with the *Schlagerfilm* and the [Italian] travelogue."[53]

Aware of these CCC crime releases but also appreciative of the skepticism surrounding the viability of the crime film (few in numbers but a powerful historical resonator with the German public), Constantin's programming adviser, Gerhard F. Hummel, submitted a complete draft of Wallace's *Die toten Augen von London* (*The Dead Eyes of London*) to Waldfried Barthel in 1955. Writing a spec script without any real market data to inform his decision was a strong indicator of Hummel's confidence regarding the feasibility of the genre. However, Barthel ultimately passed on the project, but he did not soon forget it.

As head of the Copenhagen-based Rialto Film, Philipsen had acquired the German Prisma film distributor in 1958. Included in Prisma's cinema program for 1958–1959 was the UK crime film *The Ringer* (in Germany, *Der Hexer*, 1952). This marked the third time a film was adapted from Wallace's popular play (first made in the United Kingdom in 1928, then remade in 1931). After watching the film in Munich, Barthel and Philipsen saw potential and sensed that Rialto could elevate the material and production values. With Hummel's previous enthusiasm for the genre in mind, in 1959 Philipsen acquired the German film rights to all of Edgar Wallace's novels, plays, and stories. The Wallace estate was not, however, asked for the rights to Edgar's son Bryan Edgar Wallace's works. Not recognizing Bryan as a literary copy of his father proved to be a costly oversight. Nonetheless, Rialto's rapid-fire releases of *Der Frosch mit der Maske* (*Face of the Frog*, 1959) and *Der Rote Kreis* (*The Crimson Circle*, 1959), both shot in Copenhagen at Danish studios with German casts and crew, became huge hits with the public. "After the success of the first two films, Philipsen relocated his production base, first to Hamburg where *Die Bande des Schreckens* (*The Terrible People*, 1960) and *Der Grüne Bogenschütze* (*The Green Archer*, 1960) were shot and then to Berlin."[54] These first four extremely effective and popular films would set the tone, manufacture a fan-base, and generate momentum for Rialto over the next dozen years.

Just as AIP and Constantin shared similar business strategies, readers who are familiar with the Gothic cinema of England's Hammer Films will

Figure 1.1 Klaus Kinski Prepares for His *Krimi* Debut as Edgar Strauss in the Rialto Production of *Die toten Augen von London* (*Dead Eyes of London*, 1961). Source: Stifung Deutsche Kinematek Berlin.

likely see a strong parallel with Rialto Film. This parallel is not only useful for business model comparisons, but also for gaining an appreciation of just how rapidly a few isolated films can, by capturing the public's fascination, produce an entire cycle of production that not only supersedes other units of production, but can last for years, or indeed decades. In this regard, Hammer and Rialto performed along analogous lines. Hammer claimed new territory and boldly drove a fresh stake in unhallowed ground with the watershed releases of *The Curse of Frankenstein* (1957) and *Dracula* (*Horror of Dracula*, 1958). Hammer was responding, in a sense, to the same societal stimuli that fueled the initial film noir era of the United States (1941–1958, by most accounts). Hammer, however, chose a different genre, horror rather than a crime, through which collective trauma, postwar anxieties, and repressed sexual desires could be channeled and articulated. Few could have anticipated, however, that a contemporaneous and strikingly parallel film movement would be under way in Germany less than one year later with the back-to-back (and boffo) releases of *Der Frosch mit der Maske* (*Face of the Frog*, 1959) and *Der Rote Kreis* (*The Crimson Circle*, 1959).

Both Hammer and Rialto studios harvested from rich fields of UK fiction for their films. Hammer primarily focused on the Gothic cinematic revival of Stoker and Shelley that Universal mined so efficiently and lucratively in the 1930s and 1940s, while Rialto chose the immensely popular crime fiction of Edgar Wallace (who had been banned in Germany during the Nazi era). Like Hammer, Rialto's decision also harkened back to an earlier era. True, there were previously filmed adaptations of Wallace's work in England, the United States, and Germany, but I refer specifically here to Rialto's conscious effort to revisit the Weimar screen's shadowy, dangerous, omniscient, controlling, and hypnotic underworlds of master criminals such as Caligari, Cesare, and Mabuse.

In front of and behind the camera, communities of talent populated Hammer and Rialto's modest productions creating a cottage industry coziness uncommon in larger studios. A regular team of directors, editors, cinematographers, production designers, composers, and so on were contentedly employed at both studios. Friendships developed and productivity flourished. At smaller studios, the head of the production typically doubled as producer and production manager of each film. They were largely responsible for the day-to-day operations and supervision over productions. For Hammer this position was held by Anthony Hinds; for Rialto Horst Wendlandt assumed the producing role. Wendlandt had apprenticed for Tobis Film during the Reich era and then later joined CCC. Under Brauner's aegis, Wendlandt learned virtually every aspect of the industry from the ground up. Ironically, the benefactor of that business acumen and industrial knowledge turned out to be Philipsen's

Rialto and not CCC, which only served to intensify the rivalry between the two production companies.

Hammer's constellation of notable European stars and deep bench of character actors included talents like Peter Cushing, Christopher Lee, Hazel Court, Michael Gough, Martine Beswick, Barbara Shelley, Oliver Reed, Michael Ripper, and so on. Moreover, the connection between Hammer and Rialto is all the more self-evident for the fact that Hammer regulars such as Christopher Lee and Freddie Francis actually worked for Rialto during their *Krimi* cycle.

Lesser-known internationally, but outstanding nonetheless, Rialto also boasted a repertoire of stellar performers to populate their growing catalog of *Krimis* (and their Karl May westerns). Comedian Eddi Arent appeared in a staggering twenty-three of the cycle's films; Klaus Kinski lent his budding but already formidable talent to sixteen; Siegfried Schürenberg showcased his considerable presence in fifteen (most often as Sir John of Scotland Yard); Joachim Fuchsberger employed with or for Scotland Yard, often as the leading man, thirteen times; and "*Krimi* Queen" Karin Dor starred in five.

One of the more ironic and comedic elements common to both studios (and Universal for that matter) was *where* these films actually took place. The choice of location for many of Hammer's most notable titles was usually some small town or village in rural Germany. This often amounted to adding the suffix "stadt," "stein," or "berg" to words—Karlstadt, Ingstadt, Badstein, Klausenberg, and so on. Case in point: Hammer's *Dracula* (*Horror of Dracula*, 1958) should rightly balance the majority of its story between Transylvania (then in the Kingdom of Hungary) and England; however, screenwriter Jimmy Sangster chose rural Germany as its setting. Commonplace in Hammer productions were grumpy Burgermeisters, pubs full of overflowing steins, lederhosen, schnitzel, and so on. The turnabout in this case was swift and robust; indeed, although all of the diegetic elements of the Rialto *Krimis* were British, the films were made (apart from the first two and sundry coproductions) in Germany with German casts and crews. Like Hammer, Rialto often relied on stereotypical characterizations and the taking of liberties writ large with British culture. Given the longitudinal arc of the series, it is fascinating to watch Germany's cinematic interpretation of Wallace's England evolve as cultural shifts dictated, particularly during the most transformative decade of the twentieth century, the 1960s. A salient factor that interests me is what Bergfelder describes as the challenge *Krimi* producers faced in "find[ing] narrative formulae that were accepted by different national audiences as being part of an 'indigenous' cultural framework."[55] Rialto's Edgar Wallace cycle proved "that a foreign cultural source could be successfully adapted into a recognisably 'German' film series." The forthcoming film analyses of chapters 2 and 3 bear scrutiny on this claim.

HELLO, THIS IS EDGAR WALLACE! (BUT, WHO WAS EDGAR WALLACE?)

Who was the literary source of this long and popular cycle of films from the United States, the United Kingdom, and especially Germany, and why was his work so appealing to readers and audiences? Edgar Wallace (1875–1932) was "perhaps the most popular fiction writer of his time."[56] As Neil Clark, author of *Stranger Than Fiction: The Life of Edgar Wallace, the Man Who Created King Kong*, neatly summarizes, Wallace was "the illegitimate son of a travelling actress, who left school at the age of 12 with no formal qualifications, he was also, at one point, the most widely read author in the world."[57] From bartenders to bishops, it seemed everyone was reading Wallace.

The author of 170 books that were translated into more than 30 languages, Wallace's staggering output is one of his most defining characteristics as an author. The fact that he was uncommonly prolific, however, has cloaked the true measure of the man (and author): Wallace was a gifted and beloved storyteller.

> More films were made from his books than those of any other twentieth-century writer. He was the publishing sensation of the 1920s—in one year in that decade, one out of every four fiction books bought in England was by Edgar Wallace. If that wasn't enough, he also wrote twenty-three plays, sixty-five sketches and almost 1,000 short stories.[58]

Moreover, as the title of Clark's book clearly illustrates, Wallace was an initial and forgotten architect of one of the most famous films of the twentieth century, RKO's legendary *King Kong* (1933). As film historian Tim Lucas notes, "Over the years, there has been an unfortunate tendency among scholars to downplay Wallace's contribution to the film's scenario, due in large part to the fact that he died before the film went into production."[59] Nevertheless, Wallace's early contribution to *King Kong*'s scenario is now well documented.

As with many authors, Wallace's success in Great Britain waned over time and his star power faded, particularly after his death in 1932. Conversely (and concurrently) in Germany, his star power was on a steady and ultimately meteoric rise. Film historian Kim Newman wrote about this in 2007:

> Wallace is the David Hasselhoff of vintage crime writers, proverbially popular in Germany while long out of print in the land of his birth. His eighty-year-old novels still crown bookshops and supermarket racks in Germany, and several were adapted all over again for German TV in the late 1990s.[60]

So, what were the causes of Wallace's decline outside of Germany? Several factors may have led to the Western marginalization of Wallace: writers of more popular "literary substance" were likely jealous of his success; Wallace's critique of British society (in particular, his favoring of feminism) was surely offensive to some; and his epic productivity left many contemporaries lagging behind, causing some critics to impose a "second rate" status on the author simply based on the sheer volume of his work. But as film scholar and historian Wheeler Winston Dixon points out, although Wallace is most often associated with his crime fiction or detective thrillers, he actually "wrote in a variety of narrative and/or fictive voices, producing science fiction, historical surveys, tales of feminist self-empowerment, social criticism, autobiography, as well as a number of crime and detective novels."[61]

At the same time, Wallace's work has also drawn criticism for a variety of ideological reasons, chief among them is his endorsement of British colonial rule. Dixon elaborates:

As disturbing as Wallace's jingoistic Colonial racism and homophobia rightly are to contemporary readers, within the context of work written by his contemporaries and predecessors, one is confronted by the distressing yet undeniable fact that such deplorable and unenlightened attitudes were then common social currency.[62]

Wallace's authorial intent in his crime fiction is outside the scope of this book. Tim Bergfelder echoes this critical stance when he states he does not "believe that an investigation of the ideologically problematic aspects of Wallace's fiction, or of his personal political beliefs, ultimately help explain his success with German readers and audiences."[63] Moreover, the German interpretations of Wallace's work often engage in parodies of traditional "English culture." These stereotypical jabs are not mean-spirited, but rather I see them as attempts to further open the postwar dialogue between the German and English nations. Whereas Hammer randomly assigned German locations to the stories in many of their films, Rialto is ever-conscious that they are depicting another country, its customs and norms, and thereby understood how these films could positively or negatively affect German-Anglo relations.

As noted earlier, the West German market was perfectly primed for a resurgence of crime thrillers. The motion picture industry had tentatively tested what turned out to be chilly market waters for the crime thriller in the early 1950s, but by the end of that decade the water had reached the perfect temperature. The origin of Edgar Wallace's popularity in Germany can be traced to his publisher, the Jewish-owned Goldmann. Founded in 1922, Goldmann established an entire series for Wallace's crime novels titled "*Goldmanns*

Taschen-Krimi" or Goldmann's Pocket-Thrillers, so named because of their size and low cost. Goldmann also sequentially numbered each volume (with bold red dustjackets) in the series—one, two, and so on. This numbering system is acknowledged in the title credits of the Rialto series. The *Taschen-Krimi* series proved to be (as it had been in the United Kingdom) an outstanding success with German bibliophiles.

Consequently, by the time Preben Philipsen approached Edgar's daughter, Penelope Wallace, to purchase the German film rights for her father's work, there was a preexisting demographic (one that bled across traditional markers of age, sex, and income), a built-in audience primed and ready for the films that Rialto would soon deliver.

THE WALLACE *KRIMI*

As previously noted, few English language scholarly works exist on *Krimis* in general and the Edgar Wallace adaptations in particular. The agenda of late twentieth and early twenty-first century global cinema studies, however, has fortunately expanded to accommodate previously overlooked and potentially obfuscated areas of investigation. What was once consigned to the province of populist magazines and fanzines is now fertile soil for academics to sow. Despite this, the West German *Krimis* have not been widely nor, in some cases, warmly received. For example, Wheeler Winston Dixon casts the films in a disparaging light:

> Directed by Alfred Vohrer and a series of equally indifferent *auteurs*, these cheaply produced travesties update Wallace's works to a phantom zone of 1960s London, as haphazardly recreated on sound stages in Berlin, with liberal deviations from the original texts and enormous doses of sadism and violence added which appear nowhere in the novels themselves.[64]

It is significant that Dixon, an exceptional and meticulous scholar, should dismissively write off the series. I do not share his opinion regarding the series, but, more importantly, it is unclear exactly what cinema spectrum is used to frame his basis of comparison. When placed on a cinematic timeline of similar international productions, the *Krimis* shimmer precisely because of their unique composition. Perfunctory glances at the series do not reveal what the careful textual analyses of chapters 2 and 3 of this book verify: the Rialto *Krimis* are not "travesties" (certainly not to tens of millions of Germans) but are thoroughly professional, skillfully crafted, wildly popular, influential, and valuable cultural artifacts. Along these lines, German film historian and author Joachim Kramp conducted authoritative research, gathered granular historical data, and provided insightful and vivid analyses of the filmed works of Edgar Wallace in his comprehensive and exhaustive book *Hallo—Hier sprich Edgar Wallace! Die Geschichte der deutschen Kriminalfilmserie 1959–1972*.

According to Kramp, there are four distinct phases to the Rialto *Krimis*. The first phase, films one (*Der Frosch mit der Maske*, *Face of the Frog*, 1959) through eleven (*Das Gasthaus an der Themse*, *The Guest House on the Thames*, 1962), is essentially faithful adaptations from the Wallace source material. In this first phase, efforts were made to keep the compression or outright elimination of characters to a minimum and to preserve subplots where possible, keeping to the spirit, intent, and tone of the novels. Naturally, during the translation process from one medium to another, certain aspects were unavoidably lost while others, however, were gained. The second phase, films twelve (*Der Zinker*, *The Squeaker*, 1963) through eighteen (*Das Verrätertor*, *The Traitor's Gate*, 1964), borrows from the source material but does not attempt genuine fidelity. Titles, scenarios, and characters are used or modified to suit their new cinematic scenario. The third phase, films nineteen (*Der Hexer*, *The Mysterious Magician*, 1964) through twenty-eight, (*Der Mann mit dem Glasauge*, *The Man with the Glass Eye*, 1969), produced increasingly looser adaptations of Wallace's titles while also integrating more horror elements in an attempt to compete with market trends. This stage is also marked by the self-cannibalism that would bring Hammer Films to insolvency at around the same time. Lacking the creative incentive to keep the series fresh and competing with the higher-concept movies of the burgeoning blockbuster era of the 1970s, Hammer and Rialto plundered their own libraries, recycled plots and stories, and reused tired and wobbly tropes. While extremely productive (averaging two films per year), the third phase simply, but inevitably, showed signs of genre fatigue and exhaustion. The remaining four films of the final phase (*Das Gesicht im Dunkeln / A doppia facia*, *Double Face*, 1969) through *Das Rätsel des silbernen Halbmondes* (*Sette orchidee macchiate di rosso*, *Seven Blood-Stained Orchids*, 1972) relied on international funding through coproduction means, minimizing risk but also decreasing profits. The fourth phase also marked the period when the two nationally distinctive yet intertwined genres (the German *Krimi* and Italian *giallo*) ultimately bled onto a new canvas—forming, shaping, and coloring the modern *giallo* as defined by Dario Argento, Umberto Lenzi, Michele Soave, Lucio Fulci, and Lamberto Bava, among others.

The defining characteristic of the *Krimi* is its intense criminal element, but they also offer the atmospheric flourishes of the Gothic thriller. Common and often standard archetypes populate these stories—for example, the dashing hero, a heroine in distress, a dryly humorous Scotland Yard inspector, a sidekick who serves as comic relief, and a mysterious super criminal.[65] It is

Figure 1.2 An Exciting Tunnel Chase Culminates in an Armed Face-off in 1964's *Der Hexer* (*The Mysterious Magician*, 1964). *Source: Stifung Deutsche Kinematek Berlin.*

worth noting that this basic story template, with its ready-made situations and characters, resembles that of a number of genres found in other national cinemas—for example, the Mexican luchador films featuring masked wrestlers like Santo, the Blue Demon, and Mil Máscaras in pulpy stories with elements of mystery, horror, and science fiction—which perhaps accounts for the lasting popularity of *Krimis* not only in Germany but elsewhere in the world as well.

One crucial element to the mystery formula (which Wallace thoroughly embraced) is the motley assortment of eccentric characters that inhabit the scenario—all of whom are credible suspects. This trope robustly carried over into the Wallace film franchise and was populated by Rialto's revolving troupe of actors. In addition to the constant task of keeping characters mentally organized, the viewer is also bumped and bounced from one scene to another often with little narrative causality. In a sense, this is the residue that the *Krimi* inherited from a vast majority of film noir narratives. Noir derived its strength from its visual core; the often confusing and byzantine turns of plot were totally subordinate to the genre's more primal elements. These narrative limitations, however, actually strongly anchor the *Krimi*. The *Krimi* trusted that the viewer might often be so distracted and confused that debate and discussion surrounding unresolved storylines, gaping plot holes, or logical incongruities would be abandoned or, at least, attenuated "The mandatory Scooby-Doo like revelation of the culprit's true identity [from a cast crammed with oddball characters] usually owed more to a spirit of 'bet you never saw that coming' than any due attention to narrative logic."[66]

Building off of this foundation, the Rialto Wallace adaptations employed an ever-growing collection of conventions that were consistently utilized (and modernized as cultural shifts dictated) throughout the series. These defining features included, first and foremost, a recurring cast of actors and production personnel, police-procedural plots, numerous red herrings (supernatural and non-supernatural), class conflict, estate inheritances, revenge, castles, moors, hotels, recycled shots of London (day and night, foggy, and clear), the conflation of sex and violence, bondage, unique and often gruesome deaths, and expressionist mise-en-scène and lighting (during the black and white era). The comparatively late shift to color photography with *Der Bucklige von Soho* (*The Hunchback of Soho*, 1966) transformed the genre by stripping it of its most defining characteristic, chiaroscuro lighting, and substituting in its place an eye-popping vividness commensurate to Italy's early *giallos* and Britain's Hammer films.

Once Rialto gathered fair winds and full sails, their films continued to reach wider seas of success, particularly in the early-to-mid-1960s. Rialto's *Krimis* even managed to outperform Hollywood blockbusters *The Longest Day* (1962), *Cleopatra* (1962), and the first James Bond sequel, *From Russia with Love* (1963). Tim Bergfelder elaborates on the impressive numbers:

> Gross returns of the Wallace series at the German box-office averaged at 5 million DM each, with added export revenues [mostly from Austria, France, and Italy] of 500,000 DM per film. Given that the films' production budgets rarely exceeded 2 million DM, the Wallace series' box-office performance, both in the indigenous market and through exports, was unusually healthy and stable compared with German film production in general.[67]

After the success of the first two films, Philipsen's *Krimi* factory relocated to offices and studios first in Hamburg and then Berlin. By then, the Rialto Wallace wave had officially begun, and competitors soon took notice of the swelling profits. Smelling blood in the water, Artur Brauner's CCC (who had made impressive crime thrillers a decade earlier) capitalized on the ongoing and lucrative Wallace adaptation explosion by securing the motion picture rights to Edgar's son, Bryan Edgar Wallace's, novels which were essentially indistinguishable from the works of his father. Bergfelder explains how

> Brauner's strategy to contract Edgar Wallace's son was perhaps the most ingenious in gaining a foothold in the Wallace boom. Between 1962 and 1972 CCC produced 10 Bryan Edgar Wallace films, which were stylistically exact replicas

of the "genuine" Rialto productions, proclaiming the author's name in bold letters on posters, though with the Bryan part in distinctly smaller letters. In *Der Würger von Schloss Blackmoor* [*The Strangler of Blackmoor Castle*, 1963], Bryan Edgar Wallace even appeared in the film's credit sequence, dressed identically to his father. Brauner's productions adapted the iconography of the Rialto series almost slavishly by employing directors Harald Reinl, and Franz Joseph Gottlieb, cinematographers Ernst W. Kalinke and Richard Angst, and Wallace "stars" such as Karin Dor, Barbara Rütting, and Elisabeth Flickenschildt.[68]

Regarded as epigones by devout *Krimi* fans, CCC's *Krimis*, while not considered the "genuine article" by many, nevertheless established a coveted foothold in the crime thriller market and performed well. Moreover, before Brauner could truly mobilize his *Krimi* doppelgängers, he developed "a number of generic formulae which were close enough in style to the Wallace films, yet sufficiently independent not to incur prohibitive court claims of plagiarism or copyright infringement."[69] This resulted in the resurrection of the literary and cinematic criminal mastermind Dr. Mabuse for six CCC films—*Die tausend Augen des Dr. Mabuse* (*The Thousand Eyes of Dr. Mabuse*, 1960), *Im Stahlnetz des Dr. Mabuse* (*The Return of Dr. Mabuse*, 1961), *Die Unsichtbaren Krallen des Dr. Mabuse* (*The Invisible Dr. Mabuse*, 1962), *Des Testament des Dr. Mabuse* (*The Testament of Dr. Mabuse*, 1962), *Scotland Yard jagt Dr. Mabuse* (*Scotland Yard Chases Dr. Mabuse*, 1963), and *Die Todesstrahlen des Dr. Mabuse* (*The Secret of Dr. Mabuse*, 1964)—all of which spelled competitive domestic trouble for Rialto. The CCC epigones also presented another unique challenge: they were not only stylistically similar to Rialto's *Krimis*, but they also successfully tapped into a mainstream vein of prewar nostalgia through the revival of icons like the mesmerizing criminal mastermind Dr. Mabuse.

In *From Caligari to Hitler: A Psychological History of the German Film*, German cultural theorist Siegfried Kracauer controversially asserted that the Weimar cinema of the late teens and 1920s (especially the *Dr. Mabuse* films) prefigured the rise of fascism in the 1930s. Writing in the United States in the mid-to-late 1940s, Kracauer's analyses focused not on the propaganda films of the Reich era (as one might confidently speculate), but rather on the popular post–World War I Weimar-era films that were seen and largely treasured by the German masses, films such as *Das Cabinet des Dr. Caligari* (*The Cabinet of Dr. Caligari*, 1920), *Dr. Mabuse, der Spieler* (*Dr. Mabuse the Gambler*, 1922), *Die freudlose Gasse* (*The Joyless Street*, 1925), *Metropolis* (*Metropolis*, 1927), *M* (*M*, 1931), and *Mädchen in Uniform* (*Girls in Uniform*, 1931). Kracauer essentially argued that not only are films a market commodity with exchange value (bound to demand and other mobilizing forces), but also they are an ideological product of the economic base (and thereby the society and culture) that produced them. Therefore, as a mass medium, film is the perfect vessel to transport, transmit, and expose the subconscious desires (as well as the fears and anxieties) of the masses it seeks to entertain. He writes:

> The films of a nation reflect its mentality in a more direct way than other artistic media for two reasons: first, films are never the product of an individual [...] Second, films address themselves, and appeal, to the anonymous multitude [...] General discontent becomes apparent in waning box-office receipts, and the film industry, vitally interested in profit, is bound to adjust itself, so far as possible, to the changes of mental climate.[70]

Kracauer argued that the German public was mass-hypnotized by the likes of Dr. Caligari and Dr. Mabuse, mesmerized "by the extraordinary power of the German film after 1918."[71] The films transmitted (in the wake of World War I) a subconscious desire to be controlled (and to again bring Germany to a position of prominence in the world) and, in exchange, the industry received incontrovertible evidence through box-office receipts that the public wanted more.

The late 1950s and 1960s cinematic crime wave of West Germany is entirely evocative of the late 1910s and 1920s cinematic crime wave of Weimar Germany, going so far as to resurrect infamous Weimar-era characters such as Dr. Mabuse. This begs the question of why there has been no discursive stampede to explain the *massive* spike in the crime thrillers of the 1950s and 1960s. Earlier in this chapter, I noted the shortage of domestic crime films in the civil reform era that characterized the early 1950s; but by the end of the decade, they were reproducing at a feverish rate. Was, as Kracauer suggested, the German public again engaging in mass psychological submission to state apparatus control?

The answer is no, at least not in the same way that Kracauer suggests. Both Rialto's *Krimis* and CCC's criminal escapades were thoroughly defanged of any fascist toxins. In their place, however, we see a vivid and naked postwar confluence of sex and violence that would shape the genre for decades to come. Moreover, by placing the films in England and dotting them with laugh-out-loud humor and a postmodern playfulness, they signal a *safe* activation of the same societal stimuli that had so enthralled the Weimar-era audiences.

As a cohesive series, the *Krimi* still befuddles cinephiles anxious to generically categorize them. As former *Fangoria* Editor-in-Chief Phil Nobile Jr. observes "For such a specific cinematic moment in time, what fascinates about krimi [*sic*] is all the ways they defy categorization." He concludes that "[the Krimi] sits at a very particular cinematic intersection, connecting one era with another, and discovering the krimi film is like finding a missing puzzle piece under the table, with all the satisfaction that comes from finally clicking that piece into place."[72]

Nobile's puzzle metaphor is fitting and suggests the law of closure commonly associated with Gestalt theory of visual perception. Going a step further, if we broaden our gaze to examine the entire *Krimi* family (*Krimis* often center on family histories, estates, legacies, inheritances), we see a significant house with multiple lineages. The joining of Edgar Wallace to the postwar "crime film" yielded what could be called "House *Krimi*," the immediate offspring being Rialto, the legitimate heir, and Rialto's half-sibling, CCC. Rialto later joined House Constantin and produced thirty-two of its own offspring. CCC, however, joined with several houses to sire several "bastard" children before the line died out. Rialto, however, conjoined with an Italian house to produce a number of hybridized offspring who eventually went on to form their own house, "House *Giallo*."

While consulting with archivists at Frankfurt's Deutsche Filminstitut, I was informed that while the Wallace *Krimis* were tremendously popular in their first-run theatrical releases, it was their second life on television—spanning syndication over many decades—that really cultivated generations of

Figure 1.3   No Trope Was Off-limits to Rialto's Franchise, Including Mad Scientists and Their Notorious Experiments. *Der Mönch mit der Peitsche* (*The College Girl Murders*, 1967). *Source: Stifung Deutsche Kinematek Berlin.*

fans and created the legacy that continues through today. My associates went on to explain that on nights when a Wallace thriller played on television, streets emptied, phones were left off their hooks, parking was impossible, and you would have to fend for yourself in the kitchen. No interruptions were tolerated during the broadcast.[73] This level of fandom and active celebration is what ultimately cemented Edgar Wallace as a national fixture and common German household name. Moreover, this contextual testimony gestures to a comparable model in the United States. For decades, millions of households would gather in the family room and huddle around the warm glow of their electronic fireplaces to enjoy syndicated broadcasts of *The Wizard of Oz* (1939), *The Sound of Music* (1965), *Singin' in the Rain* (1952), or a select few other "event television" evenings.[74]

Beyond their theatrical exhibition in West Germany, the European sector served as the primary export destination of the Wallace thrillers, especially Italy, the Benelux countries, and the Nordic nations. Finland, in particular, proved to be a country thirsty for West German products. As HT Nuotio has noted, "Between the years 1949 and 1963 roughly 480 German-speaking films were released theatrically (nearly five times as many as in the UK), of which about 400 were produced in the FRG."[75] He continues: "The all-time peak year for German cinema in Finland appears to be 1961: in the year of the Wall, at the height of FRG-GDR rivalry, no fewer than 58 German-language films were premiered." Among them were four new Rialto Edgar Wallace films.[76]

Lamentably, the majority of Rialto's *Krimis* never saw theatrical distribution in the United States; rather, they were sold as a television syndication package acquired by small-time distributor Roberts and Barry.[77] Roberts and Barry, described by *Variety* as an "office-in-hat operation," placed these films into syndication in 1965 under the package heading Europa 33.

> The group contained both Edgar Wallace films from Rialto such as *The Squeaker* (1965) and Bryan Wallace adaptions from CCC-Film such as *Curse of the Yellow Snake* (1963) as well as the European James Bond knockoffs *Operation Hong Kong* and *Mission to Hell with Secret Agent FX 15*, among others.[78]

A few films are listed with US release dates through smaller, independent distributors. For example, in 1965, *Die Toten Augen von London* (*Dead Eyes of London*, 1961) was paired and released on a double bill with Italy's *Lo spettro* (*The Ghost*, 1963) through Magna Pictures.[79] Ultimately, the unlicensed home video versions of these films, those found in the Sinister Cinema adverts in *Filmfax*, were culled from the 16 mm dupes that circulated from the Roberts and Barry syndication package.

READING THE SERIES: THE *KRIMI* AS SIMULACRA

While this book is structured as both a cultural history and a critical filmography, it is also informed by critical and cultural theory. And while I am curious to know what Kracauer and his Frankfurt School contemporaries would have made of the postwar German *Krimi* boom, a more practical and useful theoretical prism exists. The German *Krimi* can be read, characterized, and contextualized through the conceptual framework of what French sociologist Jean Baudrillard deemed the simulacrum (*Simulacra and Simulation*, 1981).[80] Casting the series within this particular discursive strategy aids in explaining—both culturally and economically—these rather unique films.

Jean Baudrillard famously expanded upon the Frankfurt School's contemplations of consumption, commodification, and technological domination. He was the perfect provocateur to carry on many of the school's foundational works, particularly those of Marcuse, Benjamin, Horkheimer, and Adorno.[81] Baudrillard's broader theoretical assertions and predictions are complex and move beyond postmodern theory (to what he ultimately describes as a postmodern break or rupture with history), but for our purposes, it is his "ordered simulacra" classification system, what he termed a "precession of order," that warrants our attention and merits examination.

A crucial starting point, however, is to first acknowledge the mid-century German *Krimi* as a collection of early postmodern cinematic texts that embody many of the characteristics that would come to define the postmodern theory.[82] The Wallace *Krimis* are a hybridized, self-reflexive, and intertextual group of films that often prioritize aesthetics, boast illogical and unrealistic plots, engage in pastiche, and relocate the cultural endemism of London and Scotland Yard to urban and rural Germany. While these and other deliberate textual strategies mark the series as postmodern, the German *Krimis* are also an unlikely, and therefore captivating, example of simulacra.

At its most basic, a simulacrum is a representation or imitation of something—in other words, a *copy*. Baudrillard's "precession of order" defines three magnitudes of simulation. Simulacra of the first order are simply representations of a given thing: a painting, a novel, a map of the world; these are acknowledged substitutes of the object's actual existence. Moreover, the object in reality and its representation are clearly distinguishable. With simulacra of the second order, however, the real and its representation become *indistinguishable*. The industrial revolution, and the rate and rapidity its technological innovations wrought, enabled novel large-scale manufacturing. An identical copy of an original could now be mass produced, and in immense quantities. To the naked eye, these appear to be exact copies—that which is *real*. For example, a digital photo of a sunset (a first-order simulacra) is sent as an unmanipulated file to a dozen recipients. However, the naked eye cannot distinguish the original from its eleven copies. Now then, if we imagine that those copies were to spawn copies of their own, then we have entered into Baudrillard's third order of simulation—a reality where the original referent is lost, forgotten, erased, and no longer visible.

Simulacra of the third order, however, are often more ideologically constructed rather than physically manufactured. An oft-cited example lies in the legacy of frontier journalism and the popular "Wild West Shows" (such as Buffalo Bill's Wild West Show) on the American perception of its "epic old west," which largely reinforced myth and legend over historical fact. Exaggerations of frontier life for entertainment purposes, early radio and motion picture serials, comics, and Western literature further mythologized cowboys, gunfighters, and indigenous nations. In this particular and well-known case study, a new perception of historical reality has replaced actual historical reality. This myth of the "old west" persists well into the twenty-first century and is almost entirely the product of mediated images passed down and reinforced over the past 150 years by the mass media industries.

What, then, is the relationship of simulacra to the Wallace *Krimi* cycle? Let us first remember that Edgar Wallace's numerous crime novels are, in reality, not actually England, London, or Scotland Yard, but *representations* of them that exist wholly in the imagination of the author and thereby substitute a narrativized form of reality over reality itself—resulting in simulacra of the first order. Some years later, a German preoccupation—and fascination—with these Wallace novels generated dozens of cinematic representations—more simulacra of the first order. But, crucially, as the textual matter moved from one medium to another (novel to film), and from one culture to another (English to German), a much more complex text was created. In other words, Wallace's representations were now German cinematic interpretations of Wallace's fictional interpretations of London and Scotland Yard.

Additionally, as the series progressed throughout the 1960s and into the 1970s, the films began to remake their earlier efforts (many of which were remakes of earlier pictures) resulting in copies of copies (of copies).[83] Muddying the waters further were competitor Artur Brauner's CCC epigones which were based on the works of Bryan Edgar Wallace. Just as Hammer Films had Amicus Productions continually nipping at their franchise's heels, Rialto similarly had to contend with Brauner's imitations. Formed by Americans Milton Subotsky and Max J. Rosenberg and based out of Shepperton Studios, Amicus' most popular offerings were often conflated as motion pictures from Hammer. This was attributable to the sharing of key personnel (directors, writers), the touting of recognizable Hammer actors (Christopher Lee and Peter Cushing), and similar marketing. Regardless, Amicus did manage to distinguish itself with a series of clever horror anthologies (*Dr Terror's House of Horrors* [1964], *The House that Dripped Blood* [1970], and *Tales from the Crypt* [1972], among others).

With CCC's Bryan Edgar Wallace productions, however, we fundamentally witness a *human* simulacrum. Bryan Edgar Wallace's novels were deliberately written in the not only compatible but basically indistinguishable style of his more famous father. Moreover, CCC lured away Rialto regulars (such as Karin Dor, Joachim Fuchsberger, Elisabeth Flickenschildt, and Pinkas Braun) to lend their talents and personas to CCC's attempt at gaining a respectable market share. Even more conflation and confusion enter into the equation with CCC's advertising campaigns, which were identical to Rialto's ephemera in terms of graphic layout and overall design—more copies of copies of copies. Finally, Baudrillard's third order of simulacra was realized—the so-called counterfeit had produced a viable substitute, a new reality for audiences. But what exactly was this reality? What kept audiences persistently glued to the franchise; what accounted for such substantial buy-in? Clearly, a love for Edgar Wallace and his many works provided much of the viewer's interest in seeing them brought to cinematic life by well-known and beloved personalities. But I would also argue that, in part, it was the concept of verisimilitude that powered and enabled the success of the franchise. Verisimilitude, or the *appearance of reality* and not reality itself, was crucial to the selling of Britain as a narrative locus to German moviegoers. Indeed, it was the last but most essential ingredient. With largely German locations, directors, actors, writers, technicians, and so on, the overall geographic and cultural plausibility of these productions relied upon the imaginations of millions of Germans.

Moreover, the level of verisimilitude achieved, particularly during the black and white era, might've easily replaced the *real* London and Scotland Yard with Rialto's imagined versions in the minds of moviegoers. These persistent and sustained cinematic versions of reality could then paradoxically appear more "real" to the German fans of the series than reality itself. Therefore, it is through the third order of simulacra that verisimilitude is achieved—not only because the epigones were clones of clones, but also because of the willingness of millions to suspend their disbelief.[84]

Viewing the series through Baudrillard's distinctive prism offers a clearer view of the cultural and market forces that shaped and formed these works. While the German *Krimis* reflected the aesthetics of the recent American film noir movement, those same American noirs were highly influenced (and sometimes created) by Weimar-era films and filmmakers, bringing the Teutonic connection full circle. However, as Bergfelder has argued, it was "precisely the series' strategy of blurring cultural distinctions and historical specificities that made these cultural forms internationally viable."[85]

Powering this international viability was a conceptually fresh approach toward the genre. As Steffen Hankte has rightly pointed out, after World War II Germany adopted

> a more postmodern concept of genre, a more flexible and self-conscious understanding of how a cinematic tradition positions itself toward a concept that both facilitates and enables creative expression. Genre would no longer mean an authoritative gesture of classificatory closure but rather a process of engaging with internal and external heterogeneity that helps to negotiate individual and collective identities. This reframing of the concept of genre strikes me as particularly relevant for the case of postwar Germany, a culture haunted by the historical trauma of the Third Reich.[86]

It is rational and convenient to interpolate the German *Krimi* into broader genres such as the crime film, the horror film, or the mystery film, particularly given Germany's history with these genres, but doing so ultimately does the *Krimi* a disservice. As realized and given life by Rialto, the Wallace *Krimis* are uniquely their own genus, complete with a recognizable system of signs and distinctive iconography. In essence, they create and occupy the *Krimiverse*.

FROM SAUERKRAUT TO SPAGHETTI: THE ITALIAN HANDOFF

Although early coproductions were with England and subsequently France, by the end of the 1960s and dawn of the 1970s, Rialto had found a new coproduction partnership with Italy. 1969's *A doppia facia* (*Das Gesicht im Dunkeln, Double Face*), helmed by veteran Italian director Riccardo Freda, marked their first collaboration.

Italy was an ideal coproduction partner. With Italian audiences, Philipsen and Wendlandt recognized a fertile market where the Wallace films still performed well; in the Italian film industry, they acknowledged a parallel increase in genre-driven commercial productions that followed Germany's postwar *Trümmerfilm* era and Italy's postwar Neorealist movement. Moreover, the Germans and Italians were kindred spirits in their history with, consumption of, and passion for, lurid crime narratives. Just as Germans relished their "*Goldmanns Taschen-Krimi*" (Goldmann's Pocket-Thrillers) with their bold red dustjackets, in like manner Italians cherished their *I Classici del Giallo Mondadori* (The Mondadori Yellow Classics). Rather than the bloody red covers of Germany's *Taschen-Krimis*, however, the *Mondadori* series featured bright yellow (*giallo* in Italian, also the color of fear) covers, hence the public's impulse to name them as such and, in the process, establish a literary and later cinematic genre.

Arnoldo Mondadori founded his eponymous publishing house in 1907 and launched the *Gialli* series in 1929.[87] The goal of the series was to highlight international writers who had established themselves in the areas of crime, detective, and murder mystery fiction. Authors such as Agatha Christie, Erle Stanley Gardner, Ross Macdonald, Ellery Queen, Cornell Woolrich, and Edgar Wallace saturated the series' nearly 1,500 titles.

Of the final four Rialto *Krimis*, three were Italian coproductions: *Das Gesicht im Dunkeln* (*A doppia facia, Double Face,* 1969), *Geheimnis der grünen Stecknadel* (*Cosa avete fatto a Solange? What Have You Done to Solange?* 1972), and *Das Rätsel des silbernen Halbmondes* (*Seven Blood-Stained Orchids, Sette orchidee macchiate di rosso,* 1972). By then, several hard truths emerged unvarnished. Rialto had rifled through their own graveyard to reanimate recently buried corpses—remaking their own films (some of which were international remakes from earlier eras). Facing imminent genre exhaustion and being stripped of the defining characteristics that caused their popularity in the first place, the series' partnership with Italy merely prolonged the inevitable. This, along with generational shifts in postwar culture, particularly in Europe and the United States, elicited the closing stages of the Rialto Wallace *Krimi* and, to a large degree, the once-thriving German "popular" film in general.

This period, however, also manifested significant transformation. The Oberhausen-inspired Young German Cinema movement (which began gradually nearly a decade earlier) was not so much ending as it was blossoming into the more fully formed, French New Wave-inspired, New German Cinema (NGC) era of the 1970s and 1980s. Similarly, the German *Krimi*, as defined by Rialto and CCC, did not fully disappear (indeed, it was soon reconstituted on German television) as much as it received a fresh coat of bloody red paint and innovation by both veteran and youthful Italian filmmakers. Rialto, through its coproduction partnership, effectively "handed off" the *Krimi* baton to the Italian film industry, who then ran with it for several decades in its new form, with a new cultural character, as the new Italian *giallo*.

Many of the genre conventions that would come to define the modern *giallo* (those of Dario Argento, for example) were established in the German *Krimis*—striking expressionistic composition and shadow play; stylish and prowling camerawork; deep pools of shadow; narrow, tree-lined streets or paths bathed with strong single-source lighting, employment of knives as a primary murder weapon; a revenge motive; black leather gloves; highly stylized title sequences; repressed sexual tension; numerous misdirects; red herrings; musical leitmotif (often in the form of transformed nursery rhymes); misleading editing; and strong, angular production design.

Read in this light, the mid-century German *Krimi* becomes a key progenitor of the modern horror era of the late twentieth and twenty-first centuries. The German *Krimi* drew upon long-standing thematic and aesthetic traditions from its own rich cinematic history and united them with other elements from a variety of international sources, including American film noir. The *Krimi* would consequently influence the contemporary Italian *giallo*, which in turn powered the modern American slasher genre, a bastard child that was subjected to its own evolutionary cycle—resulting in genre burn-out and parodic rebirth at the close of the century.

But for now, however, let us examine and analyze the unique and significant cinema society that is the German Edgar Wallace *Krimi*. Step right this way.

NOTES

1. *Neuordnung* refers broadly to the new political order Nazi Germany sought to impose upon its conquered nations.

2. Japan's unconditional surrender just a few months later on September 2, 1945, presented similar Allied occupation predicaments and challenges.

3. Heide Fehrenbach, *Cinema in Democratizing Germany: Reconstructing National Identity after Hitler* (Chapel Hill: University of North Carolina Press, 1995), 1.

4. Hans Wolenberg, *Fifty Years of German Cinema* (London: The Falcon Press, 1948).

5. Stephen Brockmann, *A Critical History of German Film*, 2nd edition (Melton, UK: Boydell & Brewer, Incorporated, 2020), 160.

6. Tim Bergfelder, *International Adventures: German Popular Cinema and European Co Productions in the 1960s* (New York: Berghahn Books, 2005), 20.

7. See Eric Rentschler, "The Place of Rubble in the Trümmerfilm," *New German Critique* no. 110 (Summer 2010): 9–30.

8. Fehrenbach, *Cinema in Democratizing Germany*, 51.

9. Ibid., 54.

10. Robert R. Shandley, *Rubble Films: German Cinema in the Shadow of the Third Reich* (Philadelphia: Temple University Press, 2001), 11.

11. Ibid., 12.

12. Gerd Gemünden, "In the Ruins of Berlin: A Foreign Affair," in *German Postwar Films: Studies in European Culture and History*, eds. W. Wilms and W. Rasch (London: Palgrave Macmillan, 2008).

13. Shandley, *Rubble Films*, 12.

14. Eric Rentschler, "The Place of Rubble in the 'Trümmerfilm'," *New German Critique* no. 110 (2010): 12. Accessed June 1, 2019. http://www.jstor.org/stable/40926580.

15. Shandley, *Rubble Films*, 13.

16. Fehrenbach, *Cinema in Democratizing Germany*, 68.
17. Wolfgang Schivelbusch, *In a Cold Crater: Cultural and Intellectual Life in Berlin, 1945–1948* (Berkeley: University of California Press, 1998), 137.
18. These eight studios consisted of the vertically integrated "Big Five": FOX, MGM, Paramount, RKO, and Warner Brothers and the major minors Columbia, United Artists, and Universal.
19. Ibid.
20. Schivelbusch, *In a Cold Crater*, 143.
21. Fehrenbach, *Cinema in Democratizing Germany*, 62.
22. Lyon, "Bertolt Brecht's Hollywood Years," 146–47.
23. Fehrenbach, *Cinema in Democratizing Germany*, 62.
24. Sebastian Heiduschke, *East German Cinema: DEFA and Film History* (London: Palgrave Macmillan, 2013), 45.
25. Thomas Elsaesser, *New German Cinema: A History* (New Brunswick, NJ: Rutgers University Press, 1989), 9.
26. This report proved to be false in its estimation. There were, in fact, three films in production at the time.
27. Fehrenbach, *Cinema in Democratizing Germany*, 69.
28. Ibid., 69.
29. Ibid., 71.
30. Ibid., 78.
31. Ibid., 79.
32. Ibid., 83.
33. John Sandford, ed., *Encyclopedia of Contemporary German Culture* (Milton Park, UK: Taylor & Francis, 2013).
34. David Sanjek, "Foreign Detection: The West German *Krimi* and the Italian *Giallo*," Spectator 14, no. 2 (1994).
35. Bergfelder, *International Adventures*, 172.
36. Eric Rentschler, *The Use and Abuse of Cinema: German Legacies from the Weimar Era to the Present* (New York: Columbia University Press, 2015).
37. Claudia Dillman and Olaf Möller, *Beloved and Rejected: Cinema in the Young Federal Republic of Germany from 1949 to 1963* (Frankfurt, Germany: Deutsches Filminstitut - DIF e.V., 2016), 29.
38. See Peter Ellenbruch, "Crime Pays! The West German Crime Thriller 1950–1963," in *Beloved and Rejected: Cinema in the Young Federal Republic of Germany from 1949 to 1963*, 243.
39. Bergfelder, *International Adventures*, 72.
40. Ibid., 73.
41. Ibid., 82.
42. Ibid.
43. Ibid., 83.
44. Ibid.
45. Ibid., 82.
46. Ibid., 49.
47. Peter Ellenbruch, *Beloved and Rejected*, 242.

48. Ibid., 244.
49. Ibid., 245.
50. Ibid., 248.
51. Ibid., 248.
52. Ibid., 246.
53. Ibid., 249.
54. Bergfelder, *International Adventures*, 149.
55. Ibid., 127.
56. Michael R. Pitts, *Famous Movie Detectives III* (Lanham, MD: Scarecrow Press, 2004), 34.
57. Neil Clark, *Stranger than Fiction: The Life of Edgar Wallace, the Man Who Created King Kong* (Gloucestershire, UK: The History Press, 2014), 5.
58. Ibid.
59. Tim Lucas, "Edgar Wallace and the Paternity of King Kong," *Video Watchdog* no. 126 (July/September 2006): 29.
60. See Kim Newman's "Your Pocket Guide to *Krimis* 1959–1967," *Video Watchdog* no. 134 (Sept. 2007): 20–48.
61. Wheeler Winston Dixon, "The Colonial Vision of Edgar Wallace," *Journal of Popular Culture* 32, 1 (1998).
62. Ibid., 133.
63. Bergfelder, *International Adventures*, 140.
64. Dixon, Wheeler Winston, *Colonial Vision*, 82.
65. Hantke, Steffen. "Postwar German Cinema and the Horror Film Thoughts on Historical Continuity and Genre Consolidation," in *Caligari's Heirs: The German Cinema of Fear after 1945*, 114.
66. See: *The Dark Side: The Magazine of the Macabre and the Fantastic* no. 191 (2018), for an enjoyable roundup of Rialto's "usual suspects."
67. Bergfelder, *International Adventures*, 149.
68. Ibid., 152.
69. Ibid., 151.
70. A necessary book for any initial inquiry into German cinema is Siegfried Kracauer's *From Caligari to Hitler: A Psychological History of the German Film* (New York: Noonday Press, 1959), 5–6.
71. Ibid., 15.
72. Phil Nobile Jr., "A Genre Between Genres: The Shadow World of German *Krimi* Films," *Birth. Movies. Death.*, October 11, 2015. https://birthmoviesdeath.com/2015/10/11/a-genre-between-genres-the-shadow-world-of-german-krimi-films (accessed May 20, 2019).
73. A great deal of cultural background surrounding the Wallace *Krimis* was shared with me by Deutsche Filmmuseum Archivists Christof Schoebel and Jens Kaufmann. Frankfurt am Mein, June 2018.
74. For myself and my brother, our version of "never-to-be-interrupted" televised films were the Abbott and Costello features leased to network affiliates in the 1970s.

75. See "HT Nuotio, Merry Ghosts, Hidden Memories: West German *Nachkriegskino* in Finland," in *Beloved and Rejected: Cinema in the Young Federal Republic of Germany from 1949 to 1963*, 293.

76. Ibid., 300.

77. *Die toten Augen von London* (*The Dead Eyes of London*, 1961) was released on a double bill in the US by Magna distributors with Riccardo Freda's *Lo spettro* (*The Ghost*, 1963) in 1965.

78. Kevin Heffernan, *Ghouls, Gimmicks, and Gold: Horror Films and the American Movie Business, 1953–1968* (Durham, NC: Duke University Press, 2004), 170.

79. "Supernatural Theater / Edgar Wallace Mystery '*Krimi*' Series." https://supernaturaltheater.blogspot.com/2013/04/edgar-wallace-mystery-krimi-series.html

80. Jean Baudrillard, *Simulacra and Simulation*, 1981.

81. A good place to start with the Frankfurt School of social theory and critical philosophy is with the foundational publication. Andrew Arato, Eike Gephardt, eds., *The Essential Frankfurt School Reader*, (London: Bloombury Academic Press, 1978).

82. See Frederic Jameson's *Postmodernism, or, The Cultural Logic of Late Capitalism* (Durham, NC: Duke University Press, 2013) among several other crucial texts.

83. This fate also befell England's own Hammer studios. Kim Newman succinctly states that "like Hammer, Rialto remade stories which had been done before [sometimes several times] in what was, at first, a new, rougher style—and when they ran out of such material, they started over again and remade their own remakes" in *Video Watchdog's* "Your Pocket Guide to the Rialto *Krimi* Series," 20–49.

84. Twenty-first century audiences may not necessarily read the series through the prism of verisimilitude but rather through multiple reception strategies, such as nostalgia or camp.

85. Bergfelder, *International Adventures*, 139.

86. Steffen Hantke, ed. *The German Cinema of Fear after 1945* (Lanham, MD: Rowman and Littlefield, 2006), ix.

87. At the time of this manuscript's completion, *I Classici del Giallo Mondadori* is still active and publishing titles.

Part II

THE FILMS

Chapter 2

Krime in Chiaroscuro
1959–1966

The newly established Federal Republic of Germany charted a more mainstream cinematic course to navigate during the 1950s and 1960s. One of the prominent producers of that period, Hans Abich, succinctly summarized the new strategy for German cinema by recognizing that "The public no longer wanted rubble or the problem of guilt at that time."[1] Consequently, a broad spectrum of popular and profitable commercial productions replaced the indigenous *Trümmerfilm*. These genres were dominated by *Heimatfilme* (*Heidi*, 1952; *Sissi*, 1955) which would number in the hundreds, Karl May *schnitzel* westerns (e.g., *Winnetou*, 1963, and *Old Shatterhand*, 1964), the many German spy films (e.g., the seven *Kommissar X* entries, 1965–1971), plentiful soft-core sex comedies (e.g., the *Frau Wirtin* series, 1968–1973), and the soft-core adult series, *Schulmädchen-Report* (*Schoolgirl Report*, *1970–1980*). However, it was the conflation of sex and violence offered by the beloved and time-honored crime genre, epitomized by the Edgar Wallace *Krimi* and personified by the return of Dr. Mabuse, that appeared to capture and captivate the widest demographic. Regardless of gender—teens, young adults, the middle-aged, and elderly—large segments were reading (and now watching) their beloved *Krimis*.

From 1959 to 1972, Rialto produced thirty-two *Krimis* in its Edgar Wallace series. Some were faithful adaptations of Wallace's work, some were loose, and others could best be described as "in name only." By the end of the cycle, however, the Rialto-Italian coproductions were truer in form, tone, and character to Italy's *Gialli* than to the German *Krimi*—with Wallace nowhere to be found (except on promotional materials).

This chapter focuses strictly on the black and white Rialto productions (twenty in total), which span the years 1959 to 1966. This black and white era can be further demarcated by the location of Rialto's bases of operation.

Beginning with 1960s *Die Bande des Schreckens*, Hamburg served as headquarters for both production and administrative duties until 1963 (although some films, beginning with 1962's *Das Rätsel der roten Orchidee*, were shot, at least in part, in Berlin). Thereafter, offices were relocated to Berlin which became the permanent center of operations. The utilization of CCC's various Berlin sound stages made this transition especially smooth.

Using Joachim Kramp's four phases as a general guideline, I trace the evolution of the Rialto *Krimi* from a rather tentative industry experiment to a cinematic titan and ultimately a cultural phenomenon. The mid-century Wallace boom begins in 1959 with the Danish/West German coproduction, *Der Frosch mit der Maske* (*Face of the Frog*). Given the mystery-revealing nature of these films, I have tried to provide spoiler-sensitive synopses whenever possible, but it is recommended to watch the films first. For the first few entries, I have provided slightly more muscular summaries to immerse the reader in what I have labeled the "*Krimiverse*." After this, however, they taper to basic abstracts which are intentionally brief. Unless otherwise noted, Constantin is the de facto distributor for all of the films discussed in the following chapters. Premiere dates and venues are provided where available.

Finally, a word about the box-office receipts of these films. The German term *Besucher* (visitors) is used to measure the *number of tickets sold* for theatrical releases. Therefore, each of the following entries cites the number of tickets sold rather than a specific dollar amount.[2]

DER FROSCH MIT DER MASKE / *FACE OF THE FROG* (1959)

In London, the notorious "Frog" syndicate (whose members bear tattoos of frogs on their forearms) enjoys causing general mayhem, terrorizing ports, committing various crimes—from larceny to murder—and has, most importantly, infiltrated Scotland Yard. The gang's leader, the eponymous "Frog," is a sadistic, cloaked, googly eyed, Mabuse-like criminal mastermind whose power, reach, and influence are growing. An opening fade-in pans across a large, lily pad-laden pond that broadcasts (appropriately enough) a cacophony of croaking frogs as we settle on the grounds of an aristocratic English estate. Inside the estate's chateau, a locked vault is blow-torched and looted by the "Frog" and his gang. The theft triggers an investigation and Chief Inspector Elk (Siegfried Lowitz) is summoned to the estate where the iconic "Frog" monogram was left on the vault as a calling card of sorts. This new investigation then joins a preexisting and clandestine Scotland Yard sting in which we quickly learn just how crafty, sly, and slippery a villain the "Frog" truly is. Joining the fray is the nephew of Sir Archibald (head of Scotland Yard and recurring character in the series), the young playboy and amateur detective Richard Gordon

(Joachim Fuchsberger, who becomes a backbone of the series), and his loyal valet (Eddi Arent, who would become the actor most closely associated with the Wallace *Krimis*). Gordon soon becomes interested in the young and attractive Ella Bennett (Eva Anthes), daughter of one of the prime suspects, John Bennett (Carl Lange). The "Frog," however, also has set his goggle-sights on Ella and pays her disturbing nocturnal visits. Meanwhile, Bennet suspiciously takes multiple trips to London while tightly clutching a strange, mysterious black suitcase. These plot elements, and quite a few more (including a reference to 1949's *The Third Man* arch-criminal Harry Lime), ultimately merge on a path that leads us to the Lolita Bar where the chanteuse Lolita (Eva

Figure 2.1 The Mid-century Wallace Thriller Launches with a Truly Unforgettable Villain in 1959's *Der Frosch mit der Maske* (*Face of the Frog*). *Source: Stifung Deutsche Kinematek Berlin.*

Pflug) underlines the film's English setting by singing "*Nachts im Nebel an der Themse.*" Hereafter, the film quickly ascends to a brutal and unexpected slaying and also to a satisfying and identity-revealing "unhooding" of the Frog.

Rialto chose a well-loved property with an established history to herald Wallace's postwar return to the big screen. *Der Frosch mit der Maske* was adapted from Edgar Wallace's novel *The Fellowship of the Frog* (1925) and was Goldmann's very first *Taschen-Krimi, bd.1* (*band* or volume 1) released in Germany in 1928. The novel was previously made in the United States (as a serial in 1928) and in 1937 in the United Kingdom, both titled *The Mark of the Frog*. *Der Frosch* was filmed with a principally German cast and crew in Copenhagen's Palladium studios. The film's budget was recorded at around 600,000 Deutsche marks which in 1959 converts to approximately 150,000 US dollars (bearing in mind that the economics of the Hollywood studio system differed significantly). *Der Frosch mit der Maske* was shot between April 24 and June 9, 1959, and premiered at the Stuttgart Universum on September 4, 1959. The film would sell a staggering 3.2 million tickets.

In what would become a series-defining convention (similar to, but predating, the Bond franchise's *Dr. No* by three years), *Der Frosch mit der Maske* opens with an elaborate pre-credit teaser that both sets the film's tone and also introduces its outrageous antagonist. In the years that followed, this would prove to be but one of several iconic Rialto signatures that would memorably brand the franchise in the public's perception.

From these opening minutes, the film (and the Rialto series overall) quickly distinguishes itself from many contemporaneous international efforts in similar genres. To place the Rialto *Krimis* on an international stage draws unavoidable comparisons to their competition. Dependent on an international distributor and lacking a large studio's backing, the Rialto *Krimis* are essentially equivalent to films made in America's B-movie production sector. Candidly, many late 1950s efforts from Allied Artists, AIP, or the independent circuit's exploiters (or, more broadly, titles that might be featured on MST3K) generally fail to match the intensity, technical proficiency, and artistic expression vividly on display in *Der Frosch* and its immediate successors.[3] This is in large part due to the pedigreed talent Rialto chose to hold prominent positions. From bit parts to major roles, from grip to the editor, Rialto cultivated a thoroughly professional roster of personnel, and these decisions paid off handsomely in their finished products.

Der Frosch not only boasts an impressive opening sequence, but an impressive and memorable opening to the series writ large. With perfectly exposed, eye-popping, and atmospheric low-key cinematography (marked with hard-edged chiaroscuro lighting), clever editing (particularly in scenic transitions) effective blocking-to-camera dynamics, an enthusiastic cast, and an imposing and memorable villain, (a sort of hybrid of Darth Vader and DC Comics' villain Black Manta), the fledging Rialto *Krimi* did not disappoint. The Frog's simple but menacing costume (a cost-effective one at that) conjures up images associated with Peter Lorre's insane Dr. Gogol in *Mad Love* (1935), directed by the legendary German cinematographer Karl Freund. And like Gogol, the Frog is shown to be completely insane. Indeed, his on-screen introduction, amid a blossom of white-hot sparks while he maniacally melts a safe with a blinding blowtorch, sets a powerful afterimage that sears itself into the viewer's memory and haunts the rest of the film. The picture's many assets, such as Ernst Kalinke's sparkling cinematography and Eva Pflug's delightfully manipulative Lolita, keep us glued to the screen. With its shadowy aesthetics and themes, *Der Frosch* nostalgically evokes the expressionistic Weimar cinema of the 1920s, which proved to be a touchstone for Rialto's first-phase rollout of their Wallace films. As a result of its excellent production values and pivotal timing (which resulted in outstanding box-office), *Der Frosch* set a high bar for the subsequent Rialto (and later CCC) films.

The ongoing congruity between Hammer and Rialto again proves a helpful comparison, as their respective flagship titles reveal. Hammer's *Dracula* (*Horror of Dracula*, 1958) and Rialto's *Der Frosch mit der Maske* share commonalities. Both Hammer's *Dracula* and Rialto's *Der Frosch* feature cloaked, menacing antagonists who infiltrate English communities, spread crime and violence, spill blood, and ultimately cause death for those who refuse to submit to their mesmerizing will. Both figures attack the well-established bourgeoisie, as well as state institutions such as the Holy Church and Scotland Yard. Both also pay nocturnal visits to the film's heroines and mark them as their own.

Perhaps, however, *Der Frosch*'s most significant accomplishment is its skillful combining of genuine thrills and frights with some smartly leavened occasional comedy. In this regard, the film (and the series) benefits from the dry wit and self-deprecating humor of comedian, Eddi Arent. In fact, it is this delicate mixture of thrills and tension-releasing laughs that makes the movie's climax such an unexpected jaw-dropper. As Kim Newman pinpoints, the film's "most shocking moment, announcing how far the series will go, has the Frog rough up singer Lolita, strategically tearing her blouse as if she were posing for a paperback cover, then tying her to a chair and bloodily riddling her with machine gun bullets." Tying a heroine to train tracks is a tired trope that still persists in today's modern cinema. But the cliché also carries the expectation that Dudley Do-Right will thwart Snidely Whiplash in time to untie Nell Fenwick for their eventual ride off into the sunset. Watching the train eviscerate and disembowel Nell is a violation of the agreement between the genre and its spectator. Granted, Lolita is not the film's heroine, but her sudden and brutal demise produces an unexpected rupture of the film's cinematic current. Newman's isolating of the BDSM imagery, yet again reinforcing the conflation of sex and death that would become commonplace in the Euro horror film, is letter-perfect and famously reoccurs the following year with Rialto's third *Krimi*, *Die Bande des Schreckens*. That offending scene, however, summoned the scissors of the FSK's censorship committee. In this regard, *Der Frosch* indeed goes further than most other contemporaneous efforts and therefore accurately forecasts a larger trend in the development of 1960s Euro horror.

Der Frosch mit der Maske established the *Krimi* cinematic blueprint for Rialto. While it is admittedly odd (at first) to see such cultural signifiers of Great Britain lensed through a Germanic filter (e.g., helmeted Scotland Yard bobbies conversing in German), the criminal story elements congealing around Wallace's story world (hypnotically constructed by Reinl) lets it pass the yard stick to measure the many *Krimis* that followed which was, for many, established with a quartet of bold early efforts: *Der Frosch mit der Maske* (1959), *Die Bande des Schreckens* (1960), *Der Grüne Bogenschütze* (1961), and *Die toten Augen von London* (1961). *Der Frosch*'s many virtues overcome its minor flaws: some unresolved subplots or loose-ends (typical of the genre and especially these films) and a rather ineffective score by Willy Mattes (but which finds welcome compensation with Eva Pflug's memorable performance of "*Nachts im Nebel an der Themse*," the perfect *Krimi* theme song). *Der Frosch*'s phenomenal box-office and reception paved the way for Rialto's immediate sequel.

DER ROTE KREIS / THE RED CIRCLE (1960)

Der Rote Kreis opens with morbid fanfare as murderer Henry Charles Lightman (actor's identity intentionally withheld) faces the guillotine. The execution, however, is bungled when a protruding nail—clumsily misfed through the wood by a drunk executioner—accidentally stops the guillotine mid-stroke, allowing Lightman to escape.

Eight years later in London, the "Red Circle" holds prominent citizens in the clutches of his blackmail ring. Those who refuse to pay inevitably pay with their lives instead. As for punctuation, the mysterious killer invariably leaves some clever form of a crimson Circle at the scene of his crime. We witness two attempts at blackmail. The first unfortunate target is Lady Doringham (Edith Mill), who the Circle insists replace her priceless necklace with a fake he has manufactured. He advises her that to disobey or go to the authorities would be unwise. Following this, we meet Mr. Beardmore (Alfred Schlageter), who has also received threatening letters from the Circle. Possessing little faith in Scotland Yard or its Chief Inspector Parr (Karl Georg Saebische), Beardmore prefers to solicit the talents of freelance private investigator Derrick Yale (Klausjürgen Wussow). Later, at Beardmore's estate, Yale and Parr meet Beardmore's nephew Jack (Thomas Alder) as well as his crush, Thalia Drummond (Renate Ewert). Drummond works as a secretary to the eccentric and reclusive Mr. Froyant (Fritz Rasp, who starred in the prior Wallace adaptation—1931's *Der Zinker*), and she appears to have a troubled past of her own. As with most Wallace thrillers, dead bodies accumulate quickly, subplots and misdirects abound, and a thrilling climax is hatched from this stew of tropes that will keep viewers glued and guessing.

Edgar Wallace's *The Crimson Circle* was first published in 1922 and later released by Goldmann in 1927 as *bd.35* in their *Taschen-Krimi* series. The novel had been previously adapted as a silent film in the United Kingdom (*The Crimson Circle*, 1922) and later remade as a German-British coproduction in 1927 as *Die Rote Kreis*, which was directed by Friedrich Zelnik. The latter is especially noteworthy for its transnational approach, having been released in both silent and sound-on-film versions. Rialto's new adaptation of *Der Rote Kreis* was shot in November and December of 1959 and premiered at the Stuttgart Universum on March 2, 1960; distribution was handled by Prisma.[4] *Rote Kreis* fell short of *Der Frosch*'s stellar box-office benchmark but did respectable business with 1.9 million visitors.

Figure 2.2 Branded by the Dreaded "Red Circle." *Klausjürgen Wussow and Renate Ewert in Die Rote Kreis (The Red Circle, 1960). Source: Stifung Deutsche Kinematek Berlin.*

When Preben Philipsen acquired the film rights from Edgar Wallace's daughter Penelope Wallace, he only secured the rights to two of her father's novels, *Der Frosch mit der Maske* and *Der Rote Kreis*, with the option, however, to buy more if they performed well. Consequently, *Rote Kreis* began production before the actual release of Rialto's inaugural *Krimi*. Rialto's plan was to release both films and then reassess the purchase option based upon the profit ledger. One crucial difference, however, was that *Rote Kreis* was to be released through Prisma Film (also acquired by Philipsen) and not Constantin. This was yet another metric Rialto designed to measure which distributor would be optimal for these films. As it turned out, regardless of the distributor, the films not only met but exceeded expectations.

Der Rote Kreis is an assured and solid follow up to *Der Frosch mit der Maske* possessing many of the same strengths as its predecessor while still forging and maintaining its own identity. As Kim Newman observes,

> *Der Rote Kreis* is very much a reprise of *Der Frosch mit der Maske*: again, an oddly masked crook (featureless hood, coat-collar turned up, optional hat) with a nickname ["the Red Circle"] and a secret identity is behind a series of crimes.[5]

Although shot in essentially the same tableau as its predecessor, *Rote Kreis* simply *feels* different. Foremost among the differences are newcomer Jürgen Roland's directorial approach as well as the casting of different actors in key roles. Harald Reinl, in comparison, enjoyed a measure of continuity across his first two *Krimis* (the series' inaugural *Der Frosch* and the follow up to this film, *Die Bande des Schreckens*), especially in the casting of Joachim Fuchsberger as the hero.

Several expertly crafted scenes warrant close consideration. The first occurs when a car begins tailing Lady Doringham. Unaware that the vehicle following her is actually her assigned metro police protection, she suddenly and unexpectedly takes flight. What follows is a carefully constructed and executed interplay of cuts, eyeline matches, and coverage that is on visual par with Alfred Hitchcock's famous driving sequence from 1960's *Psycho*. With both films in production essentially at the same time, ascribing inspiration or blatant theft to one or the other is not possible. The scenes prove similar though *Rote Kreis* features more coverage. For example, Roland intercuts close-ups of Doringhams's heel on the gas pedal and her hands turning the steering wheel intermixed with cutaways to fixed exterior pans that track the pursued and pursuing cars. Both scenes use and rely on the same three essential shots: a medium close-up of a woman driving, her point of view of the road in front of her, and her point of view in the rear-view mirror (reflecting the image of the chasing car). Of course, to heighten suspense, Hitchcock injects distress and paranoia in guilt-laden voice-overs, the protagonist's obvious frustration at the ineffective windshield wipers, and Bernard Herrmann's legendary minimalist (strings only) score. Conversely, Roland chooses to focus on irony. Roland shows a self-congratulatory Doringham, having evaded the chasing car, smiling as she reaches for a cigarette—only to have the viewer suddenly realize the killer is in the back seat. He raises up and strangles her.

This basic grammar of shooting car chase sequences was nothing particularly new; crime films from the 1930s and 1940s often employed a similar array of shots for such sequences. However, Hitchcock and Roland offer provocative variations on this oft-used trope.

There are many other striking sequences in the film: for example, the slow, steady, mounting tension that is felt as centripetal forces advance on Beardmore's estate; the spotlighted meeting between corrupt bank director Brabazon (Heinz Klevenow) and the Circle at a noisy railway station; the many exciting foot chases; and the film's thrilling climactic sequence. Each of these impressive set pieces add to the character of *Die Rote Kreis*.

Upon first viewing, *Rote Kreis* can give the impression that these described set pieces are merely threads of loosely related sequences hastily woven together. Keen viewers are likely to spot this occasionally annoying slack in narrative causality (something the series would eventually, but more seriously, fall victim to). Still, they are carefully crafted and entertaining sequences. Indeed, as early as this second film, a perplexing, yet highly addictive, *Krimi* "flavor" begins to infuse (and later define) the series. This *Krimi* "character" continues to inform the following productions, arguably reaching a state of early perfection with 1961's *Die toten Augen von London*.

Perhaps, in the end, the most striking detail about *Die Rote Kreis* is the tragic tale of its female lead, Renate Ewert (1935–1966). Born in Königsberg, the daughter of a grain merchant and Polish mother, the striking Ewert dreamed of becoming an actress and first entered the industry as a voice actor (a dubbing actor used to convert films to a target language for regional distribution or for ADR [automatic dialogue replacement]) in the mid-1950s. Shortly thereafter, she was cast as Barbara Bruks in the third film of the *08/15* trilogy *In der Heimat* (1955), and subsequently her celebrity blossomed. Unfortunately, Ewert's personal life, rather than her profession, became the target of tabloids sensationally covering her numerous affairs. Nevertheless, hints at a strong international career appeared in the early 1960s, but prescription pill addiction slowly took its toll on her career and personal life. She was found dead on December 10, 1966, in her Munich apartment by a friend and fellow German actress Susanne Cramer. It was speculated that she had died weeks earlier from a combination of pills and starvation. Unable to cope with his daughter's tragic death, her father, Paul Ewert, committed suicide a year later with an overdose of sleeping pills. Renate's mother, Helene Ewert, overwhelmed and suffering, also took her own life in 1969 with an overdose of pills.[6]

DIE BANDE DES SCHRECKENS / THE TERRIBLE PEOPLE (1960)

Die Bande des Schreckens opens with many of the same second unit establishing shots of London commissioned for *Der Frosch mit der Maske* and *Der Rote Kreis* (this became de facto, creating a sense of continuity in the first phase of releases) but then energetically pivots to a bank robbery gone awry. The notorious blackmailer, forger, and murderer Clay Shelton (Otto Collin) bungles the robbery and unfortunately shoots and kills a policeman during the scuffle. Later, as he is about to be hanged for murder, Shelton issues a death curse to everyone associated with his capture and execution. He raises his arm, tightly spreading his fingers, and vows that the *Galgenhand* ("gallows hand") will come for you. We learn later that Shelton ingested poison in the execution chamber, thereby robbing the hangman of his duty.

Time passes and Inspector Long's (Joachim Fuchsberger) retirement from his post at Scotland Yard happily nears. But when Shelton's threat appears to manifest and people begin to die—first the prosecutor, then the judge, and finally the hangman (ironically hung)—Long (lured back into duty now as "Chief Inspector") orders the exhumation of Shelton's body. At the graveyard, his unearthed casket contains no corpse, instead, only dozens of bricks and Shelton's death list—which features a sinister sketch of the threatening *Galgenhand*.

The investigation leads Long to the home of Mrs. Revelstoke (Elisabeth Flickenschildt) and her assistant, orphan Nora Sanders (Karin Dor in her first of five *Krimis* for Rialto). Unfortunately, Nora has made Shelton's list (she is indirectly related to his capture). The story then pivots between a kindling romance involving Long (my friends call me "Blacky") and Sanders, and Shelton's pursuit of bank president Mr. Monkford (Karl Georg Saebisch).[7] When Monkford's twin brother is mistaken for him and murdered on a train, Long and Monkford decide to strategically place Shelton's ghost in check by calling his bluff. Over a phone call, Monkford invites Shelton's "ghost" to attend the upcoming Golf Week in Little Hartsease where eventually all plots, red herrings, conflicts, and supernatural suspicions resolve.

Edgar Wallace's *The Terrible People* (1926) was previously adapted in America in 1928 as a ten-episode serial (now lost) bearing the same name. It was released in Germany as Goldmann's *Taschen-Krimi bd. 11*. Rialto's modernized version began production on June 18 and wrapped on July 23, 1960. Harald Reinl returned to the director's chair, and in doing so, the Wallace *Krimi* was gripped by Rialto's own *Galgenhand*, one of great success with 3.2 million tickets sold, when it premiered at the Europa-Palast in Frankfurt am Main on August 25, 1960. Constantin resumed distribution duties.

With *Bande Schreckens*, it's resolutely clear that Rialto's *Krimis* have gathered not only momentum but their own cadence and rhythm as well; they are clearly defining themselves. This is especially significant since there is no single corollary from which the Rialto *Krimis* derived their tone, mood, and aesthetic, but rather many. The supportive columns that hold up the *Krimiverse* are built from thriller film, mystery film, horror film, crime film, and film noir. Consequently, the popularity of the series was no mere fluke. On the contrary, in the Wallace *Krimi*, Rialto had achieved genuine success with their virtuoso creation of something simultaneously familiar and unique.

Figure 2.3 The Striking Artwork for *Die Bande des Schreckens* (*The Terrible People*, 1960) Is Uncannily Reminiscent of World War II Propaganda Posters. A Disembodied *Galgenhand* (Gallows Hand) Looms Ominously over London, Holding the City in Its Vice-like Grip. *Source: Photo courtesy of Ronald V. Borst/Hollywood Movie Posters.*

Nowhere is this better illustrated than in the now pro-forma pre-credit teaser established with *Der Frosch mit der Maske*. *Bande Schreckens*, however, raises the stakes with a gripping scene that not only powers the plot's raison d'être but also produces the picture's most provocative moment. In his cell, Shelton faces those responsible for his capture, sentencing, and looming death; in a monologue, he prophesizes each of their impending deaths. This shot in particular, low angle and low key, spotlights a deranged man raising his arm and extending his fingers in a vice-like death clutch, vowing vengeance. The image of a madman raising his arm and making implausible pledges to those in power resonates deeply and provides a current of dread to the many tense moments that unfold throughout *Bande Schreckens*. Moreover, this ominous image of a looming, black "death hand" conjures up suggestions and overtones in both F.W. Murnau's *Nosferatu* (1922) and Fritz Lang's *M* (1931).

The image of the disembodied *Galgenhand* looming ominously over London (unnervingly reminiscent of World War II propaganda posters) was effectively used in the marketing campaign for the film. Moreover, like a deadly spice accentuating each murderous meal, Shelton suddenly apparates with his "gallows hand" raised high before each killing—an act that physically approximates the Nazi "*sieg heil*" salute. Consciously or not, Reinl draws parallels between the criminals in this story world and the Nazis of the previous generation.

Atmospheric touches adorn *Bande Schreckens*. Shot in Hamburg with a keen eye for locations (which can be said of all the Hamburg-based *Krimis*), the film impressively showcases its sets and leverages its exterior locations, often producing associations with Germany's expressionist past as well as Universal's Gothic library. Several scenes visually echo with reverberations from Universal's *Dracula* (1931), *Frankenstein* (1931), *The Old Dark House* (1935), *Creature from the Black Lagoon* (1954), and the Basil Rathbone Sherlock Holmes franchise. Of course, those films themselves were the result of the collective efforts of a mass influx of European immigrant talent from, in particular, Germany. A few of these locations merit discussion.

The Landstone Avenue exterior scene, the site of the prosecutor's automobile accident, is expertly shot, composed, and choreographed for the camera. Over a cross-dissolve, a blowtorch brightly flares in the foreground while the exposed underbelly of an upended car fills the background. The camera pans and tilts down revealing the dead prosecutor who has half-spilled out of his car, his face bloodied. The camera pans further right and simultaneously pulls back to reveal photographer Anthony Edwards (Eddi Arent) setting up his tripod to photograph the scene. The flash ignites and (in a comedic device that becomes a running gag) Edwards passes out, unable to withstand the images of violence he has been assigned to document. Edwards, a former animal photographer, much prefers to "snap nice happy doggies or sweet little bunnies." Harsh, low-angle shafts of light jut upward through dense trees that frame the road. At that moment, framed between those ominously lit trees, Shelton suddenly appears with his *Galgenhand* raised high and then just as quickly vanishes. The only witness is, naturally, Edwards (who has already photographed the dead Shelton in London), a less than credible witness in Long's eyes. Aesthetically, the scene evokes early film noir location shooting with its strong source lighting and fluid and intricate camera movements that not only generate a potent atmosphere but reduce set-ups and thereby save time and money. This scene is essentially a microcosm of the movie itself: highly stylized and morbid, but with an amusing touch.

Outdoing that location for sheer atmosphere, the exhumation of Shelton's body becomes Gothic splendor on a shoestring budget. Creepily framed through the cemetery's gates, two grave-diggers shovel and carelessly toss dirt onto a growing pile. Events then play out similar to the previous roadside murder as Edwards woozily photographs the exhumation. Low-angle shots from the perspective of the casket eerily frame Long and other Scotland Yard officers. A quick cut to a close-up of the sweaty gravedigger's face and the hoisting of Shelton's casket from the grave recall iconic grave-robbing scenes from *Frankenstein* (1931) and *The Body Snatcher* (1945). The coffin is opened only to reveal dozens of bricks and, in what turns out to be an accurate prediction on Shelton's part, a freshly unearthed list of his intended victims. Although the scene appears to be shot in a makeshift cemetery with a fake stone wall and possibly plywood headstones (a step up from Ed Wood's cardboard), it hardly matters. Parallel scenes shot in similar films are often criticized for their lack of production design, staid blocking, unimaginative camerawork, uneven performances, and general incompetency. Reinl's exhumation scene clocks in at under two minutes yet manages to completely (and nostalgically) captivate the viewer. Reinl's cinematic approach and technique are thoroughly professional yet inventive and energetic, exactly the traits Constantin valued for their growing distribution catalog.

With the Elbe doubling for the Thames, the many river sequences are a welcome change of venue from the set work at Bendestorf studios or the city locations in Hamburg. For me, the scenes joyfully recall sequences from *Creature from the Black Lagoon* (1954), despite the absence of the famous aquatic missing link of the film's title. Like that film, *Die Bande* has several long sequences that rifle up and down riverbanks. One, in particular, stands out (especially, as it turned out, to the FSK). It occurs during Nora's first kidnapping (she is abducted twice). After drinking drugged tea given to her by a phony Metropolitan bobby, Nora is blindfolded, gagged, and hijacked by rowboat to a seldom-used Shelton hideout (a small boathouse) along the river. Bound and lashed to a chair (referencing Eva Pflug's demise from *Der Frosh*, but also foreshadowing an element from this film's climax), she suffers a brutal interrogation by Mr. Crayley (Dieter Eppler), who threatens her eyes with a long, pointed blade. In a rare moment of empathy, however,

Crayley ultimately uses the knife to cut her bonds and free her. This scene was shortened by the FSK to eliminate the more sadistic elements, but it has since been restored.

With a swift pace, high body count, and myriad misdirections, *Die Bande des Schreckens*, Rialto's third entry in the Wallace series, feels bigger and more finely tuned without ever losing that cottage industry atmosphere. The film boasts a stunning debut by Karin Dor, who at that time was married to the film's director, Harald Reinl (until their divorce in 1968), while veteran German actress Elisabeth Flickenschildt adds elegance and undeniable class to the ensemble. The comedy is light and sporadic but appears just at the right moments to add welcome relief. Film historian Carlos Aguilar suggests Wallace's "novels contained excellent cinematic potential simply because they balanced the sinister with the fun."[8] Indeed, the reoccurring motif of Arent's syncope-suffering crime-scene photographer provides genuine laughs (and one clever misdirect). A quieter and deliciously wry moment sees Inspector Long's post-promotion penciling in of the prefix "Chef" (Chief) to his name on Shelton's list. These moments of levity not only endear to the viewer but also signal the tongue-in-cheek aspects of the series (which would grow over time) and gesture toward the texts becoming more self-aware, more postmodern (as in the next film in the series). Like *Der Frosch mit der Maske* and *Die Rote Kreis*, *Die Bande des Schreckens* struggles to find a composer to appropriately underscore and punctuate the film's musical needs. Perhaps the film's biggest failing is simply that, as Kim Newman candidly points out, "All the English people in *Die Bande des Schreckens* drink tea without milk."

DER GRÜNE BOGENSCHÜTZE / THE GREEN ARCHER (1961)

While American millionaire Abel Bellamy (Gert Fröbe) travels abroad, his personal secretary Julius Savini (Harry Wüstenhagen) illegally organizes tours of Bellamy's legendary Garre Castle. On this tour, however, an American is shot with a green arrow supposedly fired by the "Green Archer," a spirit of English legend said to haunt the estate. Meanwhile, across the castle's property line, a neighboring estate is bought by Mr. Howett (Hans Epskamp) and his goddaughter Valerie (Karin Dor). Their intent is to search the castle for missing clues about the disappearance of Valerie's mother (who indeed is being held captive there). Enter Inspector (and potential love interest) Featherstone of Scotland Yard (Klausjürgen Wussow) and police-beat journalist (and comic relief) Spike Holland (Eddi Arent), and this Rialto stew bubbles with essential *Krimi* ingredients.

Edgar Wallace's *The Green Archer* was published in 1923 and was first adapted for the screen in 1925 as a serial for Britain's Pathé Exchange. Its second adaptation hit theaters in 1940 as a Columbia fifteen-chapters serial. Goldmann released the novel in Germany as *Taschen-Krimi bd. 150*. Shot in Hamburg and Schleswig-Holstein from October to January 1961, *Der Grüne Bogenschütze* reached German cinemas on February 2, 1961.[9] Falling somewhere in the middle of the box-office spectrum of these early efforts, *Grüne Bogenschütze* managed a respectable 1.7 million tickets sold.

Rialto staggered the directorial duties of their first four productions between Harald Reinl and Jürgen Roland. Their combined cinematic vision branded the series from its inception and largely defined this first phase for Rialto. Reinl had entered the business in 1949 as an assistant to Leni Riefenstahl on her long-shelved *Tiefland*, eventually released in 1954. Reinl kept busy in the 1950s, averaging two or three *Heimatfilme* a year until he branched off into the action genre. After directing *Die Frosch mit der Maske* (1959), he became one of the more common adapters of the works of Karl May and Jerry Cotton, as well as a realizer of "Dr. Mabuse" for CCC.[10] Reinl was married to his frequent leading lady Karin Dor until their divorce in 1968. Tragically, in 1986, Reinl was murdered, fatally stabbed by his wife, actress Daniela Delis, in Tenerife, Spain.

After the success of Reinl's *Die Bande des Schreckens*, Jürgen Roland was brought back to direct Rialto's fourth entry in their now burgeoning series. Roland's background and history differed from that of his colleague Reinl. Roland had trained with and worked for the *Propagandakompanie* (*PK* or Propaganda Company) during the war. After the war, he briefly worked for Radio Hamburg before leaving for London in 1950 where he attended the BBC Television Academy. Returning to Germany, Roland worked for the Northwest German Radio in Hamburg where he established himself as a journalistic jack of all trades, covering news, sports, and film. In 1953, however, his career path veered into television with the creation of the influential series *Der Polizeibericht meldet* (*The Police Report Reports*, 1953–1958, 1961). This series passed the torch to Roland's *Stahlnetz* (literally translated: Steel net or "Dragnet") which was West Germany's answer to the US' Dragnet. Like the American series, *Stahlnetz* was based on actual cases and was enormously popular, often featuring many of the actors from the Wallace *Krimis* (Eddi Arent, Hellmut Lange, Karl Georg Saebische, etc.). *Stahlnetz* is also considered the vital progenitor of *Tatort* (1970–), Germany's longest running television crime-scene series.

Roland starts the *Der Grüne Bogenschutz* memorably. The novelty of its opening shot, which seemingly breaks the cinematic fourth wall, also shows us the director adopting a decidedly lighter tone that will reverberate throughout the movie. Rialto's Wallace films were developing, solidifying, and perfecting a formula and *Grüne Bogenschütze* sits simultaneously within

Figure 2.4 Karin Dor Strikes a Beguiling and Mysterious Pose in This Eerie German Lobby Card for *Der Grüne Bogenschütze* (*The Green Archer*, 1961). Source: *Stifung Deutsche Kinematek Berlin.*

and somewhat apart from this formula. Despite its convoluted narrative (which became more and more integral to this developing formula), *Grüne Bogenschütze* remains a significant entry because of its especially "cheeky" attitude and its willingness to take risks. The film is a clever mix of postmodern whimsy and British satirical humor (of the [pre] Monty Python variety) which still manages to embrace its Wallace roots and preserve its overall continuity with Rialto's previous films. The next entry in the series, *Die toten Augen von London* (1961), would differ significantly in tone and mood.

Roland's *Die Rote Kreis* adopted an almost *Third Man*-esque approach for the film's darker moments, a choice that stood in contrast to his lighter approach with *Grüne Bogenschütze*. To be fair, *Grüne Bogenschütze* has more than its share of "darker" moments, yet none of them provide any frightening impact or genuine surprise. The first two acts take ample time in setting up characters and numerous plot threads (a few of which lead to brick-walled dead ends). However, patience is rewarded with the film's concluding third act, which devolves into incongruous (with the series, not itself) moments of slapstick. Depending on your point of view, this slapstick might be a welcome and spicy addition to the recipe. It certainly compensates for the film's inability to satisfactorily reconcile its overly complicated plot and underexplored and seldom seen eponym.

The most striking sequence in the film offers a showcase for Karin Dor's graceful athleticism and resilience in the face of demanding cold and wet night shoots. This protracted sequence sees the plucky Valerie nimbly traverse a cruel obstacle course beginning when she negotiates a Czech hedgehog-like protective barrier, then skillfully gondola a boat across Garre Castle's moat, then maneuvers her way through a wicked, wet, and dense thicket, and finally enters the castle through a sub-floor—only to break a ceramic vase which in turn unleashes Bellamy and his dogs. Roland carefully documents each moment of Valerie's trek from one property to the other, intercutting Bellamy's slumber, the barking dogs (there are a lot of barking dogs in this film), Valerie's father (who curiously shadows her movements) cutaways to owls, and so on. With the dogs and Bellamy now alerted, Valerie reverses course and literally sprints away from the castle (in casual, yet chic evening pants, flats, and blouse no less). At the close of this long fast-paced sequence comes a suggestion that this was all nothing more than a dream. The audience and exhausted Valerie, however, know better.

Fröbe is, as usual, unforgettable as the lumbering hulk Abel Bellamy. As film critic Danny Peary writes of Fröbe, "He treats villainy like an art."[11] This is especially true in *Der Grüne* where Bellamy spits venom at everyone, belittles everyone, manhandles or assaults everyone, and gleefully takes a front-row seat to watch everyone drown. Yet, in the talented hands of Fröbe (who actually gets to deliciously deliver the phrase "We have other ways of making you talk"), he indeed charms us with his art.

The best time for a genre to experiment is, as one would expect, during its experimental phase. The film's postmodern touches are charming, but fortunately, they also work. As conceptually drawn and executed by Roland, they reside somewhere between Bob Hope and Bing Crosby's endearing fourth-wall fractures in their durable and entertaining *Road* series (1940–1962) and the postmodern, deconstructionist approaches of Bob Rafelson's and Bert Schneider's *The Monkees* (1966–1968). Perhaps the film's best moment involves the English custom of afternoon tea (and the question of milk is raised, yet again). Like its predecessors, *Der Grüne Bogenschutz* is beautifully shot; but as a Wallace thriller, and as defined by the series' first three films, it slightly underperforms. This shortfall is arguably offset by the film's welcome ingenuity, humor, and metatextuality. Of the several columns that supported the *Krimi* genre, the series' next entry focused its spotlight specifically back on the thriller pillar.

DIE TOTEN AUGEN VON LONDON / THE DEAD EYES OF LONDON (1961)

A string of wealthy, bespectacled, and elderly men are fished out of London's famous Thames river, puzzling Sir John (Franz Schafheitlin) of Scotland Yard. Inspector Larry Holt (Joachim Fuchsberger) sees a pattern forming in these "accidental" drownings. Not at all convinced that the deaths are unrelated, Holt suspects that the Dead Eyes of London (a criminal gang of the blind) has resurfaced. When a bit of water-logged Braille parchment turns up on the most recent victim, Holt, along with his partner Sunny Harvey (Eddi Arent), begin their investigations with the aid of Nora Ward (Karin Baal), Braille specialist (and soon Holt's romantic interest). Suspecting the notorious "Blind Jack" may be at the center of the murderous mystery, Holt ends up at Jack's last-known residence, the *Blindenheim* (home for the blind), run by Reverend Dearborn (Dieter Borsche). Into the mix steps, lawyer Stephan Judd (Wolfgang Lukschy), who represents the insurance company, was charged with paying off the accidental deaths of these elderly men. Unlike the bodies found floating in the Thames, a break in the case fails to surface. What links these deaths?

Edgar Wallace's *The Dark Eyes of London* was published in 1924 and later released by Goldmann as *Taschen-Krimi bd. 181* in Germany. It was previously made into a film in the United Kingdom as *Dark Eyes of London* (1939), starring Bela Lugosi, and was released in the United States through Monogram Pictures under the alternate title *The Human Monster*. Production began on *Die toten Augen von London* in Hamburg and the surrounding area on January 16 and wrapped on February 21, 1961. Interiors were shot at the Real-film Studios in Hamburg-Wandsbek. *Die toten Augen von London* premiered on March 28, 1961, at the Turmpalast in Frankfurt am Main. Prisma handled the West German theatrical distribution, but notably a US distribution occurred in 1965 when *toten Augen* was paired and released on a double-bill with Italy's *Lo spettro* (*The Ghost*, 1963) through small independent distributor Magna Pictures.

If there were any doubts as to the series' inclination to embrace traditional horror elements, particularly after the comedic tone of *Der Grüne Bogenschutz*, *Die toten Augen von London* surely put them to rest. From the film's very first shot, an iris-out (an optical choice that reaches back to the silent era) to a traditional Victorian streetlamp, horror tropes and conventions dominate the next ninety-five minutes. Of particular note are the credits, which are boldly presented in a blood-red font even though the film was shot in black and white. The film begins on a neglected London street, bathed in fog and illuminated by a strong, single-source light. The fog in *Die toten Augen* is both a vital narrative and key aesthetic character in itself, often verbally discussed in scenes and observed creeping up and down in narrow cobblestoned streets or outside windowpanes. Enveloped in this fog, an elderly man cautiously walks down a steep street, unaware that the white delivery truck that nearly clips him will be his hearse a few minutes later.

So begins the pre-credit sequence for *Die toten Augen von London*, a film that many *Krimi* devotees consider the best of the early black and white period while others insist it is the finest in the entire series. As *Diabolique Magazine* Associate Editor, Samm Deighan, agrees, *Die toten Augen* is "one of the most famous and beloved of the early Krimi [sic] for a reason." She adds,

> What [Dead Eyes of London] lacks in eroticism or exploitation, it makes up for with the macabre. There is a basement torture chamber with a variety of unpleasant tools and implements, death by drowning and elevator, as well as the cunning use of a blowtorch . . . how you can resist that?[12]

As it turns out, German audiences could not resist such dark attractions and made *Die toten Augen* the studio's most profitable *Krimi*, yet with 3.4 million tickets sold.

While the essential ingredients for Rialto's series came together in 1960's *Die Bande des Schreckens*, they achieved precise measure and perfect execution in *Die toten Augen*. Yet, despite the series' continual evolution and impressive progress, the films were seen as failures by latter-day armchair critics. It is my contention, however, that if selected highlights of the first several Rialto *Krimis* (perhaps up to the film currently being discussed) were edited together into a montage and screened for scholars, historians, or simply fans of the genre, I am confident that responses would run from "provocative, eye-catching, and atmospheric" to bold declarative statements such as "works of serious art" or the "lost films of a post-expressionist forgotten genius," which makes Wheeler Winston Dixon's wholesale write-off of this film as "shoddy" and possessing "rock bottom production values" all the more puzzling. On the contrary, *toten Augen* is not only professionally made but also, quite simply, gorgeous to look at. An evening of Dwain Esper's *Maniac* (1934), H.G. Lewis' *Blood Feast* (1963), or Andy Milligan's *The Ghastly Ones* (1968) would more appropriately inspire such descriptors as "shoddy" or "rock bottom production values."[13]

Toten Augen importantly heralds the addition of Director Alfred Vohrer and actor Klaus Kinski (both of whom would become *Krimi* staples) to the Rialto series. In Vohrer (who would become the de rigueur interpreter of Wallace, directing fourteen[!] *Krimis* for Rialto), the Wallace *Krimi* found the perfect enunciator. His direction of the camerawork is inspiring: fluid movements, velvety pans, dramatic close-ups, dynamic blocking-to-camera,

Figure 2.5 The Austrian Restaurant Owner, World Champion Professional Wrestler, and Cult Actor Ady Berber Terrorizes Karin Baal as "Blind Jack" in *Die toten Augen von London* (*Dead Eyes of London*, 1961). Source: Stifung Deutsche Kinematek Berlin.

and some unusual point-of-view shots. In Kinski, the *Krimi* found the perfect Swiss Army knife actor. A performer capable of fulfilling any number of dramatic needs, Kinski was nonetheless often utilized as a heavy, a foil, or a red herring, but his magnificent presence and piercing blue eyes (even in black and white) kept him ever-present in the viewer's mind. In Fuchsberger, the *Krimi* found a stalwart leading man who effectively struck the right balance of tough-guy exterior and romantic lead interior while maintaining a sporadically amusing rapport with his sidekick (usually Arent). *Die toten Augen* also marks an important step in Horst Wendlandt's career; he was promoted to full Rialto partner from his previous role as production manager. All of these elements coalesced to create a perfect synergy for *Die toten Augen* which explains its popularity with fans and durability in the genre. While promoting the film, Vohrer was asked about the incredible popularity these Wallace adaptations were currently experiencing, he responded that

> Wallace's popularity is easily explained; he simply wrote what we call "*guten Kintopp*" ("good movies")—a superb mixture of suspense, surprise, sex, humor,

and deception [without harming the reader!]. He satisfies a variety of different tastes and his novels contain pretty much everything. This is even more true for his movies as the lively diversity of his plots cry out for film adaptions.[14]

Eddi Arent is in full British bloom by *toten Augen*. What strikes me as ingenious about Arent's performances from film to film is that his characterizations of "Britishness" modulate. Arent is not engaging in authentic or precise attempts at British humor per se (which are culturally determined), but rather the *German perception* of British humor, exaggerated and cleverly amplified. In *Die toten Augen*, this is taken to new and hilarious heights. His bowler hat is used like Batman's utility belt, he knits sweaters and baby clothes, he dresses loudly in an overstated sense of "British fashion," he fumbles around women he is attracted to, and he is proper and meticulous to a fault (his cracking of a poached egg richly deserves the spotlight it receives in one scene). In short, Arent provides the much-needed tension-breaking *Die toten Augen* requires because of its newly established thresholds of violence. Moreover, the film deftly weaves other subtler forms of humor into its narrative. Amusing props placed in the *mise-en-scène* provide laughter: a skull cigarette dispenser that suddenly pops open to fan-out cigarettes, a black cat statue sitting atop a bar whose eyes light up when the "speakeasy" door is buzzed. These and other light touches balance the more gruesome aspects of the film.

Several deaths (and also near-deaths) in *Die toten Augen* are particularly brutal. In most of the on-screen murders, it is the implied action rather than the act itself that is so disconcerting. A prime example of this would be the murder of Blind Jack. As Jack brings his head to the opening that separates the truck's cab and bed, he begs for his life, but because he is blind, he cannot see the gun barrel inches from his face. The audience, however, certainly does and cringes all the more as the revolver is emptied into Jack's head. Ironically, Jack slides out of the delivery truck into a garbage dump, mirroring the manner in which he slid his own weighted victims down a laundry chute into the Thames.

An even more intense and multilayered scene sees Nora's aunt Ella (Ida Honor) abducted and placed in a small sublevel cell at a remote and rather peculiar structure located in an abandoned industrial setting. A small, rectangular jail-cell-type door set on the hallway floor opens to the cell below where Ella is held captive. In what can only be described as a most unusual method of murder, the villain (identity still unknown) lights a bit of fabric and tosses it down onto a pile of oily rags. The rags quickly ignite and thick smoke gathers. Ella screams for help and begins gasping for air. Fortunately for her, Holt arrives, breaks open the pad-locked cell door, and lowers a ladder down, saving aunt Ella.

This scene in particular summons associations that are hard to overlook—the setting, the fire, the asphyxiation, the impression of death dropping from above, the shots of rats scurrying, desperately trying to escape—the complex layering of these images prompts cognitive associations with the atrocities of World War II. Conceptually, death dropping from above signifies, on one level, the dropping of burning fabric into the cell which holds Ella. But if we go a bit deeper, we access other visual cues that trigger the concept of *death from above*. Asphyxiation killed thousands during the firebombing of Dresden and other German cities. In Dresden alone, it is estimated that the Allied forces (RAF and USAAF) dropped 4,000 tons of high explosive and incendiary bombs from above resulting in a devastating firestorm.[15] Several Nazi extermination camps, particularly Auschwitz, dropped Zyklon B canisters (a cyanide-based pesticide) into gas chambers, killing approximately one million by this method.[16]

In the hands of Vohrer, however, Ella's entrapment (in what would have been her crematorium) is thwarted and she is safely returned to her home. Her impending death hinges upon an intervention, and Vohrer eagerly provides one, stipulating an alternative climax over those written in recent history. In this sequence, heroism, selflessness, and a certain type of postwar wish-fulfillment are made manifest.

DAS GEHEIMNIS DER GELBEN NARZISSEN / *THE DEVIL'S DAFFODIL* (1961)

The unsolved murders of three young women weigh heavily on Scotland Yard. A bouquet of yellow daffodils is left on each victim, linking the homicides and suggesting the work of a serial killer. Chief Inspector Whiteside (Walter Gotell) oversees the investigation for Scotland Yard. Meanwhile, an international airline sends their agent, Jack Tarling (Joachim Fuchsberger), to partner alongside Whiteside to crack the case. Visiting Chinese detective Ling Chu (Christopher Lee) confirms Tarling's theory that the drug trade is responsible and joins forces with Scotland Yard. It appears that heroin is being smuggled in from Hong Kong to England in the stems of daffodils. The investigation leads the three detectives, Tarling, Whiteside, and Chu, to the popular nightspot, the Cosmos Club. There, the questioning of shady businessman Raymond Lyne (Albert Lieven) and his protégé Peter Keene (Klaus Kinski) only result in more murders.

This German-Anglo coproduction, a first for Rialto, also had the distinction of being the first cinematic adaptation of Wallace's 1920 novel *The Daffodil Mystery*. Goldmann released *The Daffodil Mystery* with the punchier title *Das Geheimnis der gelben Narzissen* (*The Secret of the Yellow Daffodil*) as

Taschen-Krimi bd. 67. Ákos Ráthonyi, a seasoned Hungarian-born director, was hired to helm both the German and English language versions. *Das Geheimnis der gelben Narzissen* was shot from April to May of 1961 at Shepperton Studios and around London. The German language version of *Gelben Narzissen* was released in cinemas on July 20, 1961, while the English language prints hit screens the following year on May 20, 1962. As it turned out, fortune favored the bold and both parties reaped the exceptional profit. In fact, the German language version far exceeded sales expectations with a series record-breaking 3.5 million visitors. Having been fully absorbed by Constantin in August of 1961, *Das Geheimnis der gelben Narzissen* was the last German film to be distributed by Prisma Film.

Continuing to confidently experiment with the series, Rialto entered new *Krimi* territory with *Das Geheimnis der gelben Narzissen*. As Tim Bergfelder explains,

> Unlike the majority of Rialto's Wallace productions, the film was shot in London with a predominantly British crew and it was written by a British screenwriter, Basil Dawson. As in the heyday of pan–European co-productions in the early sound period, the film was shot simultaneously in two language versions, tailored to their respective markets.[17]

Each version also swapped out important lead roles with recognizable stars from within their own markets (e.g., Fuchsberger, Kinski, and the female lead Sabine Sesselmann were replaced in the English version by William Lucas, Colin Jeavons, and Penelope Horner). The German film's first shot, a night exterior that highlights Big Ben, states "*Eine Omnia Pictures Ltd. London Produktion,*" which then dissolves to: "*In Co-Produktion mit Rialto Film-Preben Philipsen Hamburg,*" promising a new binational experience for *Krimi* fans. What follows, however, is the manifestation of one fictional world realized, shaped, and formed by two different nations, with two different cultures, two different languages, and different cinematic histories. *Gelben Narzissen* marks the first of what would total eleven coproductions for the series. This begs the question: did the Rialto franchise rise to meet this innovative opportunity to create new fans and strengthen its international sales potential? And the answer is, just like a typical *Krimi* plot, complicated. In terms of box-office, *Gelben Narzissen* exceeded expectations, even outperforming Rialto's previous film *Die toten Augen von London* (which is always the desired outcome), but critical reception was generally lukewarm and occasionally negative. Still, the film's box-office remained the ultimate mediator and another UK coproduction would follow three years later.

Gelben Narzissen benefits from the return of Joachim Fuchsberger and Klaus Kinski, but noticeably absent is Eddi Arent. By now, Arent's characters and his inimitable brand of humor had become a series-defining feature. His absence is felt in what was an already oddly shaped endeavor. *Der Frosh mit Der Maske* and *Die Bande des Schreckens* were, more or less, straight crime-thrillers with humorous asides. Alfred Vohrer's *Die toten Augen von London* amped up the horror quotient yet still provided delicious moments for Arent, while *Die Rote Kreis* and *Der Grüne Bogenschütze* (although both different) bear the recognizable signatures of director Jürgen Roland. In contrast, the German version of *Gelben Narzissen* doesn't fit comfortably into the young but growing *Krimi* canon. Typical of a coproduction, the German version is neither English nor German but is, more precisely, in a state of liminality. This was targeted as a common criticism of the film. German critics complained mainly about the film's lack of visual interest via production design, cinematography, and other aesthetic choices (which were given priority in the German approach), while British critics thought the plot was implausible and preposterous (which was given priority in the British approach). The resultant film was, perhaps inevitably, a mix of different sensibilities. Rialto's next British coproduction, however, *Das Verrätertor* (*The Traitor's Gate*, 1964), would push the series further over into the English column of the ledger.

Though the German perception of the film's visuals was largely negative, I feel *Gelben Narzissen*'s visual design proves refreshingly energetic. A sense of realism (not endemic to Rialto's house style) guides Ráthonyi's direction and cinematographer Desmond Dickinson's eye. The shots, shaky camera movements, character blocking, realistic staging, and especially the negotiation of actual London exteriors (which are a welcome addition after the continuous recycling of the original second unit photography from 1959) all mark *Gelben Narzissen* as absolutely unique to the first wave of Rialto *Krimis*. Some critics echoed this sentiment. For example, the *Stuggarter Zeitung* praised the camerawork and its emphasis on "cold objectivity."[18] Nowhere is this better expressed than with the murder of Katja (Dawn Beret) in Piccadilly Circus. Shot and choreographed during actual London street and foot traffic, her murder unfolds like a verité assassination.

Another unique murder occurs late in the third act. The scene reflects the expressionist and film noir bloodlines that flow through the *Krimis*. Anne's wheelchair-bound landlady, Mrs. Rider (Grace Denbeigh-Russell), is quite literally frightened to death by the film's off-screen villain. His menace is reflected in her terrified countenance as a knife blade slowly rises into the frame. This set-up is reminiscent of the unforgettable wheelchair murder in 1947's *Kiss of Death* (minus the psychotic cackling of murderer Tommy Udo [Richard Widmark]). In this case, however, it is actually Rider's frisson that ultimately causes her wheelchair to roll down several steps to her death.

Actors are supposed to know their lines, invest in their roles, and be collegial and professional (on and off set), among other exacting duties. To do this in one's native language can be challenging, but to do it in entirely

Figure 2.6 Expressionistic Shadow Play Was an Enduring Hallmark of Rialto's Black and White Period. *Das Geheimnis der gelben Narizzen* (*The Devil's Daffodil*, 1961). *Source: Stifung Deutsche Kinematek Berlin.*

another language is considerably more demanding. Christopher Lee's command of German is impressive (Lee was a well-known polyglot), and he gives a strong performance (twice, in fact, as he is in both language versions); but it's one largely defined by action. Ling Chu's dialogue is unflatteringly laced with Chinese aphorisms that may have some relevance to the discussion but not to any narrative or character arc, and are annoyingly overemphasized. Instead, notwithstanding Lee's commanding baritone, he decided to play the part visually; his imposing height and gestured mannerisms aided him in doing so. In what occurred a number of times throughout his career, Lee played Ling Chu in yellow face. While older generations are familiar with Caucasian actors portraying Asian characters (particularly Fu Manchu and Charlie Chan), unacquainted modern viewers will likely be uncomfortable.

While the German-made *Krimis* managed to sidestep any explicit discussion of World War II (which would narratively equate to a West German production speaking on behalf of a former adversary during a period of extended peace), Rialto's series still acknowledged the war, just not manifestly so. Encoded into the cinematography and mise en scene of such films as *Die Bande des Schreckens*, *Die toten Augen von London*, and *Die Tür mit den 7 Schlössern* the specter of war haunts the celluloid.

In contrast, *Gelben Narzissen* screenwriters Basil Dawson and Donald Taylor do not hesitate to discuss the war. We learn that Peter Keene's father was Lyne's squadron commander during World War II but was killed in action. Lyne took Peter (who had turned delinquent) under his guidance and financial support, but not with wholly pure intentions. Up until this point, the Rialto *Krimis* (perhaps weary of the messages from the *Trümmerfilm* era) avoided explicit references to the war. *Gelben Narzissen*, possibly because of its English environment, marks the first time World War II surfaces as a subject.

The score by newcomer Keith Papworth is an improvement over the previous efforts by Willy Mattes and Heinz Funk. Given more time, Funk might have developed memorable and binding motifs, but as it was, the excellent and prolific Martin Böttcher was hired for the next Rialto *Krimi*, *Der Fälscher von London*, and it was clear the series had found an ideal composer. For the first time since *Der Frosch mit der Maske*, a nightclub act is incorporated into the scenario. While not as captivating as Eva Pflug's spicy *"Nachts im Nebel an der Themse,"* Ingrid van Bergen's number *"Bei mir ist alles Natur!"* proves a most welcome (re)addition and provides a memorable moment by offering a modest striptease (in front of a metro bobby, no less). Although, in terms of titillation, van Bergen's act seems rather staid compared to Pflug's seductive nocturne. Regardless, the sequence was popular enough to commission another *Krimi* anthem—tantalizingly intoned by Elisabeth Flickenschildt—in the following year's *Das Gasthaus an der Themse*. All in all, considering the essential architecture of the series was fundamentally altered with *Das Geheimnis der gelben Narzissen*, it performs admirably combining the best of both German and English traditions.

DER FÄLSCHER VON LONDON / *THE FORGER OF LONDON* (1961)

Wealthy man about London Peter Clifton (Hellmut Lange) and his fiancée Jane Leith (Karin Dor) harbor misgivings, insecurities, and secrets from one another. Regardless, they marry and spend their honeymoon at Longford Manor. Complicating matters, Jane witnesses Peter operating a printing press hidden behind a bookshelf façade suggesting that he maybe the criminal of the film's title, the infamous counterfeiter of five-pound notes. Jane's old admirer, Basil Hale (Robert Graf of the German POW classic *The Great Escape* [1963]), surfaces at the castle and refuses to take no for an answer by continually pestering Jane and threatening Peter with secrets from his past. Tensions escalate until eventually the two come to blows in an impressive donnybrook. Unfortunately, Hale is later found dead, and Jane wipes away all traces of what she suspects is a murder committed by her husband. Enter Inspector Bourke (Siegfried Lowitz) who, for some reason, aids Jane in her efforts to protect her husband. Friends and family begin to gather at Longford

Manor in an effort to help the young couple. But everyone's motives are questionable, as indeed so are their psychological states of mind.

Edgar Wallace's *The Forger* was published in 1927 and made its cinema debut the following year in Great Britain with the silent film *The Forger* (1928). In Germany, Goldmann released the book as *Taschen-Krimi bd. 67*. Director Harald Reinl returned for his third Rialto *Krimi*, joined by his wife Karin Dor as the female lead. Production began on May 2 and concluded on June 6, 1961. *Der Fälscher von London* was shot in Hamburg, most notably, at Herdringen Castle (as Longford Manor) in Arnsberg. The film premiered on August 15, 1961, in the New Bavaria Theater in Aachen. *Der Fälscher* performed well with two million tickets sold.

For the seventh Rialto Wallace adaptation, production returned to Germany and began shooting in May of 1961. For the first time since 1959's *Der Frosch mit der Maske*, the series welcomed back Siegfried Lowitz in the role of Inspector Bourke (known as the "bomb" in Scotland Yard for his slow methodical collection of prosecutorial evidence until he suddenly strikes with an explosion—"boom!"). Also returning to the series was comedic icon Eddi Arent, whose absence in the previous *Das Geheimnis der gelben Narzissen* was conspicuous. With Lowitz fulfilling the Scotland Yard position, newcomer Hellmut Lange capably filled the romantic male lead role of Peter Clifton (Fuchsberger often fulfilled both requirements). Lang brings an "everyman" vulnerability to the leading man role that is missing from the prototypical, Bond-like Inspectors animated by Fuchsberger. The returns of Karin Dor (her third outing) and Siegfried Lowitz (his second) are audience pleasing not only for the talent and charisma they bring to the screen but because each has well-written characters to inhabit. Dor gives an excellent performance in a strong role (proactive, fearless, and loyal). Moreover, it is predominantly through her eyes that the film unfolds making her rather than Lang, the protagonist of the story. Siegfried Lowitz is paternal, authoritative, kind, and charming—a scene-stealer in every regard.

The film's other major creative addition was composer Martin Böttcher. Trained as a jazz guitarist, the young Böttcher eventually became an in-demand arranger for several popular film composers in Germany, including Michael Jary and Hans Martin Majewski. By this time, the progression to writing his own compositions for the film was only natural, and in 1955 Böttcher scored his first motion picture, *Der Hauptmann und sein Held* (*The Captain and His Hero*).

Along with German composer Peter Thomas (more on Thomas later), the *Krimis* had finally found their ideal house composers. Beginning with *Der Fälscher von London*, Böttcher aurally defined these early scores with an identifiable signature, something lacking in the first several pictures. Like the James Bond series, the *Krimi* now had a recognizable motif-driven style—not

Figure 2.7 Krimi Newcomer Hellmut Lange Brings Vulnerability, but also Intensity, to the Role of Peter Clifton in *Der Fälscher von London* (*The Forger of London*, 1961) with Walter Rilla and Karin Dor. Source: *Stifung Deutsche Kinematek Berlin.*

a theme song per se, but a tone, a vibe, a groove, and stylish hipness. I am not disparaging the previous scores, all of which were semi-effective in their own way, but with Böttcher at the musical helm, the difference was like night and day. The series would later commission Peter Thomas as the series' court composer with Böttcher occasionally submitting a score.

After's Böttcher's innovative theme ends, *Der Fälscher* gets off to a somewhat sluggish and expository start. Fortunately, relief comes via a clever credit sequence that features a magnifying glass continually hovering over a suspicious bank note. Once the newlyweds arrive at Longford Manner, however, we are in firm *Krimi* country. The series continually benefited from atmospheric locations. From opulent manors, castles, boarding schools, and chateaux, to rotting dungeons, fetid dockyards, and sleazy nightclubs, Rialto continually worked magic with their locations, choosing their settings with a scrutinous eye, and *Der Fälscher* is no exception. A large portion of the film takes place at Arnsberg's Herdringen Castle, an extraordinary Gothic revival structure that appropriately adds menace at every turn.

Der Fälscher is yet another prime example in the initial wave of Rialto *Krimis* that managed to stay consistent with the agreement it had made with its audience yet still introduces new material. The core characteristics are present, but there is some brave risk-taking, too. For instance, in *Der Fälscher*, tension is primarily supplied through psychological rather than physical means, which is a refreshing addition. Too much change, however, opens the door to overstatement, and this lamentably happens in *Der Fälscher*. For example, in one very amusing scene, Karin Dor's character Jane provides some metacommentary about the film's "multiple mental madness" plot device by rhetorically and frustratingly asking, "Who *isn't* mad now?" Then, to add the perfect button to the scene, she adds, "*it's all so confusing.*" All that is missing is a wink to the camera (which Arent would have no doubt supplied).

One particularly effective recurring motif is the Mabuse-like two-way mirror and intercom employed by The Forger. He puts it to good use in his lair for order-giving, strong-arming, false negotiations, and so on. It is a nice touch that allows for some clever edits between locations to keep the audience off guard and guessing The Forger's true identity.

In the end, the surprises prove predictable, but nonetheless disturbing. Later films such as Polanski's *Rosemary's Baby* (1968) or Wendkos' *The Mephisto Waltz* (1971) would similarly, but more seriously, meditate on issues of trust, madness, and safety—places that *Der Fälscher* successfully takes us. A satisfying slow burn to the film's revealing climax powers *Der Fälscher*. Though the death toll remains decidedly low for a Wallace thriller, Reinl gives us atmosphere, setting, character, and room to let that all breathe. An underrated early entry from Rialto, *Der Fälscher von London* is beautifully shot and perfectly confusing, and therein lies its charm.

DIE SELTSAME GRÄFIN / *THE STRANGE COUNTESS* (1961)

Margret Reedle (Brigitte Grothum), secretary to lawyer Rechtsanwalt Shaddle (Fritz Rasp), leaves her current employment with the practice to assume a new position as personal live-in secretary to the aristocratic Countess Moron (Lil Dagover). At the same time, a strange man, Bresset (Klaus Kinski), begins to harass Reedle; she receives bizarre phone calls, she is physically stalked, and the menacing man is suspiciously present when she is almost killed near some street construction. Enter (from seemingly nowhere) Mike Dorn (Joachim Fuchsberger) of Scotland Yard, who has, in fact, been hired on "special assignment" by Shaddle to protect Reedle—from the strange man, or the Countess, or both. Meanwhile, in a nearby prison, convicted murderer Mary Pinder is released after a twenty-year sentence. As a liaison to the parole board, the Countess has arranged for Mary to take a housekeeping position at the estate. Along with the Countess' hovering coterie of odd professional associates is her mollycoddled, eccentric, but sincere son, Selwyn (Eddi Arent). Unfortunately, the attempts at Margret's life continue. On her first night at (the regrettably named) Castle Moron, she nearly plunges to her death (a favorite fate in Wallace fiction) from a collapsing balcony. To complicate matters dramatically, Margaret finds out that poisoner Mary Pinder is actually her birth mother. As with *Der Fälscher von London*, questions of sanity take over the narrative in this Gothic Wallace thriller.

Edgar Wallace's *The Strange Countess* was first published in 1925. Goldmann released this Wallace thriller in Germany as *Taschen-Krimi bd. 49*. With no prior adaptations, Rialto was the first studio to bring the story to the silver screen. Completed between August 28 and September 29, 1961, *Seltsame Gräfin* marks the first Rialto *Krimi* to be shot in Berlin rather than the usual location of Hamburg. Over time, this became a cost-cutting method for Rialto, renting studio facilities from CCC's Spandau location (a suburb of Berlin) or *Ufa*'s facilities in Tempelhof. The other major location used was Castle Ahrensburg (last featured in *Der Grüne Bogenschütze*) as the Countess' home. The film premiered on November 8, 1961, in the Capitol Theatre in Trier. The film did strong business, surpassing its predecessor with an impressive 2.6 million tickets sold.

As a *Krimi*, *Seltsame Gräfin* sits askew from its contemporaries; as a standalone thriller, however, it is an effective, eerie, and, at times, disturbing Gothic thriller not dissimilar in tone and narrative structure to such films as *Jane Eyre* (1943) and *Uncle Silas* (1947). *Seltsame Gräfin* surprisingly begins *sans* a pre-credit sequence, which by then had become a de facto introduction to each entry in the series. This notable absence also sends a clear signal to the audience that what is about to unfold may not be a traditional Wallace *Krimi*, and indeed, it is not.

Seltsame Gräfin is, first and foremost, a clear and affectionate tribute to the cinema of Germany's Weimar era. The selection of novel, the choice of director, the eclectic cast, and the overall approach deliver an affectionate valentine to a recent and cherished German cinematic past. From the casting of major *Ufa* star Lil Dagover (*Das Cabinet des Dr. Caligari*, 1919) as the Countess and Fritz Rasp (*Metropolis*, 1927) as her solicitor, to the choice of veteran Austrian Hungarian director Josef von Báky (this was to be his last film and an appropriate coda to his career), *Seltsame Gräfin* luxuriates in its Weimar-esque touches. Many intentional echoes of the past penetrate this film, especially through the optical transitions (intercutting through panned wipes) and the numerous scenes of institutional madness vis-à-vis strait-jacketed asylum patients, and sinister syringes.

Indeed, it is in these unsettling scenes where the film successfully channels the insanity often found in expressionist work. Kinski is in especially good form in this regard, though his interpretation of a homicidal mental patient at times bears more than a slight resemblance to Dwight Frye's iconic portrayal of R.M. Renfield (a part Kinski would later play for Jess Franco) from Universal's *Dracula* (1931).[19] I found that several scenes in *Seltsame Gräfin* lingered in my mind for days. These scenes almost always revolved around the gaslighting of Margret. The audience cheers for Margret when she finally manages to escape the Countess' clutches (as if replying to the often audience-posed "why doesn't he or she *just leave*?" level of immersion/ scrutiny), but the happiness soon fades when she is found and brought to Dr. Tappatt's ominous asylum.

The Countess, Dr. Tappatt (played with sinister fussiness by Rudolf Fernau), and the madman Bresset, among others, have all conspired to slowly and steadily drive Margret insane. Von Báky's handling of the asylum and its horrid Victorian dungeon is skillfully executed and disturbingly real. Like Dagover, Fernau gives a highly mannered performance, and his sadistic doctor remains one of the most unsettling villains in the entire *Krimi* canon. Even Fuchsberger's heroic Dorn succumbs to Tappatt's syringe, which does, however, lead to one of Blacky's very best moments in the entire series—his capture is thwarted via a finely executed and perfectly staged Harry Houdini-esque escape.

Although he had been scoring for German television for several years, this was Peter Thomas' first score for a Rialto *Krimi*, and it is disappointing. While it is true that Thomas, along with Martin Böttcher, would come to define the *Krimi* sound, he struggles to find the right tone and approach in *Seltsame Gräfin*. Thomas alternates between music that is too heavy, melodramatic, or simply obtrusive for scenes that require a subtler approach. Conversely, he composes cues that are too light and whimsical for scenes that require dark tonal color. The score feels too episodic and lacks a memorable central theme. Overall, Thomas' scores, while never dull, are inconsistent in their ability to enhance the material.

Die Seltsame Gräfin is better than its reputation might suggest. There are very strong forces imposing their wills on this movie: legends from a golden era of artistic expression in Germany—when anything was possible—and *Ufa* was one of the great motion picture studios of the world.

DAS RÄTSEL DER ROTEN ORCHIDEE / SECRET OF THE RED ORCHID (1962)

Chicago infiltrates London as rival gangs engage in turf wars in 1962's *Das Rätsel der roten Orchidee*. Threats are dispatched in the form of letters demanding protection money to the upper crust of London's citizens. This extortion and blackmail racket, however, had recently turned deadly. When the elderly Elias Tanner (Fritz Rasp) receives the form letter, his secretary Lilian Ranger (Marisa Mell) informs the police. Goons posing as Scotland Yard protection arrive at Tanner's home and slaughter him in his study—directly in front of Miss Ranger and Tanner's butler, Parker (Eddi Arent).

Scotland Yard's Inspector Weston (Adrian Hoven) is assigned to the case with Chief Inspector Tetley (Wolfgang Büttner) overseeing the investigation. The Chicago connection prompts Scotland Yard to partner with American FBI agent Captain Allerman (Christopher Lee) in an advisory capacity. Some unlikely coincidences, such as the butler Parker's employment with each of the targeted patrons or the fact that they all had accounts at the same bank, bring additional intrigue to the plot.

Edgar Wallace's popular thriller *When the Gangs Came to London* was first published in 1932. Goldmann later released the book in Germany with the new title *Gangster in London* as *Taschen-Krimi bd. 178*. Rialto was the first studio to adapt the novel for the big screen, again under a new title, as *Das Rätsel der roten Orchidee*. Production began at Real-film Studios in Hamburg-Wandsbek on December 15 and wrapped on January 15, 1962. Additionally, this production saw second unit photography capture some fresh exterior shots in London. The film premiered in German cinemas on March 1, 1962. The movie underperformed financially, with attendance dipping to 1.5 million visitors.

A hotel situated on the stark, rain-soaked streets of Chicago provides the unusual setting for the pre-credit teaser in *Das Rätsel der roten Orchidee*. Audiences were then treated to a "that's the Chicago way" greeting as the film begins with a bang (literally) from machine-gun fire (plus a grenade tossed into the room for good measure) when one organized crime gang slaughters another rival syndicate as they unsuspectingly play poker. Segue to credits that roll over fluid establishing shots of our new location in London—suggesting this Chicago consortium (in this case, specializing in extortion and blackmail) will spread to England. Composer Peter Thomas provides a jazzy, travelogue-esque score over the title credits.

Of particular note in these credits, however, are the detailed descriptors given to Rialto regulars Eddi Arent as "*Todesbutler* Parker" (Death Butler Parker) and Klaus Kinski as "*der Schöne Steve*" (Beautiful Steve)—which is unusual. In the case of the former, the name is a running gag in which Arent's rich employers continually wind up dead. In the case of the latter, the moniker and performance from Kinski lean toward coded homosexuality.

Thus, from its very introduction, *Das Rätsel der roten Orchidee* sets itself apart as an atypical entry in the black and white *Krimi* era; what it ultimately lacks is the chilling atmosphere it compensates for in originality. It's an American gangster film with noir tendencies displaced to England and shot in Germany. A newcomer to the series, Austrian cinematographer Helmuth Ashley, helmed *roten Orchidee*, which helps explain the freshness of its approach and the complexity of several prominent set pieces (the railroad-construction site sequence, the train milieu, various night-street scenes), in addition to the film's overall visual sophistication. Apparently, Ashley was not, however, well received by a significant portion of the cast, which led to zero additional work from the studio and being excluded from the Christmas party. Rialto was, after all, a close-knit, small-scale studio dependent on collegial working relationships.

British actor Christopher Lee makes his second appearance in a Rialto Wallace outing—this time as tough American FBI agent Captain Allerman. Always an aurally commanding and physically imposing actor, Lee is the most dynamic character in the film. Fans of the actor are encouraged to watch the German language version of the film in which Lee again delivers his lines in fluent German.

Sharing far less screen time, but equally significant, is German actress Christiane Nielsen's portrayal of mafia moll Cora Minelli. Nielsen's scene-stealing mannerisms and her critical role in the film's plot make her one of the series' more memorable characters despite her minimal screen time and sole appearance.

Figure 2.8 England's Christopher Lee Delivered His Lines in Fluent German While Portraying an American FBI Agent in His Second *Krimi* for Rialto, *Das Rätsel der roten Orchidee* (**Secret of the Red Orchid,** 1962). *Source: Stifung Deutsche Kinematek Berlin.*

Another memorable addition to the cast was Austrian actress Marisa Mell. Mell's performance as Lilian Ranger adds distinction to the movie's notable cast. Although very early in her career, and inhabiting a typically underwritten female supporting role common to the genre at that time, her striking presence and hypnotic gaze command the viewer's full attention. Mell would complete her *Krimi* cycle by circling back to accept another role in 1972's *Das Rätsel des silbernen Halbmonds* (*Sette orchidee macchiate di rosso, Seven Blood-Stained Orchids*), Rialto's last *Krimi* production.

Peter Thomas' score offers an assortment of melodies—some of which are more effective than others. One highlight, in particular, is the leitmotif Thomas establishes with the delivery of the extortion letters. Thomas heralds the arrival of the ominous missives with a harsh brass motif that repeats in staccato triplets (presumably with an Echoplex). Doom-laden and heavy, they are an effective display of Thomas' creativity. Less effective are his travelogue-esque cues that accompany the main titles and other sequences, which seem far too bright and cheery for what essentially amounts to a gangster film. One could argue, however, that the music hints at the comedic elements present in the scenario. In either case, the score is typical of Thomas's asymmetrical approach to these early *Krimis*.

There are several "nice touches" in *roten Orchidee*, particularly with the orchestration of murders. For example, the barren train-track-trap sequence is starkly but thrillingly shot and choreographed—with negative space playing a dominant role. A coda is provided by a sentry machine-gun that automatically opens fire on the construction site below. Another memorable sequence occurs when the well-off Mrs. Moore (Sigrid von Richthofen) refuses to pay protection money. Her death pays homage to a classic murder scenario in which an oversized mirror is used to give the false impression to unsuspecting motorists that a head-on collision is imminent. This was perhaps most memorably and ghoulishly utilized in Roland West's *The Monster* (1925).

Perhaps *roten Orchidee*'s greatest asset is its straightforward story line, one that doesn't require mental calisthenics. To be sure, as a Wallace motion picture, the story has its customary flaws, but the plot remains mercifully easy to grapple with. Several rich men and women choose to dismiss extortion threats and are summarily murdered. A token identity mystery (one that is not difficult to crack, particularly to those who pay close attention to the pre-credits teaser) is thrown in, and the rest (in Wallace fashion) writes itself.

Das Rätsel der roten Orchidee's strengths lie in its unconventional approach to the series, its outside of the box casting, and its technical values. While an underperformer theatrically, it is nonetheless an unusual and therefore noteworthy production in the Rialto Wallace canon.

DIE TÜR MIT DEN 7 SCHLÖSSERN / LA PORTE AUX SEPT SERRURES / THE DOOR WITH SEVEN LOCKS (1962)

Petty thief and locksmith Lew Pheeny (Klaus Kinski) is found dead after confessing to Scotland Yard Inspector Richard "Dick" Martin (Heinze Drache) about a job he was to have completed. The job in question involved opening seven locked doors with seven unique keys. Meanwhile, at London's Victoria Station, a poisoned priest lay dead. A seemingly random doctor (Pinkas Braun) emerges from the crowd, rummages through the priest's attire, while pretending to examine the stricken man, and produces a key. Fortunately, an intervening bobby seizes the key as potential crime-scene evidence before the doctor can abscond with it. Head of Scotland Yard Sir John (Siegfried Schürenberg) is baffled by the two bizarre murders and assigns top man Inspector Martin and his assistant Holms (Eddi Arent) to the case.

Acting off of the first and only clue (a quick sketch of a family crest provided by Pheeny before his death), Martin enlists the help of the film's heroine, librarian Sybil Lansdown (Sabine Sesselmann). Lansdown immediately identifies the crest as belonging to the Selford family, as she herself is distantly related to the Selfords. It would appear that the door with seven locks is likely housed somewhere in Selford Manor. Into the fray comes the diabolical Dr. Staletti (last seen hovering over the poisoned priest), Bertram and Emely Cody (former member of Lord Pierce Selford's household staff), and chauffeur Tommy Cawler (well-known by Inspector Martin as a former thief).

As for the rest of the story, as Kim Newman observes, by the time we learn of Staletti's bizarre human experiments in his Dr. Frankenstein-like laboratory, "any pretense at proper plotting has been dropped in favor of whatever sensationalist fun can be had, with a constant stream of surprises, gimmicks and gags like a gun concealed inside a false hand." Newman pinpoints the narrative trend Rialto had by now perfected. Scrutiny of story, plot, logic, and narrative causality bear little gratification with these elements frequently jettisoned in favor of excitement and sensationalism.

Edgar Wallace's *The Door with Seven Locks* was published in 1926 and later adapted for the screen by Pathé in Great Britain as *Chamber of Horrors* (1940). Dripping with atmosphere and a palpable sense of menace, *Chamber of Horrors* proved to be a strong vehicle for its leads Leslie Banks and German actress Lili Palmer. One of Wallace's more popular novels, *The Door with Seven Locks*, was released by Goldmann in their pocket crime series as *Taschen-Krimi bd. 21*. Filmed in West Berlin and Hamburg from February 26 to March 30, 1962, Rialto's adaptation premiered on June 19, 1962, in the Europa-Palast in Frankfurt am Main. The film was one of Rialto's top performers, with over 3.2 million tickets sold.

Continuing to invest in their profitable coproduction sector, Rialto decided to initiate another bilateral production. This time, however, rather than another Anglo-German project, Rialto chose to partner with the French production company Les Films Jacques Willemetz—with Constantin handling distribution. The result is a confusing but enjoyable and important early entry in the Wallace cycle.

Like *Die Seltsame Gräfin*, *Die Tür mit den 7 Schlössern* begins without the usual pre-credit sequence. Instead, and for the first time, machine-gun fire rings out and seven blood-red bullet holes puncture the screen to gruesomely blossom (via an animation) into seven blood-red keyholes. Over this, we hear glass shattering and the rough, creaky sound of a crypt door opening. Post-credits, the action begins in typical *Krimi* fashion with the murder of a priest in London's renowned Victoria Station. The Hamburg-Altona Bahnhof convincingly doubles for London's famous landmark. The usual collection of recycled London stock shots accompanies the film's set-up, and, as evidenced through the use of the Altona railway station, Rialto was still reliant on their Hamburg studio (and Hamburg exteriors) for its productions. The new production arrangements in Berlin, however, were proving successful. This time, the Berlin-Spandau studio used for *Die Seltsame Gräfin* was not utilized, instead, *7 Schlössern* was filmed in and around the *Ufa* Film Studios in Berlin-Tempelhof and on the extraordinary Berliner Pfaueninsel (Peacock Island) and its Palmenhaus (Palace) on the *Havel* River in Berlin.

7 Schlössern benefits from a uniformly gifted cast (although Kinski's role amounts to a cameo), particularly with the addition of German cinema stalwart Siegfried Schürenberg as Sir John of Scotland Yard, intense Swiss actor Pinkas Braun as the shrewd but cool Dr. Staletti, and series newcomer Heinz Drache as Inspector Richard "Dick" Martin (the lead detective role was often filled by Fuchsberger). Each actor would go on to star in numerous Wallace *Krimis* thereby nurturing and cultivating the *troupe* environment associated with the series. Also returning was Ady Berber as the brute Giacco (last seen as Blind Jack in Vohrer's debut *Krimi Die toten Augen von London*). This time around, however, Berber's physical size and mental deficiencies are apparently the results of bizarre scientific experimentation orchestrated by Staletti. Eddi Arent reprises his ongoing function as a comedic sidekick. His character in *7 Schlössern*, *Kriminalassistent* Holms, does not share his namesake's (minus the "e") ability for the logical deduction, but that does not stop him from constantly positing absurd theories and stating the obvious. And yet Arent manages to somehow keep his delivery and the material fresh. Moreover, his rapport with new co-star Drache is easy, natural, and full of chemistry.

Perhaps the most radiant presence in the film is veteran German actress Gisela Uhlen. In her first of three films for the series, Uhlen portrays Emely

Cody as the perfect icy manipulator. She is stern, controlling, manipulative, secretive, dangerous, seductive, alluring, and cruel. Moreover, all of these character traits are given life by one of German cinema's most distinctive speaking voices (honed to perfection by over one hundred stage roles). Lightly delicate or unexpectedly harsh, Uhlen's intonations are commanding, persuasive, and mesmerizing. Unsurprising given that the Leipzig-born Uhlen (*née* Schreck) came from an exceptionally talented family. Gisela Friedlinde Schreck was the daughter of an opera singer and the niece of legendary silent film star Max Schreck, known for his masterful and terrifying portrayal of the vampire Count Orlok in *Nosferatu—Eine Symphonie des Grauens* (*Nosferatu—A Symphony of Horror*, 1922). *7 Schlössern* delivers its best set pieces when the Codys are featured—as blackmailers, kidnappers, and torturers they really do steal the show.

While the previous year's German-Anglo coproduction *Das Geheimnis der Gelben Narzissen* (1961) exposed the cultural fingerprints of its German and British constitution, *Die Tür mit den 7 Schlössern*, conversely, completely synchronizes with the Rialto *Krimi* tradition. This is primarily due to Vohrer's growing collection of stylistic signatures: the prowling camerawork,

Figure 2.9 Ady Berber Reprises His Role as a Brute Henchman in *Die Tür mit den 7 Schlössern* (*The Door with Seven Locks*, 1962). This time, however, his physical size and appearance are the unfortunate result of scientific experimentation "gone wrong."
Source: Stifung Deutsche Kinematek Berlin.

subjective point-of-view shots, attention to detail, and subtle directorial touches. For example, the L trains that roar by Inspector Martin's apartment window are not only a great atmospheric touch, but they are also accurately constructed and convincing. On that same apartment set, Vohrer adds additional weight and dimension to what could have otherwise been a rather straightforward and one-dimensional character by emphasizing Martin's hobbies (his love of magic, his love of radio crime serials, etc.). With *Die Tür mit 7 Schlössern* (his second *Krimi* for Rialto) Alfred Vohrer solidified his relationship with the studio by marrying the existing Wallace "house" style to his own creative sensibilities as a director. Like Vohrer's *Die toten Augen von London*, *7 Schlössern* is visually inventive and energetic, but strikes a decidedly lighter tone, which would become a touchstone to his long tenure on the series.

The major set piece of the third act centers on Dr. Staletti's laboratory and the results of his experimentations. While the trope of the "mad scientist" and his "human subject experiments" is endemic to a certain branch of horror films, particularly titles from Columbia, Monogram, PRC, and Universal's B-movie sector, it is equally true that these *Krimis* were exorcising some demons from Germany's recent past. Yet even this painful subject is given a light touch by Vohrer, who manages to successfully tap into the ethical madness that gives the trope its traction while brushing the sequence with a playful pastiche varnish that facilitates (intentionally or otherwise) a form of catharsis.

Peter Thomas' score is an improvement over the semi-chaotic cues composed for *Die Seltsame Gräfin* but still fails to convincingly congeal around the characters, the atmosphere, and the action. It is, however, effective in parts, less contrary, and more confident. Indeed, Thomas' subsequent scores for the series began to coalesce and blend with Martin Böttcher's musical approach, and by the mid-1960s the scores functioned less as adornment and more as fully formed themes and motifs, particularly with the credit sequences (which thanks to Vohrer and *Die Tür mit den 7 Schlössern* now had an iconic signature all their own). Vohrer would add one final touch to the Krimi's cinematic handshake in his next film for Rialto, *Das Gasthaus an der Themse*.

DAS GASTHAUS AN DER THEMSE / *THE INN ON THE RIVER* (1962)

As its title would suggest, *Das Gasthaus an der Themse* opens on London's famous Thames River. Foggy riverbanks slowly reveal a small rowboat, its captain quietly and steadily approaching the shore, unaware that he is stalked from *above* by a shark. The *Hai* (the "Shark," a serial killer in scuba gear and wetsuit), the terror of the Thames and the focus of an ongoing Scotland Yard investigation, launches *Das Gasthaus an der Themse* in typical Wallace fashion—with a murder. A speargun enters the frame, takes aim, and fires its deadly bolt. The rowboater turns out to be a whiskey runner, but, more importantly, he was an occasional informant (in German, *"zinker"*) for Inspector Wade (Joachim Fuchsberger) of the Greenwich River Police.

As the murder occurred near the seedy harbor bar "Mekka," Wade focuses his investigation on its suspicious, cunning, and hardened owner Nelly Oaks (Elisabeth Flickenschildt) and her salty bartender Big Willy (Rudolf Fenner). One of the bar's boarders, the skulking Russian "spice merchant" Gregor Gubanow (Klaus Kinski), immediately warrants our attention. His activities suggest that he has something to hide. The subplot involves Nelly's attempt to marry her indentured foster daughter Lila (Brigitte Grothum) to the unscrupulous Captain Brown (Heinz Engelmann). Lila stands to come into a sizable inheritance on her eighteenth birthday. These, and many more Wallace staples, escalate into a thrilling third act in 1962's *Das Gasthaus an der Themse*.

Wallace's 1929 novel *The India Rubber Men* provided director Alfred Vohrer with excellent cinematic potential for his third *Krimi*. Goldmann released the book in Germany as *Taschen-Krimi bd.* 88 under the new title *Das Gasthaus an der Themse*. No prior filmed adaptations of this novel existed. *Das Gasthaus* was shot from June 6 to July 11, 1962, in Hamburg with the Elbe River (doubling once again as the Thames) providing a remarkable locale for one of the most atmospheric entries in the entire series. *Das Gasthaus an der Themse* premiered on September 28, 1962, in the *Ufa* pavilion in Berlin, and with over 3.6 million tickets sold it is the most successful film in the Edgar Wallace series.

Nine films and nearly four years had passed since the series began with *Die Frosch mit der Maske* (1959). During this period the series had undergone some changes, refinements, and, to its benefit, experimentation. Alfred Vohrer was largely responsible for charting new *Krimi* waters with his visually sophisticated and gruesome interpretation of *Die toten Augen von London*. Likewise, his rendering of *Die Tür mit den 7 Schlössern* bears many of the same graphic signatures, despite it being a more uneven effort than *toten Augen*. Vohrer moved the *Krimi* forward by embracing new perspectives, and deepening and increasing the brand (and thereby the marketing) of the series. For example, *Das Gasthaus an der Themse* added the final pre-credit teaser "defining touch." Following the barrage of machine-gun fire, we now hear for the first time: "*Hallo! Hier spricht Edgar Wallace!*" ("Hello! This is Edgar Wallace speaking!"). Many may be unaware that the voice is not Edgar Wallace but actually that of director Alfred Vohrer (made to sound like a tinny early sound recording). Additionally, like its recent predecessors, *Das Gasthaus* presents

Figure 2.10 Nelly Oaks (Elisabeth Flickenschildt) as the Mecca Club's Shadowy *hausfrau* in 1962's *Das Gasthaus an der Themse* (*The Inn on the River*). Source: *Stifung Deutsche Kinematek Berlin.*

color credits over a black and white film (the font is an incongruous mixture of red and green, prefiguring Freddy Krueger's unsettling striped sweater).

With *Das Gasthaus an der Themse* Vohrer achieves a depth of immersion into the *Krimiverse* that earlier efforts didn't quite plumb. I have argued that verisimilitude was a crucial component to the success of the Rialto Krimi. Indeed, a series set in England with British characters but shot in Germany with German actors undoubtedly presented some initial mental obstacles. For me, however, verisimilitude is perfectly realized in *Das Gasthaus*. This illusion of reality is rooted in Vohrer's inspired use of sets and locations. His orchestration of the river police headquarters, the ports, the ships and boats, the foghorns, the bars and nightclubs, and (for good measure) the Oxford rowing team are dexterous and enthralling. Vohrer creates a maritime ambience that permeates the movie—one that would not have been possible in their new production setting of Berlin.

Hamburg, Germany's largest seaport and critical to Germany's war effort, was decimated during World War II. It had endured Allied bombing since September 1939, but in 1943 Operation Gomorrah unleashed hell on Hamburg—killing an estimated 35,000 civilians and destroying most of the city.[20] During the *Wirtschaftswunder* ("economic miracle") era of the 1950s, Hamburg developed a reputation for being a sin-filled port of excess, vice, rock n' roll, dancing (and stripping), drugs, prostitution, and endless "good times." Often, these good times were powered and prolonged by taking "Prellies" or Preludin (Phenmetrazine), an appetite suppressant that was commonly used as a form of "speed," particularly when paired with alcohol. Prellies were used most famously by the Beatles, who perfected their act in Hamburg (playing over 250 shows in that city). Indeed, George Harrison literally came of age in Hamburg (arriving at age seventeen) and famously dubbed it "The naughtiest city in the world."[21] This type of adult entertainment was, of course, not uncommon in port and harbor-based cities, but Hamburg was perhaps the Mecca (coincidentally the name of the nightclub in *Das Gasthaus*) of turpitude.

In a sense, Hamburg is the main attraction in *Das Gasthaus*, which is only fitting because it was the last Rialto *Krimi* whose principal photography was completed there. Much of this shooting occurred in and around Hamburg's *Holzhafen* (a port and harbor complex), and this authentic backdrop provided a mockup of London that was not only credible but perhaps made Hamburg the more ideal and desirable location.

Vohrer's debut *Krimi, Die toten Augen von London*, embraced an overall chilling and severe tone, while his follow up, *Die Tür mit den 7 Schlössern*, was lighter and boasted an overly sensational third act. Like Goldilocks, Vohrer's experimentation led him to strike just the right balance with *Das Gasthaus*. To be sure, the location was ideal and flawlessly choreographed to the camera, but the narrative and especially the cast are also first rate. Fuchsberger and Arent are in top professional form. Each has ample opportunities to flex their acting talent as well as bring more physicality to their roles. Fuchsberger nimbly jumps from ship to dock, slides down coal chutes, and ducks spear gun attacks, while Arent preps for the Oxford University Boat Club (he actually has a mid-Thames collision with the escaping "Shark") and energetically twists the night away at the Mekka.

Kinski's Russian "spice merchant" Gubanow, arguably the actor's best Wallace role, on the other hand appears to spend "all his on-screen time duded out like a refugee from the cover shoot for Led Zeppelin's *In Through the Out Door* album."[22] Appearances can be deceiving, however, as Vohrer utilizes macro focal length cinematography (in a nod to Hitchcock's *Psycho*, 1960) to bring us extreme close-ups of Kinski's penetrating Aqua Velva eyes as he habitually gazes through peepholes. Is Gubanow a chronic voyeur, eavesdropper, scopophiliac, or merely a Russian spice merchant surveillant? The answer to these questions provides *Das Gasthaus* with one of the series' best and multi-valanced climaxes.

Veteran actress Elisabeth Flickenschildt lent gravitas to 1960s *Die Bande des Schreckens*, and she successfully does so again in *Das Gasthaus*—perhaps even more so given the prominence of her character's role. From her very first scene, Flickenschildt anchors the film by reviving the series' on-again, off-again love affair with a diegetically driven presentation of a song. As Nelly, the matron of Mekka, Flickenschildt delivers the catchy and melodic chanson "*Besonders In der Nacht*" ("*Especially in the Night*") with just the right amount of allure and danger. The Wallace series memorably began with Eva Pflug's performance of "*Nachts im Nebel an der Themse*" in *Die Frosch mit der Maske*, which set a fitting tone for the scene, the film, and the series. It is unfortunate that Rialto chose not to continue integrating songs or cabaret-nightclub acts as focal points in each additional entry à la the integrated musical approach (where musical numbers serve the narrative). From a marketing standpoint, these tunes (particularly when composed by Martin Böttcher) could have been an additional source of revenue as standalone singles. Composer Böttcher outdoes himself with *Das Gasthaus*, providing one of the series' most memorable main themes (which is used as the motif for *Besonders In der Nacht*), what the Germans would call an *ohrwurm* (literally "earwig"), a catchy tune that sticks in one's head. Moreover, Böttcher's "Mekka Twist" offers the film another fun and energetic set piece—with Arent in peak performance.

Das Gasthaus an der Themse was not only the series' biggest moneymaker but was also commensurate in terms of quality and entertainment value. It was also the only film in the series to amass the collective and iconic talents of Joachim Fuchsberger, Eddi Arent, Klaus Kinski, and Siegfried Schürenberg in one motion picture. This alone should prompt viewers to take a keen interest in this exceptional entry in the series.

DER ZINKER / L'ÉNIGME DU SERPENT NOIR / THE SQUEAKER (1963)

Both Scotland Yard and London's underground criminal network clamor for the true identity of notorious informer "the Squeaker." However, those who dare to pursue him, or, more fatally, double-cross him, ultimately taste the venomous toxins of his preferred method of murder—a Black Mamba snake. Rival criminal Larry Greame (Michael Chevalier) sets a trap for the *Zinker*, but Greame is only poisoned and killed for his troubles. Inspector Elford (Heinz Drache) of Scotland Yard takes the case and, as usual, there is no shortage of suspects. Elford's first investigatory lead brings him to the office of Mr. Sutton—Günter Pfitzmann, the proprietor of a pet store that carries various exotic species, including poisonous snakes. Through reporter Joshua

Harras (Eddi Arent), an effective "journalist covering-the-story" subplot is launched.

Eventually, the case leads the inspector to the Mulford estate where its wise but eccentric matriarch, Nancy Mulford (Agnes Windeck), and her niece Beryl (Barbara Rütting) provide Elford some crucial background on the case. Beryl works as a court reporter to nourish her imagination for her true vocation as an author of crime stories—which, in a self-reflexive turn, are identical to those of Edgar Wallace. As the list of suspects narrows, the usual Wallace allotment of affairs, betrayals, jealousies, and murders complicates matters and escalates the stakes.

Edgar Wallace's *The Squeaker* was published in England in 1927, promptly followed by a Goldmann release in Germany as *Taschen-Krimi bd.* 200 under the new title *Der Zinker*. Producers clearly saw cinematic potential in *The Squeaker*; three adaptations preceded Rialto's definitive version in 1963. The UK's British Lion Films was first to adapt the novel for the screen in 1930 as *The Squeaker*. The following year, the German production company Ondra-Lamac-Film adapted a German language version, *Der Zinker* (1931), and in 1937 London Screen Productions produced the third pre–World War II adaptation under the same name (with the alternate US title being *Murder on Diamond Row*). For 1963, Rialto chose to shoot the property as another coproduction allying with France's Les Films Jacques Willemetz. Completed between January 22 and February 28, 1963, at CCC's Berlin-Spandau Studios, *Der Zinker* enjoyed its new Ultrascope format premier on April 26, 1963. A very respectable 2.9 million tickets were sold.

Building upon the excitement, momentum, and record-breaking box-office of *Das Gasthaus an der Themse*, Rialto decided not to rest on its laurels—especially given the encroaching competition from Artur Brauner's CCC. Brauner had just produced his first Rialto *Krimi* clone, *Der Fluch der Gelben Schlange*, in February 1963. With *Der Fluch*, lensed at 1:66 and starring Rialto *Krimi* icons Fuchsberger and Arent, as well as series regulars Pinkas Braun and Brigitte Grothum, CCC had officially—and successfully—begun its epigone campaign designed to exploit and cash in on Rialto's success. Moreover, as discussed in chapter 1, CCC's efforts at creating simulacra simultaneously confused and conflated the audience's expectations by imitating the graphic design and art layout consistently used by Rialto for its advertising. Not to be outdone, Rialto quickly responded by hyping its new technological upgrade: for the first time, a Rialto *Krimi* was shot in the 2:35 film format, with this new presentation patented as "Ultrascope." CinemaScope, the anamorphic process made popular by the twentieth-century Fox, commanded high royalties, whereas Ultrascope (created by Munich-based camera manufacturer Arnold & Richter) delivered the same anamorphic ratio without the costly expenditure. The lenses were manufactured by *Ultra Gesellschaft für Optik* in Munich (hence Ultrascope). This decision, however, necessitated new second unit London exterior shoots. The London footage that had been used (and reused) prior to *Der Zinker* was shot in 1:37 Academy ratio and was therefore no longer compatible. The format change also required Vohrer and cinematographer Karl Löb to adopt a different approach to frame composition with respect to lighting, lenses, filtering, blocking, and set design.

Karl Löb, Rialto's exceptional in-house director of photography for the Wallace thrillers (and several Karl May westerns), apprenticed in Berlin under the aegis of the prolific Austrian cinematographer Willy Winterstein (*Der Hund von Baskerville* 1937, *Die Fledermaus* 1946). Perhaps more than any other single individual, Löb was responsible for preserving the franchise's aesthetic from film to film and director to director, from academy ratio to widescreen, and from black and white to color film stock. Moreover, Löb needed to simultaneously accommodate various directors and their stylistic signatures while maintaining an overall visual consistency to the series. If there is an unsung hero to the epic German *Krimi* narrative, it is surely Karl Löb.

Director Alfred Vohrer wastes no time presenting Klaus Kinski's lethal, snake-loving Krishna, a character that literally starts *Der Zinker* with a bang (one from Kinski's pistol). Continuing the tradition established with *Die toten Augen von London* (1961), the movie then opens its new expansive film format with red and green title credits that segue to (newly shot) downtown

Figure 2.11 Series Stalwart Eddi Arent Delivers His Own Brand of Tension-breaking Humor on the Set of *Der Zinker* (*The Squeaker*, 1963). *Source: Stifung Deutsche Kinematek Berlin.*

London exteriors. At this point, the traditional Rialto/Wallace dramaturgy takes over.

What sets *Der Zinker* apart from a fair-to-middling effort, however, are the new film format, full-throated performances from its cast, and the movie's overall aesthetic. Anchored by series regulars Drache and Arent, *Der Zinker* heralds the first appearance of the well-known and much-admired actress Barbara Rütting, who would go on to star in Rialto's *Neues vom Hexer* (1965), as well as CCC's Bryan Edgar Wallace adaptations *Das Phantom von Soho* (1964) and *Der Todesrächer von Soho* (1972). While Karin Dor remains the unmatched leading lady of the German *Krimi*, Rütting joins the family of iconic actresses to grace the series, which includes Karin Baal, Elisabeth Flickenschildt, Uschi Glas, Brigitte Grothum, and Gisela Uhlen.

Of the initial dozen or so offerings from Rialto, *Der Zinker* stands alongside *Die Bande des Schreckens*, *Die toten Augen von London*, and *Das Gasthaus an der Themse* as a prime example of *Krimi* aesthetics and atmospherics. Indeed, all the Wallace *Krimis* are "atmospheric" to some degree—the broader genre to which they belong requires certain aesthetic physiognomies—but *Der Zinker* charms us with an almost ski-resort vibe. The notoriously brutal European winter of 1962–1963 left Berlin covered in snow for several months. This perpetual blanket of snow lent the film a "cozy" *Krimi* vibe, particularly felt at the Mulford estate, complete with digestifs and stories told around a crackling fire in the hearth. This coziness is complemented and balanced by a certain level of Anglo-realism provided by the actual London locations.

Another asset is the film's score. With *Der Zinker*, composer Peter Thomas reaches a new high. As one of the two major musical interpreters for Rialto's series, Thomas' scores were largely inconsistent; however, his work here is hip, fun, energetic, and appropriately distressing in just the right places. He manages to provide themes and cues that enhance the material and also tap into the popular musical zeitgeist typified by the John Barry Seven, Ennio Morricone, and Henry Mancini—especially in the emphasis of staccato guitar twangs.

Der Zinker is first and foremost a transition effort, a film that embraces the series' recent past but also foreshadows a "style over substance" path that Rialto would soon traverse. Wallace's works, and Rialto's subsequent adaptations of them, were not exactly known for their narrative sophistication, but they nonetheless balanced attention-grabbing aesthetics with narrative consideration. *Der Zinker* signaled Rialto's gradual entrance into this transitional phase, a phase that more or less ends with the *Krimi*'s shift to color photography in 1966. At that point, the series, and its erstwhile approach, diverged.

Both *Der Zinker* and the next film in the series, *Der Schwarze Abt* (1963), exhibit some atypical casting decisions. Siegfried Schürenberg (who would become synonymous with the role of Sir John) tries on the role of pompous and surly newspaper editor Sir Geoffrey Fielding, a part Schürenberg plays effectively but not affectionately. His repartee with Arent, however, tends to work because of their chemistry together and because of Arent's inimitable brand of humor (which by now was completely synonymous with the series). Similarly, Fuchsberger's role in *Zinker*'s follow up, *Der Schwarze Abt*, is a risky break from his traditional and likable persona as a Scotland Yard inspector. Rialto should be applauded for casting Schürenberg and Fuchsberger in atypical roles. Both actors are more than capable of inhabiting these characters as written, but in the end, Schürenberg and Fuchsberger's on-screen and off-screen personas proved too heavy for these characters.

Der Zinker builds to a satisfying climax with a customarily humorous denouement that showcases the series ever-growing self-reflexivity. The film's climax really belongs to veteran actress Agnes Windeck, who showcases her formidable talent and camera presence in a tightly written conversational cat and mouse game. This is followed by a meta-denouement that, tongue firmly in cheek, explicitly winks at the series' creator Edgar Wallace. Overall, *Der Zinker* is a taut thriller with some unique attributes; it provides a suitable coda to the first wave of Wallace *Krimis* but also heralds winds of change for Rialto's voyage.

DER SCHWARZE ABT / LE CRAPAUD MASQUE / THE BLACK ABBOT (1963)

A mysterious cloaked figure stabs a man (Kurd Pieritz) during a midnight stroll among the ruins of Fossaway Abbey. It is rumored that the long-lost legendary Chelford treasure is buried somewhere among these ruins and that a ghost, the eponymous Black Abbot, fiercely guards this treasure. Meanwhile, at Chelford Manor, we learn through the skulking ex-con butler Thomas Fortuna (Klaus Kinski) that Dick Alford (Joachim Fuchsberger)—cousin to Lord Harry Chelford and administrator of Chelford Manor—has already discovered the body in the crumbling Abbey but has failed to act appropriately (which in turn casts ambiguity on his guilt or innocence in the matter).

Arriving at Chelford Manor are Scotland Yard Inspector Puddler (Charles Regnier) and his assistant Horatio W. Smith (Eddi Arent) who take up residence during their investigation. The officials are naturally skeptical of a story that suggests that a family ghost committed the murder, but they try to keep an open mind as they interview suspects and chase down leads.

The cast of suspicious characters is, as usual, quite long. The young and attractive Leslie Gine (Grit Boettcher) is engaged to the older and rather peculiar Lord Harry (whose mental faculties are deteriorating rapidly) but is actually in love with the Lord's cousin Dick Alford. Leslie's brother Arthur, the architect of this engagement, soon finds himself blackmailed by his accountant Fabian Gilder (Werner Peters). It turns out that Guilder was masquerading as Arthur's gambling bookie to whom he now owes a considerable sum of money. Mary Wenner (Eva Ingeborg Scholz), former secretary to Lord Harry, finds herself sacked but then teams with Gilder to search for the fabled lost Chelford treasure in the tunnels beneath the Abbey. And with this sordid coterie of characters the numerous blackmails, red herrings, additional murders, and other sundry Wallace tropes begin.

Edgar Wallace's novel *The Black Abbot* was published in 1926 and, as it turned out, became an evergreen property. The following year Wallace adapted the novel for the stage as *The Terror* (1927). The stage play was then adapted by Warner Brothers in 1928 as the first "all-talking" horror film, *The Terror* (1928). Warner's motion picture proved successful enough to warrant a partial sequel/remake in 1934 from First National, released as *Return of the Terror*. Moreover, Wallace's stage play was filmed an additional two more times (bringing the total to four versions): in addition to Warner's production of 1927, the Associated British Picture Corporation remade it in 1938 under the same title, and Rialto would later adapt *The Terror* as *Der Unheimliche Mönch* (*The Sinister Monk*, 1965).

In Germany, Goldmann published *Der Schwarze Abt* as *Taschen-Krimi Bd. 69*. Principal photography commenced on April 17 and was completed on May 28, 1963. CCC's Berlin-Spandau facilities, along with the Klein-Glienicke Park in Berlin-Wannsee, provided the film's locations. Arnsberg's splendid Herdringen Castle (last seen in *Der Fälscher von London* as Longford Manor) makes its second Wallace appearance, this time as Chelford Manor. The premiere took place on July 5, 1963, at the Universum in Munich, again featuring the 2:35 Ultrascope format. *Der Schwarze Abt* performed slightly less robustly than its predecessor's 2.9 million tickets sold but still accumulated a respectable 2.7 million—supporting the rationale for further Wallace adaptations.

Another German-Franco coproduction, this time with France's Les Films Jacques Leitienne, *Der Schwarze Abt* altered the successful formula that was perfected during the first roll out of Rialto releases. Beginning, albeit subtly, with *Der Zinker* (1963), a slow but perceptible transformation began with the series. *Zinker*'s adaptation, for example, eliminated and substituted large-scale portions from Wallace's novel. The novel's protagonist, Inspector John Leslie, does not appear in the film (emphasis was shifted to his assistant, Inspector Elford). Another major alteration was the upcoming wedding between Beryl Stedtman and Frank Sutton; indeed, this was a central focus of the novel, yet this storyline was eliminated in the screenplay. And some characters, like matriarch Nancy Elford, were created for the adaptation (a wise decision, as she provided the real fireworks for the film). These, among additional changes, were made to *Zinker*'s adaptation for the screen. As noted in chapter 1, Joachim Kramp delineated his second phase of Rialto *Krimis* with the release of *Der Zinker*. Kramp stressed that less fidelity toward the source material was emphasized during this transition, and I agree with his assessment. While this change is most keenly felt with the series' inevitable shift to color, it nonetheless began with *Der Zinker* and *Der Schwarze Abt*.

To this point, many Wallace *Krimis* were burdened with confusing plots; over time, this simply became a semi-endearing trademark of the series. *Die Tür mit den 7 Schlössern*, for example, jettisoned plot in favor of sensationalism, and *Der Grüne Bogenschütze*'s third act cleverly evolved into what could be best described as a German interpretation of British humor. But this was not the de rigueur attitude toward adaptation at Rialto. In sharp contrast, *Der Schwarze Abt* has an exceptionally murky and puzzling plot without the absurdist underpinnings (which lend the other films a sense of charm).

Figure 2.12 Reading over Eddi Arent's Shoulder, This London Constable Cannot Resist an Open Copy of a Goldmann Pocket Krimi. Promotional still for *Der Schwarze Abt* (*The Black Abbot,* 1963). *Source: Stifung Deutsche Kinematek Berlin.*

Multiple love interests, multiple blackmails, multiple abbots, multiple spaghetti strands of plot and subplot (attempting to conceal a weakly written main storyline) hinder the film's considerable potential and frustrate viewers earnestly trying to follow along.

More's the pity, since *Der Schwarze Abt* possesses several first-rate qualities. Among them, the film's atmospherics top the list. For the first time since *Der Grüne Bogenschütze*, a Wallace *Krimi* advanced a supernatural premise, and *Der Schwarze Abt* delights in this ruse. The combination of locations like Arnsberg's Herdringen Castle and the spookily constructed studio catacombs are effectively leveraged and lend the film a fully Gothic aesthetic. Yet, at the same time, an area where overuse led to overstatement was the film's ubiquitous placement of strong, usually single-sourced, low angle, backlit, nighttime set-ups. As a result, the desired low-key lighting effect is effectively neutralized. Indeed, with this approach, less proved to be more in earlier and more deftly handled set-ups from directors Vohrer and Reinl and their cinematographer Karl Löb. Given the picture's confusing narrative, prioritizing the aesthetic over the story can be read as a tell-tale sign that change for the series was imminent. Ultimately, the aesthetics, atmospheric as they are, cannot compensate for an emphatically muddled narrative.

In a bold move, Rialto hired director Franz Josef Gottlieb, fresh off of helming the *Krimi Der Fluch der Gelben Schlange* (1963) for rival production company CCC. Gottlieb, a gifted scenarist, emphasizes style but unfortunately overlooks narrative congruity in his shooting script. His cast, however, is uniformly excellent (by now a pretty common occurrence), despite the recent odd casting decisions by Rialto. In a rare turn, Joachim Fuchsberger does not portray an inspector for Scotland Yard but is actually a murder suspect—and also quite possibly the Black Abbot! Nevertheless, Rialto should be recognized for taking some degree of risk with these recent decisions regarding casting and directing. The *Krimi*'s fanbase (and, for that matter, any fanbase), however, had established relationships with directors and actors. As such, Blacky Fuchsberger had become synonymous with the role of a Scotland Yard inspector, and Alfred Vohrer was the fan-favorite interpreter of Wallace's work, so the risk was genuine.

Another high point is composer Martin Böttcher's score. While Peter Thomas occasionally struggled to find the right approach, Böttcher rather effortlessly defined and refined the *Krimi* sound despite working on fewer films.

Still, notwithstanding its strong atmospheric touches and earnest cast, *Der Schwarze Abt* ultimately provides a less than satisfying experience. Rialto would unequivocally rebound, however, with its next production.

DAS INDISCHE TUCH / THE INDIAN SCARF (1963)

The heirs (legitimate and otherwise) of Lord Edward Lebanon are summoned to "Mark's Priory," Lebanon's stately manor in northern Scotland, to attend the reading of his will. The recently deceased Lebanon, however, has a surprise for his avaricious relatives. The nine heirs (a coterie of exceptional German actors) gather as Lebanon's lawyer Frank Tanner (Heinz Drache) explains to the family that he is actually reading Lord Lebanon's penultimate will. Before any inheritances can be communicated, the Lebanon clan will need to live together peacefully at the castle for six days and six nights. At that point, and only that point, those who remain will hear Tanner read Lebanon's *final* will and testament. Unaware that Lebanon was murdered, they all agree.

As if on cue, a sudden and violent storm strands the "mourners" at the Priory, cutting them off from the outside world. The murders begin that night. One by one, heirs are picked off—strangled with an ornate Indian scarf. Suspicions arise and fingers are pointed (only to be retracted just as quickly after each suspect turns up dead). In fact, bodies accumulate so rapidly that the Priory's chapel in the cellar becomes a makeshift morgue. Scarf strangulations predictably repeat until only a few characters remain. Then, with tongue again firmly in cheek, *Das Indische Tuch* ends in similar postmodern fashion as *Der Zinker*—bestowing a nod to Edgar Wallace.

Putting the coproduction approach temporarily on hold, Rialto chose wisely for its next Ultrascope entry in the series. Edgar Wallace's stage play *The Case of the Frightened Lady* (1927) had been a hot property in decades past. Based on the popularity of the play, Wallace adapted and released it as the novel *The Frightened Lady* in 1933. Goldmann, in turn, released that adaptation in Germany as *Taschen-Krimi Bd. 189*. Cinematically, it was initially adapted for the screen in the United Kingdom by Gainsborough Pictures as *The Frightened Lady* (1932) and later remade by Pennant Pictures (George King's outfit) as *The Case of the Frightened Lady* (1940)—both distributed by British Lion. Furthermore, the BBC adapted the play for television twice, first in 1938 and again in 1983. The Wallace property clearly had a rich exhibition history when Rialto decided to add their voice to the chorus in 1963. Filming took place in the Berlin-Spandau studios from July 8 to August 13, 1963. The film premiered on September 13, 1963. Attendance was down 800,000 spectators at 1.9 million compared to *Der Schwarze Abt*'s 2.7 million tickets sold, despite *Das Indische Tuch* being one of the series' finest entries.

Das Indische Tuch is unlike any prior *Krimi* produced by Rialto. The movie's narrative engine is powered by the "on one condition" trope so common to the thriller/mystery genre in both fiction and film. The "on one condition" scenario generally requires one or more people to spend the night (or nights) at the (usually) "haunted" mansion of a wealthy, deceased relative in order to be eligible to receive any inheritance. Numerous films have embraced this plot-driving convention, including Germany's own *Geheimnis Des Blauen Zimmers* (1932) and Universal Studios' swift remake of this title the following year, *The Secret of the Blue Room* (1933). Universal flogged that same property for an additional two remakes, 1938's *The Missing Guest* and 1944's *Murder in the Blue Room*. That same year, Paramount jumped on the bandwagon with the amusing *One Body Too Many* (1944). More well-known titles include producer William Castle's *House on Haunted Hill* (1959) and perhaps the film that *Das Indische Tuch* most resembles, Agatha Christie's *And Then There Were None* (1945).[23] This timeworn plot device was also played for laughs in Abbott and Costello's *Hold That Ghost* (1941) and parodied in Neil Simon's *Murder by Death* (1976).

Rialto's treatment of the "on one condition" scenario is delightful. Alfred Vohrer returned to helm the series after Franz Joseph Gottlieb's rather uneven *Der Schwarze Abt*. Vohrer proved to be in top form for *Das Indische Tuch*, which easily rates among the best Wallace titles. The film begins with strong echoes of the turn of the twentieth-century cinematic technique. For example, the picture opens over a tapestry-like title card that raises like a curtain and announces our location as "Mark's Priory." What follows is a tableau-inspired production of close quarters and intimate relationships. The dramatic scenario of the reading of a will, the mysterious castle setting, and the "everyone's a suspect" sensibility skillfully blends together elements from the "whodunit," "haunted house," and *Kammerspiel* (or German chamber play) sub-genres while retaining a strong Wallace *Krimi* identity—thanks to Rialto's iconographic cast, crew, and aesthetic flourishes.

Indeed, *Das Indische Tuch* is a compendium of the series' most successful strategies and highpoints up until that point in time. Wendlandt assembles a first-rate cast culled from Rialto's roster of considerable talent. Present and in fine form are Heinz Drache, Eddi Arent, Ady Berber, Elisabeth Flickenschildt, Klaus Kinski, Gisela Uhlen, and Siegfried Schürenberg. Peter Thomas' main title music is light, fun, and mood appropriate. At times, however, Thomas falls back into the habit of using incongruous cues for scenes they aspire to underscore. Fortunately, Thomas' score is complemented by piano classics from Chopin, Beethoven, Tchaikovsky, and Rachmaninov.

Rialto predictably reduced operational costs during this transitional phase in the series. Moving the production base from Hamburg to Berlin was the first major step in this process. Beginning with *Der Schwarze Abt.*, less location shooting and more emphasis on studio production would amount to some

Figure 2.13 The Butler of Mark's Priory, Richard Maria Bonwit (Eddi Arent), and . . . Friend. *Das Indische Tuch* (*The Indian Scarf*, 1963). *Source*: Stifung Deutsche Kinematek Berlin.

below the line savings. This initial belt-tightening, however, produced mixed results with the finished *Krimi* products. On the one hand, Rialto's previous release, *Der Schwarze Abt*'s reliance on-set construction provided an elevated level of control over the prominent elements of its mise-en-scène, producing a Gothic ambience that effectively permeated the Abbey sequences. On the other, these budgetary short-cuts resulted in many perceptible shortcomings. *Schwarze Abt*'s ridiculous-looking rubber bats and thin layers of gravel over a plywood trap door, among other tell-tale signs of cost-cutting, betrayed the production's palpable parsimony. Despite being a near total studio production with only two exterior shots, *Das Indische Tuch*, however, possesses none of these frugal indicators. Likewise, since the diegesis of *Das Indische Tuch*'s script confines all three acts to Mark's Priory, Rialto could effectively shoot the film entirely on-set in Berlin. This cost-saving strategy would benefit the material and its thematic and aesthetic treatment, not least by leveraging filmic space in new and imaginative ways. *Das Indische Tuch* is one of the most stylishly crafted efforts in the series, with ample humor, clever set pieces, inspired camera work, and a well-oiled ensemble cast of veteran actors.

ZIMMER 13 / ROOM 13 (1964)

When an elderly woman is brutally murdered (with a straight razor!) on a railway embankment near House of Commons member Sir Robert Marney's (Walter Rilla) manor, Scotland Yard mobilizes to find the murderer. Meanwhile, at Paddington Station, recently released crime boss Joe Legge (Richard Häussler) reunites with his gang of crooks. Of all people, Legge then pays prominent citizen Sir Robert Marney a visit. Apparently Marney, for reasons of his own, aided and abetted Legge in a heist that went wrong twenty years prior. Legge has returned to blackmail Marney and threatens to harm his daughter Denise (Karin Dor) should Marney not do exactly as instructed. Marney agrees, but also clandestinely hires private investigator/bodyguard Johnny Gray (Joachim Fuchsberger) to watch over Denise.

Using the Highlow nightclub as a front and base of operations, Legge summons Marney to "room thirteen" where he explains an intricate train robbery and Marney's role in this heist. Meanwhile, Gray and Denise attend a striptease in the nightclub's bar below. Suddenly, at the climax of the dancer's routine, an unseen assailant slashes her throat with a straight razor and a torrent of arterial blood splatters the dressing screen. The dancer, Wanda (Elfi Estell), is actually an undercover Scotland Yard officer (confirmed by her regulation metro police underwear!). This second, very public, murder of a police official intensifies the investigation.

Scotland Yard criminologist and scientist Dr. Higgins (Eddi Arent) joins Gray and Sir John (Siegfried Schürenberg) as they simultaneously try to thwart Legge's heist and discover the straight razor killer's identity. *Zimmer 13* is especially rife with plot twists and turns, and lest spoilers enter into the summary, it is best to end here.

Room 13 was published in 1924 and was the first Wallace novel to feature the recurring character of J.G. Reeder, a self-effacing but brilliant sleuth (renamed Johnny Gray in Rialto's filmed adaptation). Goldmann later released *Room 13* with the identical German language title *Zimmer 13*, as *Taschen-Krimi Bd. 14*. The novel was first adapted for the screen in 1938 as *Mr. Reeder in Room 13* (US title *Mystery of Room 13*) for British National Films and was directed by Norman Lee. *Zimmer 13* marked the fourth (and final) Franco-German coproduction (this one with the French *Société Nouvelle Cinématographie*). The film was shot from November 25, 1963, to January 16, 1964, and was directed by series veteran Harald Reinl on location in Denmark and West Berlin. The film enjoyed its Ultrascope premiere on February 20, 1964, in the Lichtburg Cinema in Essen and performed on par with Rialto's last feature, *Das Indische Tuch*, drawing 1.8 million visitors. *Zimmer 13* is an important entry in the *Krimi* canon and thus requires commensurate analysis and context.

The Great Train Robbery of 1963 dominated headlines all over the world; it was a spectacularly planned and executed heist worthy of a big-screen adaptation. The robbery occurred on a Royal Mail train heading from Glasgow to London on August 8, 1963. The fifteen gang members managed to get away with 2.6 million British pound sterling (roughly the equivalent to £55 million in 2019).[24] Timing would be crucial, however, if a studio wished to capitalize on its newsworthiness. With market competition from CCC, Rialto saw an ideal opportunity to leverage the story into *Zimmer 13*. Consequently, the next four Wallace *Krimis* scheduled for production, *Der Safe mit dem Rätselschlossm* (*The Curse of the Hidden Vault*), *Das Verrätertor* (*Traitor's Gate*), *Der Unheimliche Mönch* (*The Sinister Monk*), and *Der Hexer* (*The Mysterious Magician*), were postponed until the 1964 and 1965 production years.[25] The script for *Zimmer 13* was greenlit and took immediate priority. Moreover, this major revision of the novel inserted *Zimmer 13* into two beloved sub-genres, the heist film and the train film.

Zimmer 13 also marked a homecoming for Rialto productions—a return to the Danish soil that sprouted the first two Rialto *Krimis*, *Der Frosch mit der Maske* (*Face of the Frog*, 1959) and *Der Rote Kreis* (*The Red Circle*, 1960). Copenhagen, and especially Vallø Castle on the island of Zealand, provided photogenic locations and some appreciated relief from the by then well-known German locations and sets.

Following an intense but brief pre-credit teaser (more on that later), *Zimmer 13* opens with an unusually stylish credit sequence. After the customary "*Hallo! Hier spricht Edgar Wallace*," smartly chosen production stills from the film—bathed in hues of red, blue, and green (the primary additive color model)—accompany title cards that feature the series' traditional multicolored darting text from various screen directions. This effective new template was used for the next several productions.

The substance of the pre-credit teaser, however, is crucial to the development of the series and warrants examination. From *Zimmer 13*'s opening image on a railway embankment—a black-gloved hand wielding a raised straight razor, waiting for its victim, ready to strike—the connection between Italy's evolving *gialli* and Germany's *Krimis* becomes clear. For both nations, the appetite for these kinds of stories proved insatiable, although each employed different thematic and aesthetic treatments in their execution. Both industries certainly trafficked in the genre's requirement of blood and violence but with culturally distinct approaches. Tim Bergfelder has addressed this cultural distinction.

> Like the Wallace films, the *giallos* directed by Mario Bava, Umberto Lenzi, or Massimo Dallamano had deliriously convoluted plots featuring masked killers

and elaborately staged murders, and an excessive visual aesthetic, characterized by a highly mannered cinematographic style and flamboyant *mise en scene*. Unlike the Wallace films, their depiction of violence was quite graphic. They were also fairly sexually explicit where the Wallace films had been comparatively prudish, and they lacked the comic distractions that were such an integral element of the Wallace films' appeal.[26]

The West German *Krimi* predates the birth of the Italian *giallo* by several years, but beginning with Italian *auteur* Mario Bava's *Krimi*-inspired *giallo*, *Sei donne per l'assassino* (*Blood and Black Lace,* 1964), a back-and-forth cross-cultural impact was keenly felt—more so as the films continued to mature and evolve. As Stefano Baschiera and Francesco Di Chiara explain:

> Film *gialli* share with their literary counterparts the characteristic of having foreign ancestors; we are thinking, in particular, of the German *Krimis* films: filmic adaptations of Edgar Wallace's stories, mostly set in London. Indeed, Bava's second *giallo*, *Blood and Black Lace* (*Sei donne per l'assassino*, 1964), is an Italian and German coproduction. It is a film that can be considered the main model for the giallo over the next decade, as it set the structural standards for the subsequent entries in the genre.[27]

Figure 2.14 Dr. Higgins (Eddi Arent) "Searches for Clues" in Director Alfred Vohrer's *Zimmer 13* (*Room 13,* **1964**). *Source: Stifung Deutsche Kinematek Berlin.*

Even more to the point, *Blood and Black Lace*'s narrative takes several significant plot cues from the actual Edgar Wallace novel *White Face* (1931), particularly in the creation of the film's iconic villain.

Blood and Black Lace is an influential, stunningly staged, composed, and shot motion picture that owes much to its German progenitors; but in Bava's hands, the material is elevated to heights that Rialto and CCC never considered. The Expressionist signatures that mark the Wallace *Krimi*, principally the chiaroscuro lighting, camerawork, and set design, had only been created for the abstract, chromatic universe of black and white cinematography. Bava, in contrast, detonated an effulgent big bang all his own resulting in the new *color* universe of the *gialli*. This proved to be a huge evolutionary step for Italy, but also for Germany.

Both films were shot at the same time, from November 1963 to January 1964, so the amount of cross-pollination is difficult to measure. Nevertheless, the cross-cultural *influence* is naked to the eye. Many of the sequences in *Blood and Black Lace* mirrored the camera set-ups and lighting designs from numerous *Krimis*. Now, however, they were bathed in luxuriously saturated color. This crucial transformation was not the result of a simple change of film stock; Bava's use of color for aesthetic as well as the psychological effect is masterful. Similarly, *Zimmer 13* borrows from Bava's toolbox by including a graphic depiction of an element the series, more or less, shied away from in its current black and white format. It comes in a moment film historian Kim Newman describes as a "*giallo*-style" shocking of the audience. Newman is correct on two counts. Indeed, the audience situated in the nightclub are horrified by what they have witnessed, but we, the audience of *Zimmer 13*, are equally shaken. This violence, which had not been seen with such intensity (and realism) since the series launched with *Der Frosch mit der Maske* (1959), is especially jarring because, as Newman points out, "it segues from comedy to horror as swiftly as it does from sex to violence" while also neatly fulfilling the promise of the Chekhovian straight razor of the film's teaser.[28] He continues, "The solution to the psycho murders is a much bigger surprise—prefiguring the genuinely twisted twists of Dario Argento's early *gialli*."[29]

Given all this background and context on *Zimmer 13*, how does it measure up within the *Krimi* corpus? It is exceptionally well made in every respect. The script unfolds with mounting tension from both the main and subplot—the identity of the murderer and the train heist, respectively. The "room thirteen" of the film's title is located above the Highlow Club and contains a hidden vault that reverberates with strong echoes of World War II map rooms—the same type of strategic room found in Churchill's underground bunkers, the ground floor of Roosevelt's White House administration, and Hitler's *Felsennest* (Rocky Nest) near Bad Munstereifel. Like in those strategic chambers, Legge's room-sized map features scale models of forests, rivers, bridges, estates, and railways. This set piece (later repeated for comic effect in *Der Bucklige von Soho*, 1966) highlights the meticulous planning and rehearsing that went into the actual Great Train Robbery of 1963.

Director Reinl and cinematographer Ernst Kalinke make inspired use of the Danish locations—particularly the tree-lined drive of Vallø Castle—where we witness a truly melancholy final scene. Composer Peter Thomas not only provides a strong score but develops an unsettling "leitmotif" whenever a straight razor appears on-screen. The ensemble is in spectacular form. Schürenberg delivers one of his best Sir John performances, and the Fuchsberger/Arent teaming in the third act allows for genuine laughs amid the mounting tension and excitement. *Zimmer 13* is an important and first-rate entry in the *Krimi* canon.

DIE GRUFT MIT DEM RÄTSELSCHLOSS / *THE CURSE OF THE HIDDEN VAULT* (1964)

A man is shot during the climax of an unremarkable *Krimi* (*not* a Rialto) in a London cinema—the sound of the actual gunshot is masked by an on-screen gunfight. The man is later identified as one of a group of criminal croupiers that worked for über-wealthy retired casino owner Mr. Real (Rudolf Forster). Guilt-ridden and dying, Real is riddled with regret over his less than scrupulous business practices throughout his career. In the case of one individual, a Mr. Kent, Real's tactics to manipulate his "bad luck" drove Kent to financial ruin and suicide. Real has now decided to leave his vast fortune to Kent's daughter Kathleen (Judith Dornys). He summons her to England from Australia.

On a train to London, Kathleen and her family attorney, Ferry Westlake (Eddi Arent), meet the mysterious Jimmy Flynn (Harald Leipnitz), a former croupier with ties to Scotland Yard. Upon arrival, Kathleen and Ferry are kidnapped by Connor (Ernst Fritz Fürbringer), yet another former casino employee, who plots to block Kathleen's meeting with Real and claim the fortune himself. The vast riches, however, are locked up tighter than Fort Knox in the extremely deadly vault of the film's title (one greedy victim is poisoned, electrocuted, and breaks his neck). Only the secret code known by Real can allow safe passage into the vault. Predictably, Scotland Yard is activated when the kidnapping occurs, and series newcomer Inspector Angel (Harry Meyen) is assigned the case.

Die Gruft mit dem Rätselschloss was adapted from the early (his second) Wallace novel *Angel Esquire* (1908), which was then adapted, produced, and distributed as the 1919 silent film *Angel Esquire* by Gaumont-British Picture Corporation. The first German edition was published in 1927 under the title *Der verteufelte Herr Engel* by Josef Singer Publishing. Goldmann would not enjoy publishing rights until 1954 when it was released as *Taschen-Krimi Bd. 47*. Film production began on February 18 at the CCC Berlin-Spandau and

Ufa Tempelhof studios, and wrapped on March 26, 1964. *Die Gruft mit dem Rätselschloss* enjoyed its Ultrascope premiere on April 30, 1964, at the Gloria-Palast in Berlin. It opened to mixed opinion and comparatively low box-office.

Die Gruft mit dem Rätselschloss is a curious mid-era entry that begins with a clever film-within-a-film premise (reinforcing the series postmodern tendencies) but then never quite lives up to its potential. The strengths of *Rätselschloss* are its fine ensemble cast and the inspired camera unit dynamics. These elements are additionally supported by a few excellent set pieces; aside from these, however, there is little to recommend. The process here feels rather routine after the evolutionary developments of its superior predecessors, including recent efforts like the inventive *Das Indische Tuch* and *Zimmer 13* and the concurrent *Der Hexer*. In comparison, *Rätselschloss* feels regressive and out of step with its contemporaries. If *Rätselschloss* had been produced and released earlier, as part of the 1962/1963 catalog, it would likely feel less anachronistic. However, given that *Zimmer 13* was hurried into production to capitalize on the topical train heist of 1963, *Rätselschloss* gives the impression of a backslide and thus performed in likewise lackluster fashion—only bringing in 1.2 million visitors.

A major contributory factor to the film's incongruity is, as Kim Newman points out, that *Rätselschloss*

> is the first of the Rialto series to be vague about precisely which Wallace story, novel, or play is being adapted. From now on, many of the series are loose remakes of earlier films or cobbled together bits from various works with new material thrown in to create an essential "Edgar Wallace" feel.[30]

Moreover, the film struggles to shake its 1908 origins, resulting in an excessively staged and "talky" nature rather than the action-oriented direction the series delighted in. This is not to suggest that the film is devoid of a discernable narrative, tense action sequences, or a sense of the series' unique charm. On the contrary, Real's booby-trapped estate, the scenes involving the multichambered death vault and its ornate codex lock, and the utterly gruesome millstone murder are set pieces that linger (unsettlingly in the case of the windmill sequences). In fact, so intense was Connor's millstone "death crunch" that the FSK demanded the scene be considerably shortened (it has now since been restored). The hideout location of the windmill (where Real takes cover from his gang of former employees) and its massive, rolling millstones were so central to the film that the original suggested (but rejected) title was *Die Mühle des Grauens* (*The Mill of Horror*)!

Die Gruft mit dem Rätselschloss features a fine ensemble cast but unfortunately doesn't harness all of its formidable talents. Arent's lawyer, Ferry Westlake, comes off as annoyingly preening and fastidious, Schürenberg's Sir John is simply too severe, and Kinski plays his minuscule part mute and is therefore mostly forgotten. Our heroine, Kathleen, is given exceedingly little to do (it's impossible to imagine Karin Dor in the part; her athleticism combined with her sophistication requires much more vision and ink devoted to the page). However, legendary *Ufa* thespian Rudolf Forster is in fine form, as are Ernst Fritz Fürbringer, Harald Leipnitz, and newcomer to the series, Harry Meyen. Also appearing in her first of several Rialto *Krimis* is Ilse Steppat (as Real's caretaker Margaret Clayton), but most cinephiles will recognize the smoky-voiced German stage and screen star from her most infamous role as Irma Bunt in 1969's *On Her Majesty's Secret Service*. Her memorable role as Blofeld's villainous sidekick was sadly to be her last, as she died of a heart attack two days after the film's West German premiere.

Peter Thomas' score is proportionate to the overall merit of the film. The music is uninspired and, at times, annoyingly obtrusive (his musical cues for the hidden vault's coming to life excessively grate on the nerves). This remains all the more disappointing given that Thomas composed such an effective score for *Zimmer 13*.

Die Gruft mit dem Rätselschloss is a competently made but uninspired *Krimi* where ultimately the spectacle of a diabolically deadly vault and sinister rolling millstones overpowers an otherwise weak constitution.

DER HEXER / THE MYSTERIOUS MAGICIAN (1964)

Gwenda Milton (Petra von der Linde), secretary to the London lawyer Maurice Messer (Jochen Brockmann), is murdered, her body found floating in the Thames. The murderers, however, are blissfully unaware that Gwenda Milton was the sister of the notorious English vigilante Arthur Milton, a.k.a. *der Hexer* (The Ringer), a chameleon-like avenger for those whom justice has failed. So manipulative is *Der Hexer* that he often drives his victims to commit suicide, a technicality that shields him from murder charges. His identity remains unknown, but his vengeance is certain, and he remains a wanted man in the United Kingdom.

Sir John of Scotland Yard (Siegfried Schürenberg) quickly assigns Inspector Higgins (Joachim Fuchsberger) to the case. Higgins begins by questioning the Attorney Messer (who turns white when he learns that Gwenda was the sister of Arthur Milton). Meanwhile, Milton's wife, Cora Ann Milton (Margot Trooger), arrives from Australia for the funeral of her sister-in-law. Messer and his gang of criminals receive death threats from *Der Hexer*, and aged inspector Warren (Siegfried Lowitz) comes out of retirement to aid in the investigation (he has prior experience with Der Hexer), presumably because Higgins is overly preoccupied with his fiancé Elise Penton (Sophie Hardy). At the same time Cora Ann arrives in London, a mysterious

Australian named James W. Wesby (Heinz Drache) also arrives in England. Could he be *Der Hexer*?

One of Edgar Wallace's most popular—and indeed most adapted—works was the 1925 novel *The Gaunt Stranger*. Wallace adapted it for the stage as *The Ringer* in 1926, which proved so successful that he revised the novel to match the stage version and re-issued it under the new title *The Ringer*. Goldmann later published it in Germany as *Der Hexer, Taschen-Krimi Bd. 30*. The story was then adapted for the screen no less than six times beginning with the English-made silent version released by British Lion in 1928.[31] This was followed by the Gainsborough remake in 1931, the German Ondra-Lamac release in 1932 (as *Der Hexer*), Ealing Studios' *The Gaunt Stranger* (released as *The Phantom Strikes* in the United States, 1938), the Guy Hamilton-directed 1952 version from London Film Productions, and Rialto's 1964 version *Der Hexer*. Production began on *Der Hexer* on June 3 and concluded on July 11, 1964. It was shot at the Berlin-Spandau complex at CCC Studios and various other outdoor locations in Berlin. *Der Hexer* would be the last of six *Krimis* that enjoyed the Ultrascope format. The movie premiered on August 21, 1964, in the Capitol and Alhambra cinemas in Düsseldorf. Ticket sales performed above expectations (considering the low returns of *Die Gruft mit dem Rätselschloss*), bringing in more than 2.6 million visitors.

Indeed, *Die Gruft mit dem Rätselschloss*' comparatively poor earnings prompted Rialto to take drastic measures for their next production. The decision was made to launch Wallace's most popular and best-selling novel into production and afford it some extravagant treatment. The first script was rejected, however, as it bore too close a resemblance to its stage origins and also to its numerous big-screen adaptations. Another problem arose due to the property's most attractive and potentially lucrative asset— its popularity. The question of how to deliver some element of surprise to an audience overly familiar with the novel's plot proved a mystery all its own. The solution was to hire journalist, author, and screenwriter Herbert Reinecker to smartly redress Harald G. Petersen's initial treatment.[32] The other response was to take a cue from Universal's successful monster rally films of the 1940s (e.g., *House of Frankenstein*, 1944, *House of Dracula*, 1945, and *Abbott and Costello Meet Frankenstein*, 1948) by packing the production with stars of the series. Rather than multiple franchise monsters, however, Rialto front loaded its most popular franchise detectives into the film.

With *Der Hexer*, director Alfred Vohrer unequivocally created one of the most popular and highly regarded of all the Rialto *Krimis* (generating an immediate sequel). Yet, precisely because of its popularity and esteemed ranking among critics and fans, it also attracts a lot of attention and criticism—some warranted and fair, some unnecessary and pedantic. This entry explores this significant title in light of these wide-ranging value judgments.

Series director Alfred Vohrer often demonstrated a penchant for dispatching victims in uniquely cinematic ways (dating back to his Wallace debut with the über–sinister *Die toten Augen von London*), and *Der Hexer* opens with similar dastardly designs. The film features one of the more concise and memorable pre-credit teases from the series. It begins with the common Wallace trope of the eavesdropping (and often blackmailing) secretary, Ms. Milton. This time, however, she is caught in the act and strangled (by that old Wallace chestnut) the unholy priest—more shades of *Die toten Augen*—and diabolically disposed of via a James Bond-like submersible craft in an underground cavern. The submarine cruises into a tunnel as we hear the customary "*Hallo! Hier spricht Edgar Wallace!*" Her body is jettisoned by Messer's hasty henchman into the Thames, hoping that any patrolling London metro police would conclude drowning as the cause of death. Unfortunately for Messer, the autopsy determines homicide by strangling, which triggers the Scotland Yard investigation and also springs the cat and mouse revenge game by the victim's brother, Arthur Milton (alias *Der Hexer*).

Figure 2.15 A Scene-stealing Mini-submarine Awaits Another Poor Unsuspecting Victim. *Der Hexer* (*The Mysterious Magician*, 1964). *Source: Stifung Deutsche Kinematek Berlin.*

The post-teaser credit sequence, a long-established and crucial part of the *Krimiverse*, is among the best (if not a strong candidate for *the* best) in the series. Peter Thomas finally hits a long-awaited home run with his unconventional musical approach for *Der Hexer*. The scoring throughout the film is mood evocative and remarkably effective, but Thomas' title track is truly special and a paradigmatic example of not only the Wallace *Krimi* cycle but stylish crime films of that era in general. A droning lounge-style vocal ("da-dada-da-da-dada-da") and twangy guitar provide a supportive, repetitive pedal point that is accompanied by terrifying screams, gunshots, maniacal laughs, dissonant brass, sensuous "oohhs and aahhs," and a cacophony of voices uttering *"Der Hexer."* This is played over a continuous shot of the water's shimmering reflection painted against the submarine bases' concrete wall as the film's credits dash in and out.

Beyond the exceptional teaser and opening credits, *Der Hexer* quickly sets up and showcases what might be called the "holy trinity" of *Krimi* leading actors: Siegfried Lowitz, Joachim Fuchsberger, and Heinz Drache. Being drugged, being tied-up, being betrayed, getting bruised (emotionally and physically), these three icons shouldered the lion's share of deductive reasoning, fist-fights, gun battles, pursuits, tongue lashings from Sir John, and the general wearing out of shoe leather in virtually every *Krimi* since the series' launch in 1959. What's the result of putting them in one extravaganza? By most critical yardsticks, success.

Conceptually, the return of the three investigative personas that launched the series paid off handsomely. As written, each role fulfills a different dramatic requirement. Fuchsberger is distracted—drunk with love—and therefore apparently "off his game" as a detective. Lowitz is the retired gumshoe who has tangled with Milton in the past and is brought back to active duty as a "ringer" in his own right. And Drache is the enigmatic outsider who may, or may not, be *Der Hexer*.

The film's detractors often point to several reasonable but debatable problems with *Der Hexer*. One such criticism concerns Fuchsberger's investigative incompetence as Inspector Higgins. From a craft perspective, it is plausible and, more importantly, rational that Lowitz, Fuchsberger, and Drache's roles be sufficiently distinct from one another while fulfilling a specific dramatic purpose. In this regard, the script is successful. Audiences, however, often have difficulty separating on-screen personas with off-screen identities; it is both unusual and odd to witness the steadfast Fuchsberger portrayed as a schoolboy in perpetual puppy love rather than the man of action the series had presented. Fuchsberger's Inspector Higgins essentially bungles his way through the film, which results in, above all else, his life needing saving from the clutches of death on numerous occasions. Still, it is refreshing to see the typically macho, capable, proto-Bondian Fuchsberger humbled by his clumsiness, incompetence, and infatuation. Moreover, the script would surely crumble under the weight of two male heroes. In this case, the series was simply "having a go" at Fuchsberger's image, and he knowingly played along. Much more worthy of criticism is the unfortunate "dumb blond" mold in which Fuchsberger's love interest, Elise Penton (Sophie Hardy), is cast. The stereotype not only damages the capable Hardy, but the film as well. Recurrent series heroine Karin Dor frequently balanced the many often dichotomous requirements demanded of her (athletic but elegant, resourceful but frequently in distress, vulnerable but resilient, etc.) in far better-written roles earlier in the decade.

In my estimation, some complaints, however, amount to trifles. For example, a common grievance leveled at the film is the rather shoddy looking process shot used for the London traffic scene featuring Fuchsberger and Hardy. It's fair to point out that many composite shots of this era, in Germany and elsewhere (particularly rear-projected background plates of driving footage), were *never* all that convincing. In truth, some were merely better shot, projected, and integrated than others. So, while *Der Hexer* is undeniably guilty of mediocre rear projection, it also compensates with an amusing complement of Vohrer's well-known trick shots. These shots are meticulously executed and include Drache's spying on Fuchsberger and Trooger through a point-of-view foreground hole in a newspaper, an exigent phone call shot through rotary dial holes, and even the handing (or rather, footing) off of a cigarette from Hardy to Fuchsberger (and in a nice bit of parallelism, through a hole in a newspaper). Vohrer's passion for memorable props yet again comes to the fore; two such examples are a piano that houses a bar rather than a soundboard and strings, and a stuffed bear with a hidden pull chain in its ear that activates a hidden door. Vohrer delights in populating *Der Hexer*'s *mise-en-scène* with these ornate flourishes.

To offset the film's rather lavish treatment, certain parsimonious details can be detected upon close inspection. An obvious grain and exposure mismatch reveals a dubbed and reused Trafalgar Square news hawker shot seen previously in *Der Zinker* (1963), and a musical cue from *Zimmer 13* (1964) is also recycled, among other minor inconsequential matters. However, Rialto, like Hammer, was notorious for penny-pinching (even more so since relocating from Hamburg to Berlin), yet *Der Hexer* does not suffer from these cost-cutting practices.

Warmly imitating the theatrical gimmicks endemic to American producer William Castle's films of the 1950s and 1960s, *Der Hexer* surprises with an unexpected narrative break just moments before the film's climax. The screen goes black and a title card suddenly appears that asks the audience, "*Wissen sie schon jetzt wer Der Hexer ist?* (Have you guessed who Der Hexer is?)." Of course, the main problem with *Der Hexer* is simply that once Arthur

Milton's identity is revealed, repeat viewings yield diminishing satisfaction (true of most films of this type). It is also possible that careful observers and amateur sleuths will be surprised but also frustrated with the film's climax. Regardless, watching with friends, particularly those who are uninitiated in the Wallace *Krimi* cult, will make for a pleasure-filled evening. Many, many television broadcasts seeded this film deeply in the consciousness of several generations of German citizens and so created a gateway production. Echoing this sentiment, the 1964 review of the *Stuttgarter Nachrichten* proclaimed the film "a delicacy for the friends of the crime thriller. If you don't count yourself among them, you can easily become one here."

DAS VERRÄTERTOR / TRAITOR'S GATE (1964)

Prominent English businessman Trayne (Albert Lieven) has devised an elaborate plan to steal the priceless Crown Jewels of the United Kingdom from the Tower of London. Aiding him are his companion in crime Dinah (Margot Trooger) and a motley assortment of underlings, headed by the orally fixated Kane (Klaus Kinski) and an escaped prisoner (Gary Raymond) who bears a striking resemblance to a Yeomen Warder (Gary Raymond in a dual role with an assist from his twin brother Robin Rodney). Along the way, Trayne must reckon with Scotland Yard, the treachery of his closest confidants, and an annoying German tourist Hector (Eddi Arent) who photographs Trayne's posse and their movements.

Edgar Wallace's *The Traitor's Gate* was published in 1927 and adapted for the screen a short time later by British International Pictures as *The Yellow Mask* (1930). This earliest adaptation, however, was reportedly a Yellow Peril film that offered an uneven mix of comedy, thriller, and musical elements. Goldmann later published Wallace's novel in Germany under the title of *Das Verrätertor* as *Taschen-Krimi Bd. 45*. When it was time for Rialto to step up to the plate in 1964, the company smartly partnered with Summit Film Productions in the United Kingdom. This union brought veteran Hammer scribe Jimmy Sangster (writing under his John Sansom pseudonym) on board to pen the script and cinematographer-turned-director Freddie Francis to helm the production. The picture was shot entirely in London from August 18 to September 21, 1964. *Das Verrätertor* opened in German cinemas on December 18, 1964, and drew in approximately 1.5 million visitors—a disappointing sum.

Of all the Rialto Wallace productions and coproductions, *Das Verrätertor* is, without doubt, the most *British* in terms of personnel, tone, subject matter, presentation, and, of course, setting. Rialto's coproductions made with France were essentially indistinguishable from the solely produced German titles. The Anglo-German coproductions, however, differed in several significant ways. For example, *Das Geheimnis der gelben Narzissen* (1961) was shot in dual language versions for both the English-speaking and German-speaking markets. The Italian coproductions discussed in chapter 3, however, would diverge significantly from their Franco-German and Anglo-German counterparts. Tim Bergfelder has observed that

> French involvement in these cases appears to have been limited to financial aid in return for distribution rights, while Rialto's incentive for such cooperations was to get access to French subsidy money. In co-productions with Britain and Italy, however, the Wallace series underwent sometimes significant stylistic and narrative transformations.[33]

This was certainly true of the 1961 Rialto-Omnia coproduction *Das Geheimnis der gelben Narzissen*, but in the case of *Das Verrätertor*, exponentially more so. *Das Verrätertor* begins with a common (and often annoying) Rialto trope—the unremitting cacophony of barking hounds. The object of their chase is an escaped prisoner from Dartmoor. Of course, this introduction would be equally at home in an archetypal Wallace thriller, but what unfolds is anything *but* a pro-forma Rialto thriller. Given that Sangster's (*The Curse of Frankenstein* [1957], *Horror of Dracula* [1958]) and Francis' (*Paranoiac* [1963], *Nightmare* [1964]) Hammer pedigrees were well-steeped in horror and the macabre, it is logical to assume that they would combine their talents on a more horrific title, yet *Das Verrätertor* is, first and foremost, a heist film.

The "heist film" had proven to be quite popular during the 1950s. Numerous Hollywood studios produced (with both A and B units) many titles—typically under the larger genus of the "crime film." Europe also embraced the subgenre with one continent trying to out-heist the other. Diverse efforts such as *The Asphalt Jungle* (1950), *Armored Car Robbery* (1950), *The Lavender Hill Mob* (1951), *The Ladykillers* (1955), *Bob le Flambeur* (1956), *Rififi* (1955), and *The Killing* (1956), among others, drew audiences and admirers.

In the 1960s, however, the heist film went quite mainstream with star-studded extravaganzas like *Ocean's 11* (1960) and *The Pink Panther* (1963). Yet, the decade also opened with smaller, fascinating productions like the UK's *The League of Gentlemen* and *Seven Thieves* (both from 1960). Nevertheless, the heist film had become *en vogue* and continued to ascend in popularity during the 1960s, often commanding substantial budgets and stars. Lush productions like *How to Steal a Million* (1966), *Gambit* (1966), the underrated *Grand Slam* (1967, also with Kinski), *The Thomas Crown Affair* (1968), and *The Italian Job* (1969) were some of the most popular and profitable.

Figure 2.16 With a Predominantly German Cast, Authentic London Locations, and Hammer Film Veterans Freddie Francis (Direction) and Jimmy Sangster (Screenplay) on Board, *Das Verrätertor* Makes for a Wild Hybrid of Anglo and German Sensibilities (*Traitor's Gate,* 1966). Source: Stifung Deutsche Kinematek Berlin.

Das Verrätertor is closer in tone and execution to the scaled-back black and white productions of the previous decade. In many ways, the movie is a kindred spirit to 1962's *Das Rätsel der roten Orchidee*. Both films are outliers in the *Krimiverse*, both are directed by newcomers to the series (who were also former cinematographers) who had recently made the transition to directing, both films play greatly with genre (the blending of Wallace theatrics with the gangster and heist films, respectively), and both earned a substandard number of tickets sold (at 1.5 million each).

Das Verrätertor possesses several admirable qualities; foremost among them is Francis' perfectly captured London atmosphere. Francis and his camera unit cleverly and creatively alternate between a daytime street realism and a more formal London nightscape. The use of depth of field in certain exterior sequences provides the viewer with the most immersive London experience found in any Rialto *Krimi*. And with a fairly brisk running time of under ninety minutes (more on this later), the planning and execution of the heist, buoyed by the ensuing action, are taut enough to keep the audience absorbed and invested.

Arguably the film's most memorable sequence is not connected to the heist at all, but rather occurs when Hector asks a newsstand vendor if he carries the

German newspaper *Der Spiegel*. He explains that he is a German tourist and is anxious to see some "unusual landmarks" not often found in guides (a fun reversal for Arent, who usually played a caricature of a *British* blunderer). The vendor, deciding to have some fun at Hector's expense, suggests he visit Soho and check out the "Dandy Club." Hector obliges. Still clueless after paying two attractive hostesses a hefty sum for his ticket, Hector finally enters the theater. This is where Francis achieves lasting verisimilitude. What transpires is a salacious sequence that conflates sex, death, and slapstick humor into cinematic splendor. This Soho seediness is further enhanced by Peter Thomas' hip-grinding music, which is completely synchronous with its situation, setting, and context. The final button to the scene occurs when Hector darts from the theater and the hostess yells, "If you don't like real art, why don't you just go visit the Tower?!" The sequence is unforgettable.

The "Dandy Club" scene proved risqué enough to be cut from the West German release print—thus acquiring a broader release rating from the FSK for ages twelve and up. This cut, however, shortened the film by several minutes. *Das Verrätertor*'s television edit ran even shorter. The official DVD and Blu Ray releases restored the missing footage, the color leader, and revised the FSK rating to age sixteen and over.

The Anglo-German cast assembled for *Das Verrätertor* is first rate. Of special note is Margot Trooger, who returns for her second (of three) *Krimi* appearances. This time, however, Trooger is freed from the role of Der Hexer's spouse Cora Ann Milton (last seen in 1964's *Der Hexer* and appearing next in *Neues vom Hexer*) and plays the part of Dinah with a detached and determined cool. Self-absorbed and obsessed with masterminding the heist, Trayne does not suspect that behind Trooger's Mona Lisa smile lies an unscrupulous betrayer.

Das Verrätertor's images of blowtorches and masked men trying to forcibly remove safely guarded items nostalgically returns the viewer back to the beginning of Rialto's Wallace journey à la the opening sequence of *Der Frosch mit der Maske* (1959). *Das Verrätertor* is unlike any entry from series regulars Reinl or Vohrer, which is precisely why it is an appealing venture. *Das Verrätertor* is also a very respectable heist film, one that proves suspenseful, enjoyable, and *unique*.

NEUES VOM HEXER / AGAIN THE RINGER (1965)

In an elaborate scheme involving cellar target practice and a wheelchair ramp, patriarch Lord Curtain (Wilhelm Vorwerg) is murdered by his nephew Archie Moore (Robert Hoffmann) with the help of the family's butler, Edwards (Klaus Kinski). As in many of Wallace's novels, a sizable inheritance appears to be the motive. Inspector Wesby's (Heinz Drache) plans to return to Australia (after the events of *Der Hexer*) are halted by Sir John (Siegfried Schürenberg) who recruits Wesby to replace Inspector Higgins, an otherwise occupied newlywed. Murder charges are leveled (yet again) at Arthur Milton, a.k.a. *der Hexer*. Milton travels to London with his wife Cora Ann (Margot Trooger) and butler Finch (a newly bearded Eddi Arent) to investigate the case and prove his innocence.

Meanwhile, members of the Curtain family are being picked off. Matriarch Lady Curtain is first on the list (Lia Eibenschütz), followed by nephew Archie. Grandson Charles is kidnapped and taken to a remote windmill. Lady Curtain's sister, Lady Aston (Brigitte Horney), recognizes the voice of the assassin orchestrating the murders over a radio ear receiver and begins her own parallel investigation. In addition to young Charles, rounding out the list of heirs is estranged niece Margie Fielding (Barbara Rütting), an artist who has rejected the family, its history, and its values. Lastly, of course, the estate's lawyer Bailey, (Heinz Spitzner), casts doubt on aspects of the proceedings while drawing some suspicion of his own. Will an unlikely partnership between *Der Hexer* and Scotland Yard thwart the diabolical machinations that could systematically wipe out an entire family?

The enormous success of Wallace's novel *The Ringer* prompted a sequel, titled *Again The Ringer*, in 1929. Rather than a single narrative work of fiction, the book is actually a collection of seventeen short stories featuring the character of Henry Arthur Milton, a.k.a. the Ringer. The volume was released in Germany as *Taschen-Krimi bd. 103* as part of Goldmann's ongoing *kriminalroman* series. No prior filmed adaptations are known to exist. *Der Hexer*'s screenwriter Herbert Reinecker was again on hand to pen the script, which was not based on any particular story or stories contained in *Again the Ringer*, but rather was a bricolage of themes, motifs, and characters. Production began on March 15 and wrapped on April 27, 1965. Shooting occurred at CCC's Berlin-Spandau Studios; among the exterior locations were Pfaueninsel (Peacock Island, last seen in *Die Tür mit den 7 Schlössern*) and the Westhafen port in West Berlin. The exterior shots of the windmill appear courtesy of *Die Gruft mit dem Rätselschloss*. *Neues vom Hexer* premiered at the Passage-Kino in Saarbrücken on June 4, 1965. *Neues vom Hexer* reverted back to the pre-Ultrascope format of 1.6:1, the common European widescreen standard at that time. While performing slightly better than its coproduction predecessor *Das Verrätertor*'s anemic 1.5 million, *Neues vom Hexer* tallied only 1.8 million (well below *Der Hexer*'s respectable 2.6 million) visitors.

Neues vom Hexer possesses one of the series most iconic openings (reportedly missing from several circulating prints, but since restored). The teaser, essentially a non-sequitur, features an ornate foreground coffin flanked by a single candleholder. A doorway—bathed in low-key, chiaroscuro fog—becomes visible in the deep space of the frame. Nephew Archie Moore emerges from the mist, slowly approaches the casket, knocks three times on the coffin, and waits. Edwards (a bearded Kinski) opens the lid, slowly sits up, and dryly intones, "It fits, sir." It's unclear what this means precisely, but it's implied that this is where Edwards will sleep (much sooner than he anticipates). In any case, the co-conspirators are suitably set-up for the post-credit murder sequence. The teaser is in fact *so* formally composed that it honors the mannerist works of Lang, Pabst, and Murnau. With Kinski's punch line, the credits begin. As Rialto saw no reason to stage and score a new credit sequence, *Neues vom Hexer* presents the same credits used for *Der Hexer*, modified only to add new color tints and, naturally, new title cards. The credits happily divulge that most of the original cast from *Der Hexer* is indeed on hand in this entertaining but uneven sequel.

Continuing some of the gimmicky hucksterism displayed at the climax of *Der Hexer* (the title card: can you guess the identity of *Der Hexer*?), *Neues vom Hexer* similarly engages in some ballyhoo of its own. Not unlike the notorious marketing deployed by Universal Studios for Alfred Hitchcock's *Psycho* (1960), a vow of secrecy was issued—not for audiences this time, but rather reversed back on the production itself. Actors were not permitted to discuss the film's unique twists with the press, family, or friends. This

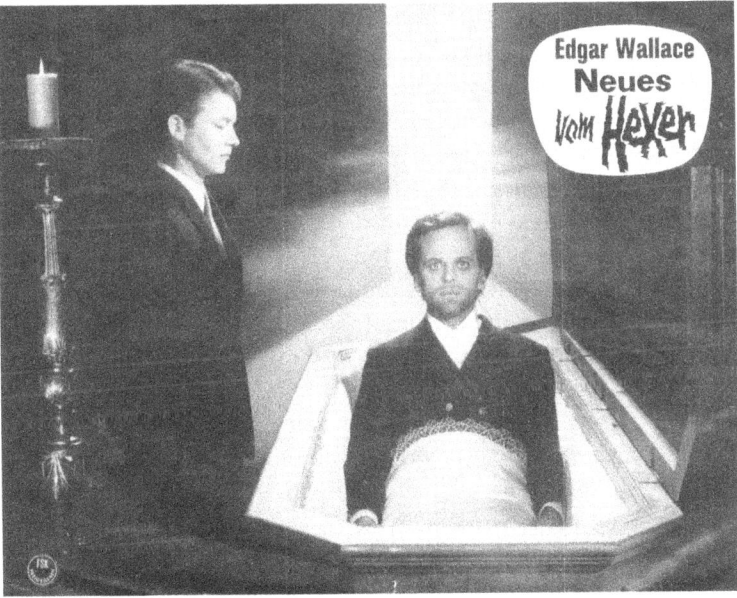

Figure 2.17 The Highly Formalist Pre-credit Teaser from 1965's *Neues vom Hexer* (*Again The Ringer*) Remains One of the Series' Most Famous and Beloved. *Source: Stifung Deutsche Kinematek Berlin.*

was a clever bit of publicity aimed amplifying the most salient feature of both *Hexer* entries, their strikingly acrobatic reveals. Several other "cheeky" moments dot the film with postmodern humor and make for a lot of knowing grins, particularly among fans of the *Krimiverse*. One such scene reveals Arthur Milton fast asleep on a lounge chair, a copy of Goldmann's *Neues vom Hexer* (featuring Wallace and his iconic cigarette holder) visibly resting on his lap. Finch enters and quickly rouses Milton, who asks "What is the matter, why did you wake me?" Finch trails off—unable to remember the film's next scene. He quickly snatches and consults the novel, exclaiming "Ah, page ninety-eight!" Milton replies "Oh my god, the boy's in danger!" They bolt from the room.

Alfred Vohrer is, yet again, in fine form in what would be the last black and white Rialto *Krimi* for the director. The ongoing partnership between cinematographer Karl Löb and Vohrer resulted in an incredibly smooth camera unit, easily on par with some of Europe and Hollywood's most celebrated pairings. Whether with exterior action sequences, intricate interior set-ups, or suspenseful milieus with expressionist echoes, Vohrer and Löb deliver perfectly operated, blocked, and lit visuals, time and again. Vohrer also continues his authorial signature of densely dressing his sets with an accompaniment of bizarre props and oddities. The Curtain mansion, in particular, is adorned in true Vohrer fashion, but his flourishes also extend to other locations. For example, niece Margie's art studio contains a stuffed stag (the *entire* stag) whose antlers double as a coat and hat "rack," and, of course, a door buzzer that triggers a light somewhere (a Vohrer favorite). Another ingenious moment showcases what appears to be a menacing syringe (a villainous instrument common to the series) which turns out to be used as a corkscrew.

Unfortunately, Vohrer fell ill during the production of *Neues vom Hexer*, requiring producer Horst Wendlandt to temporarily hire Will Tremper as a replacement. Tremper, a jack of all trades, shot around Vohrer's health problems and the film was completed without incident.

Neues vom Hexer really belongs to celebrated German actress Brigitte Horney. With the film offering aspects of the police procedural (a sub-genre unevenly applied to the series *in toto*), Horney's Lady Aston shines as the primary investigator. We learn far more from her excursions, observations, and actions than we do from any official at Scotland Yard. She provides the complex story a steady throughline. Her inscrutable visage is softened by her tired, sorrowful eyes—eyes that have seen a lot in their lifetime. Born in 1911, Horney grew up in a suburb of Berlin where she became deeply involved with the celebrated Volksbühne Theater (the People's Theater). Her childhood classmates included such future actresses as Ilka Grüning and Lilli Palmer (Horney formed a lifelong friendship with the latter). At age six, Horney developed tuberculosis and would periodically travel to Switzerland for treatment throughout her life (including during World War II). Often portraying women of power and authority, Horney was a gifted and consummate actress in the German film and television industry; her career spanned a remarkable seven decades. Her return to the screen in *Neues vom Hexer*, however, ended a period of relative inactivity for the actress, which happily led to the acceptance (a gift for fans) of more work in film and TV. Fortunately, this included another *Krimi*; Horney accepted the role of Sister General in the Rialto-UK coproduction *Das Geheimnis der weissen Nonne* (*The Trygon Factor*, 1966). Perfectly fluent in English (a tremendous industry asset), no dubbing was required.

Expectations ran high for the sequel to one of Wallace's most beloved works and one of Rialto's most popular *Krimis*. Overall, *Neues vom Hexer* did not disappoint, especially in its first and third acts (it's not often you get to see a villain literally tie someone to the train tracks). The production begins with a (literal) bang and culminates with a thrill-ride ending. But like any good sandwich, there should be some protein in-between, and *Neues vom Hexer* is often slow, (intentionally) convoluted, and malnourished, yielding a middle act of unfulfilled potential. Moreover, audiences were disappointed with the killer's identity, feeling as if they had been slightly cheated. Regardless, the film remains a staple of the series and for a good reason. With the studio's next feature, its twentieth in the series, Rialto was about to bid a final fond farewell to the massively popular and influential black and white era of the Edgar Wallace *Krimi*.

DER UNHEIMLICHE MÖNCH / *THE SINISTER MONK* (1965)

From his death bed, the Lord of Darkwood Castle amends his last will and testament, witnessed and documented by his notary (Wilhelm Vorwerg). The Lord's daughter, Lady Patricia (Ilse Steppat), is the inheritor of the castle where she will continue to run a private boarding school for girls. Estranged granddaughter Gwendolin Gillmore (Karin Dor), however, is named sole heir of the remaining Darkwood fortune, leaving his conniving sons, lawyer Sir Richard (Siegfried Lowitz) and doctor Sir William (Dieter Eppler), disinherited. Upon leaving the castle, the notary's windshield is shattered by a hurled rock. The car spins out of control, slams into a tree, and bursts into flames, but not before a dark figure snatches the will from the vehicle.

Out of concern for her niece, Patricia invites Gwendolin to Darkwood, but Richard and William have other, more sinister plans for their niece. Such plans include coercion, "accidental" harm, and perhaps even death. Shortly after arriving at the estate, Gwendolin befriends the school's caretaker, "Smitty" (Eddi Arent), and also meets pigeon wrangler-cum-death mask "artist" Alfons Short (Rudolf Schündler). The notary's death has unsurprisingly triggered Scotland Yard's arrival in the form of eager Inspector Bratt (Harald Leipnitz) and ambivalent Sir John (Siegfried Schürenberg), the latter merely antagonizing Patricia by not taking the threat to the school, or the girls, seriously. The strange resident artist—who obsesses over pigeons and begs girls to let him take death mask molds of their faces—bumps into Gwendolin and tells her the story of the ghost monk that haunts the grounds of Darkwood castle, which had previously been a monastery. Shortly, thereafter, a Scotland Yard sentry actually apprehends and arrests the monk, catching him while departing the castle grounds. Carelessly, the Scotland Yard man lets his guard down for a moment, and the monk breaks his neck with the crack of his weighted whip. Apparently, Potter was investigating rumors that the school is conscripting students into the sex trade. Inspector Bratt leads the investigation into uncovering the identity of the monk and ascertaining the reason behind the disappearance of the academy's students.

As discussed in this chapter's entry for *Der Schwarze Abt* (196), Wallace adapted his novel *The Black Abbot* (1926) for the stage as *The Terror* in 1927. The stage play was then adapted back into novel form under the same title in 1929. Rialto's *Der Unheimliche Mönch* (*The Sinister Monk*, 1965) takes its basic narrative cues from this novel. Goldmann published *The Terror*, with the German title *Der Unheimliche Mönch*, as *Taschen-Krimi bd. 203* in 1961. Production on the film began on October 6 and wrapped on November 17, 1965. Not unlike the initial *Krimis* produced by Rialto, the picture was shot in a variety of locations: West Berlin, Hamburg, the port of Hamburg-Harburg, Lower Saxony, and London. Castle Hastenbeck in Lower Saxony is especially well-leveraged for the film's spooky setting and the Hittfelder Mühle bei Hamburg scenes (with windmill and trap doors) provide ample menace. Most interior works were completed at the CCC Film studios in the Berlin-Spandau complex. *Der Unheimliche Mönch* premiered on December 17, 1965, at the Passage-Kino in Saarbrücken.

With Reinl's *Der Unheimliche Mönch* (1965), Rialto completed its cycle of black and white productions (begun with Reinl's *Der Frosch mit der Mask* in 1959)—bringing down the final curtain on this well-defined and much-loved *Krimi* era. *Unheimliche Mönch* actually foreshadows this imminent switchover from black and white to color stock very early in the film. For the first time, an *all-color* title sequence (the teaser and actual film are still in black and white) was presented to the public. Over these tantalizing credits, composer Peter Thomas wrote an effective composition with his own unique signature sound (which, perhaps consciously or unconsciously, echoes Jack Marshall's theme for *The Munsters*).[34] Apart from this main theme, however, the rest of the score offers a progressively schizophrenic platter of odd tracks that set a new standard in mood inappropriateness. As Kim Newman observed, *Der Unheimliche Mönch* "boasts the craziest score of all the *Krimis* (a Peter Thomas riot of over-orchestration and mixed-in choral effects)."[35]

Krime in Chiaroscuro 129

How did Rialto decide to "kill off" its black and white period? Appropriately enough, with a return to "proper" horror. Indeed, *Unheimliche Mönch* feels very much like a film from the "classic" era of production—the early years of 1959, 1960, and 1961. Upon first consideration, this does not appear to be a significant span of time. True, only six years had passed since the series began, but the rate of change and innovation over a frenzied production schedule of twenty films *in six years* is truly staggering.

To allow for the Gothic horror scenario to fully develop, Rialto wisely chose a book that unfolds at a remote, rural location—far enough away from the urban sprawl of London but close enough for day trips into the city. At times, the aesthetic of *Unheimliche Mönch* (previously tested with mixed results in 1963's *Der Schwarze Abt*) is dazzling. The nighttime castle courtyard sequences featuring the ominously backlit monk are especially striking. Moreover, the London excursions from Darkwood resulted in freshly shot footage of the capitol—which always lent realist value to the films while also making the concept of the white slave trade more plausible as a plot device. The London exterior scenes provide welcome relief, especially since Rialto had been become a more set-oriented production unit after relocating to Berlin.

Figure 2.18 Krimi Queen Karin Dor Demonstrates Why She Would Soon Be Cast as One of James Bond's More Memorable Villainesses in *You Only Live Twice* (1967). Promotional still for *Der Unheimliche Mönch (The Sinister Monk, 1965)*. *Source: Stifung Deutsche Kinematek Berlin.*

Unheimliche Mönch playfully amps up the horror tropes endemic (but frequently attenuated) to the series; indeed, the very first shot firmly sets the movie's tone with a panoply of common horror characteristics: a foggy night, a foreboding castle, and a shadowy figure. Moreover, the presence of a unique and menacing villain (with an even more unique method of murder) luridly recalls the series' earliest efforts (*Der Frosch mit der Maske*, *Der Grüne Bogenschütze*, *Die toten Augen von London*). Without question, the monk's deadly Australian stockwhip (a whip with a leaden ball secured to its end) becomes a major star of the film and provides Reinl a fetishistic device to spotlight. Reinl did not share Vohrer's playful love of ubiquitous props and symbolic mise-en-scène, so he fittingly compensates with the addictive spectacle of the sinister monk snapping necks like twigs. The film also has its share of truly absurd, laugh-out-loud moments. Perhaps this is most aptly demonstrated in not one but *two* scenes where a helicopter chases a carrier pigeon.

The real challenge for *Unheimliche Mönch* lay in its atypical casting. Series stalwarts Fuchsberger and Drache are absent, and Lowitz is uncharacteristically cast as a villain. The likable Harald Leipnitz, last seen as the duplicitous Jimmy Flynn in *Die Gruft mit dem Rätselschloss*, steps up to fill the lead inspector shoes but registers an at times stilted performance and lacks the genuine chemistry with co-star Karin Dor that Fuchsberger effortlessly engendered. Nevertheless, Ilse Steppat and Rudolf Schündler (in the typical Kinski role) shine and deliver first-rate performances.

By this point, it seems obvious that the series was gradually setting up Eddi Arent to become a villain, with the first steps taken as the valet for antagonist Arthur Milton (alias *Der Hexer*) in the two *Hexer* films. So, in *Unheimliche Mönch* it should come as no surprise that "Smitty" is not at all what he pretends to be. This progression is taken to its logical conclusion in the series' next picture, *Der Bucklige von Soho* (1966).

Der Unheimliche Mönch not only marks the end of the black and white era but also the end of Karin Dor's *Krimi* career. By 1965, Dor's international stock was soaring due to her unwavering commitment to Rialto's *Krimis*, Karl May westerns, and other continental and intercontinental coproductions. *Zimmer 13*, in particular, can be identified as a career turning point. Her sympathetic portrayal of a trauma-ridden child, now a trauma-repressed adult, showed impressive versatility and range. Dor, a stunningly beautiful, dark-eyed brunette easily possessed the "looks" to establish a foothold in the European production sphere, but it was her untapped talent and dedication to her craft that elicited such strong reactions in fans. Dor's real gift was her ability to generate genuine concern for her characters' safety and sincere wishes for their romantic happiness. She had an effortless ability to get you rooting hard for her vulnerable yet resourceful leading ladies. With such popularity, she soon found herself in more prominent parts in larger international productions, including perhaps her most well-known role (ironically bucking her traditional darker image with a coiffure of fiery red hair) as seductive assassin Helga Brandt in the James Bond film, *You Only Live Twice* (1967). With the newfound international status that frequently accompanies a Bond credential, more roles materialized, including a major offer from director Alfred Hitchcock, who called upon Dor to star in his 1969 espionage thriller *Topaz*.

In the final analysis, director Harald Reinl bookended the black and white productions with an influential debut and a distinguished exit (this was to be Reinl's last *Krimi*). *Der Unheimliche Mönch* provided a strong coda to this era of filmmaking and also afforded a graceful *Krimi* finale for its leading lady and her husband/director. With Rialto's next production, the series would experience a radical transformation.

NOTES

1. *Daß das Publikum die Trümmer und auch die Schuldabtragungsfrage zu dieser Zeit nicht mehr wollte*, Lichtspielträume. Kino in Hannover 1896–1991, ed. by the Society for Film Studies e.V., Hanover 1991. A conversation with Hans Abich, pp. 57–68.
2. Ticket sales are sourced from Joachim Kramp's *Hallo—Hier sprich Edgar Wallace! Die Geschichte der deutschen Kriminalfilmserie 1959–1972*. However, these numbers are approximations. European sales figures from this era are notoriously difficult to calculate due to "creative" bookkeeping by studios, distributors, and exhibitors.
3. *Mystery Science Theater 3000* is commonly abbreviated as MST3K.
4. Exact production dates are not known for this title.
5. Newman, *Video Watchdog* 134, 24.
6. Retrieved from: http://www.webarchiv-server.de/pin/archiv00/4400ob21.htm 7/20/19
7. Several stories exist about the origins of Fuchsberger's internationally known nickname of "Blacky." One account claims that a fellow soldier misheard his nickname of "Jackie" as "Blackie" and it stuck. Another tale asserts it was earned while working in coalmines after World War II. Yet another story, told by Fuchsberger himself in an interview with the *Frankfurter Rundschau*, declares it was the nickname he earned while working as a Bavarian broadcaster. A more detailed account can be found here: https://www.merkur.de/boulevard/joachim-fuchsberger-spitzname-blacky-warum-herkunft-zr-3853552.html
8. Interview with author in his home. June 2018. Madrid, Spain.
9. Exact production dates are not known for this title.
10. *Screen Series: Germany An Illustrated Guide and Index*, 1970, 146.
11. Danny Peary, *Cult Movie Stars* (New York: Simon & Schuster, 1991), 199.
12. Samm Deighan, *Smooth Kriminal: The Dead Eyes of London (1961)* https://diaboliquemagazine.com/smooth-kriminal-the-dead-eyes-of-london-1961/
13. I include myself in a category of viewer that would enjoy such a triple feature.

14. Press materials for *Die toten Augen von London*. Accessed through the *Deutsches Filmmuseum* archives in Frankfurt, Germany. June 2018.

15. Joseph W. Angell, *Historical Analysis of the 14–15 February 1945 Bombings of Dresden*. USAF Historical Division (1953). https://media.defense.gov/2011/Feb/08/2001329907/-1/-1/0/Bombings%20of%20Dresden.pdf

16. Peter Hayes, *From Cooperation to Complicity: Degussa in the Third Reich* (Cambridge, UK: Cambridge University Press, 2004).

17. Bergfelder, *International Adventures*, 157.

18. *Stuggarter Zeitung*. Review of the film, 1961.

19. For more on Jess Franco's *El Conde Dracula* and, more broadly, the Spanish horror film, see Nicholas G. Schlegel, *Sex, Sadism, Spain, and Cinema: The Spanish Horror Film* (Lanham, MD: Rowman & Littlefield, 2015).

20. Noble Frankland and Charles Webster, *The Strategic Air Offensive Against Germany, 1939–1945*, Volume II (London: H. M. Stationery Office, 1961), 260–261.

21. *The Beatles Anthology*, directed by Bob Smeaton and Geoff Wonfor (Episode 1, 2003); DVD.

22. *The Dark Side: The Magazine of the Macabre and the Fantastic* no. 191, 2018.

23. Internationally, this tradition continued with Mexico's *El Fantasma de la Casa Roja* (*The Phantom in the Red House*, 1956) and *Echenme al Vampiro* (1963; released in the United States in 1964 as *Bring Me the Vampire*), Italy's *Danza Macabra* (*Castle of Blood*, 1964), and the UK's *What A Carve Up!* (1961; released in the United States in 1962 as *No Place Like Homicide!*).

24. For more on the topic, please see: https://www.btp.police.uk/police-forces/british-transport-police/areas/about-us/about-us/our-history/crime-history/great-train-robbery/

25. As recounted in Joachim Kramp's entry for the film.

26. Bergfelder, *International Adventures*, 160.

27. Stefano Baschiera and Francesco Di Chiara, "Exotic Landscapes and Italian Holidays in Lucio Fulci's Zombie and Sergio Martino's Torso," in *Cinema Inferno: Celluloid Explosions from the Cultural Margins*, eds. Robert G. Weiner and John Cline (Lanham, MD: Scarecrow Press, 2010).

28. Newman, *Video Watchdog*, 34.

29. Ibid.

30. Newman, *Video Watchdog*, 36.

31. Additionally, there were three television adaptations of *Der Hexer*: 1938, 1956, and 1963.

32. Herbert Reinecker (1914–2007) was a prolific novelist, television writer, and screenwriter—often employed as the latter for Rialto's Wallace adaptations. Reinecker was also a former Nazi SS officer. For more on his career, please see https://www.welt.de/kultur/article13604688/Derrick-und-sein-Schoepfer-der-SS-Offizier.html

33. Bergfelder, *International Adventures*, 157.

34. The score also resembles, but predates Vic Mizzy's iconic score for the popular Don Knott's vehicle, *The Ghost and Mr. Chicken* (1966).

35. Newman, *Video Watchdog*, 38.

Chapter 3

Krime in Single-Strip Color
1966–1972

While the first half of the 1960s proved profitable for Rialto's popular productions, the second half of the decade presented new challenges. The production company had made several economic, logistical, and stylistic modifications to their two most lucrative properties—the ongoing Wallace *Krimis* and the Karl May westerns. Still, the most extreme change had yet to occur. In the face of declining ticket sales, Rialto abandoned the *Krimi* series-defining black and white look in favor of a hip, more contemporary color motion picture stock. *Der Bucklige von Soho* (*The Hunchback of Soho*, 1966) would be the flagship production for this final "color stage" of the cycle's lifespan.

To be sure, Rialto was gambling, but on its present course, the franchise was destined to suffer an anachronistic fate. Cultural shifts in Europe, the United States, and the globe writ-large necessitated prescient change—something Hollywood learned the hard way with the collapse and eventual demise of its studio system in the same decade. For Rialto then, the changeover to Eastmancolor was borne more of market share necessity imposed on the series by competing productions in Europe and the United States (particularly those that pushed a prurient agenda of sex and violence in vivid color) than a deliberate artistic choice. As we will see, however, the new format and approach would have a profound impact on the series.

Motion picture color cinematography and processing underwent a radical change in the 1950s. Although Technicolor had become the dominant luxury process, the three-strip camera (with three strips of red, blue, and green film running through the complex camera simultaneously) was cumbersome, the dye transfer printing process proprietary, and the focus soft.[1] Furthermore, as Russell Merritt has noted, "because the Technicolor apparatus was leased—never sold—filmmakers were obliged to use Technicolor's camera, its labs, its custom-made negative and print stock, and the Technicolor support staff."[2]

Competitor Eastmancolor's single-strip process, however, was unencumbered by these entanglements. As a result, "by 1954, virtually all Hollywood color films were shot in Eastmancolor negative. And as far as Eastman was concerned, studios could do with their stock whatever they wanted."[3]

As a result of this widespread migration to color photography, color movies and later television became far cheaper to produce. Indeed, in the United States, ABC, CBS, and NBC unveiled full-color prime time schedules for the 1966–1967 broadcast season. In Europe, production companies like Rialto could budget for color stock (which also required more light during production and more laboratory timing in post) without incurring prohibitive expenditures. Indeed, Rialto was no stranger to color cinematography. For example, *The Treasure of Silver Lake* (1962), the first Karl May western for the studio, was attractively rendered in Eastmancolor.

The Wallace *Krimis*, on the other hand, had remained loyal to the DNA of their ancestors—the most significant characteristic of which was the stark black and white photography. However, by the mid-1960s, this defining trait was simply incongruous with the current state of the genre. Overtaken by the color productions of England, Italy, and the United States, the *Krimi* was put on notice to either adapt or disappear.

Rialto would produce a total of twelve color films between 1966 and 1972, at which point the Wallace *Krimi* series had atrophied and faded from the cinemas. It has been widely circulated and often accepted that the introduction of color prompted the series decline and eventual disappearance. To be clear, it was not actually "color" that heralded the beginning of the end for the Wallace *Krimi*, but rather a confluence of culturally, economically, and politically determined factors that accounted for the genre's decline.

DER BUCKLIGE VON SOHO / *THE HUNCHBACK OF SOHO* (1966)

Soho "showgirls" are turning up dead, strangled by an individual of considerable strength. Inspector Hopkins of Scotland Yard (Günther Stoll) heads the investigation but struggles to find any solid leads apart from strong chemicals—detergents—found on the victims' hands. Meanwhile, US citizen Wanda Merville (Monika Peitsch), the daughter of the late Lord Donald Perkins, has returned to England to claim her inheritance. Shortly after her meeting with the executor of the estate, Harold Stone (Joachim Teege), she is kidnapped by the ruthless Allan Davis (Pinkas Braun) masquerading as a taxi driver. Davis places Merville in a halfway house for ex-cons which doubles as a Dickensian laundry workhouse. He then arranges to have his partner in crime Gladys Garnder (Uta Levka) impersonate Wanda Merville.

Considering Stone knows the real identity of Merville, they drum up an untrue blackmail accusation to ensure his cooperation with the inheritance proceedings.

Meanwhile at Castlewood estate, the eccentric brother of the late Lord Donald, General Perkins (Hubert von Meyerinck), bunkers in his basement (in full regalia) and recreates daily the Battle of Tobruk with his butler (Albert Bessler). His wife, Lady Marjorie (Agnes Windeck), is the benefactor of the halfway house for troubled girls, which is administrated by Davis. The Janus-faced Reverend David (Eddi Arent) along with his strict, whip-toting doyenne Mrs. Oberin (Hilde Sessak) supervise the girls as they toil in the house's underground laundry—which resembles a Roman slave galley. When a girl revolts or tries to escape, she is "ratted out" by the pet fact-totem, which prompts the eponymous hunchback's vice-like grip to crush their escaping necks. Conversely, if the girls behave, they can "graduate" to working for the demanding madame Mrs. Tyndal (Gisela Uhlen) in the Mekka nightclub (a casino and brothel) as "company" for guests. More murders, double-crosses, red herrings, and fake suicides ensue until events converge at the Castlewood estate. The film then becomes an endurance test for Wanda Merville; will she survive long enough to claim her inheritance?

As Rialto entered its last phase of production, it also ended any attempts at adapting Edgar Wallace novels. This trend began toward the end of the black and white era but with this entry, any pretense of literary fidelity was abandoned, closing the long-standing tradition of the Goldmann *Taschen-Krimi* novel tie-in (which was smartly marketed on the German posters). *Der Bucklige von Soho* was not based on any particular novel (no such Wallace title exists), but rather reflected common motifs used in several of Wallace's books and many of Rialto's productions. As Kim Newman observes, *Der Bucklige von Soho* is "an instant redo of *Der Unheimliche Mönch*" and "makes by-now standard references to earlier films."[4]

Despite the solid box-office performance of *Der Unheimliche Mönch*, Rialto decided to move up their color timetable, as their overall profit trend was sloping downward. *Der Bucklige von Soho* was originally announced as a black and white production along with the other titles slated for release in 1966: *Das Geheimnis der weissen Nonne* (*The Secret of the White Nun*) and *Der Hexer 66* (a planned but abandoned sequel to the popular *Der Hexer* and *Neues vom Hexer* pictures). When preproduction stalled on *Das Geheimnis der weissen Nonne*, *Der Bucklige von Soho* vaulted into the pole position and was completed between June 1 and July 13, 1966. The film was shot in West Berlin, primarily at the CCC Berlin-Haselhorst Studios and the Spandau Citadel (a fortress in Berlin that provided the exteriors for Castlewood). The conversion to color film also necessitated some new establishing and transition shots of London. The movie premiered on September 27, 1966, at the

Mathäser Filmpalast in Munich. Ticket sales were exceptional, with over 2.2 million visitors.

After penning the generally well-received script for *Neues vom Hexer*, Herbert Reinecker was hired again to rewrite a draft by Harald G. Petersson. As this film was not based on a Wallace novel or short story, Reinecker enjoyed a great deal of creative freedom in crafting the scenario. And, indeed, everything about *Der Bucklige von Soho* is clearly intended to prime audiences for a different aesthetic and thus a different theater-going experience. The gambit largely succeeded. Apart from the obvious novelty of Eastmancolor, there were several other crucial changes made—some of which were controversial. The much-loved, venerable Wallace teaser (a workhorse of exposition and style whose only real analog would be found in the James Bond series) is unusually brief and does not begin with the typical, elaborately staged Wallace murder but rather with the blunt milieu of a showgirl in an overcoat frantically escaping the Mekka nightclub by ducking into a phone booth for help, where she's brutally strangled by a limping, caricaturist hunchback. Absent is the thrilling machine-gun fire that would normally pepper the screen with the bloody letters E-D-G-A-R followed by the rapid-fire W-A-L-L-A-C-E. Like a call to a congregation of worship, the response to the machine-gun fire was always, of course, "*Hallo, hier sprich Edgar Wallace.*" This essential and iconic aural cue happily remains intact. But this opening unequivocally signaled that business would not be quite as usual from now on.

The imposing of color on the Wallace *Krimis* was responsible for several initial casualties. Foremost among them was the loss of the series-defining chiaroscuro lighting. Eastmancolor required more foot candles and faster lenses than the ISO (ASA in the United Kingdom and United States) of black and white stock. As a result, the majority of the sets are lit with a high key design. This imbued the film with a pronounced flatness, absence of depth, and appreciable lack of saturation that deprived *Der Bucklige von Soho* of one of the series' most striking, recognizable, and culturally resonant attributes—its visuals. Certain exterior shots do fare better, with more contrast and saturation present. The Mekka casino similarly makes for a handsome set, and the laundry facilities and tunnels are impressively dressed and shot, but overall the lighting design is one found more typically in motion picture comedies. Perhaps this is the film's most profound tell, for above all else, *Der Bucklige von Soho*'s humor far outweighs any serious attempts to shock or frighten.

This would become the basic resting pulse for the remainder of the series: a greater emphasis on cheeky humor, larger amounts of brightly colored blood, and bolder exploitation elements. A curious commentary on this new approach occurs within the first few minutes of the film. Sir John (Siegfried Schürenberg) enters the city morgue where Inspector Hopkins (Günther Stoll) awaits his counsel. Upon passing a completely naked female body (a recent victim of the strangling hunchback) lying on a mortician's slab, Sir John shields his eyes

Figure 3.1 *Der Bucklige von Soho* Marked the Last Rialto *Krimi* for Veteran Stage and Screen Star Gisela Uhlen (Who Was also the Niece of *Nosferatu's* Max Schreck). *Der Bucklige von Soho* (*The Hunchback of Soho*, 1966). Source: *Stifung Deutsche Kinematek Berlin*.

from the corpse by quickly raising his bowler to use as a peripheral blinder. It's a revealing gesture considering Sir John's character is the archetypal "dirty old man" who ogles women at every opportunity, even opining later in the film "I don't like to look at *dead* women." There is an explicit willingness to conflate sex and death here—boldly declaring their union (a common Euro horror trope) in vivid Eastmancolor. Sir John's fey repudiation is a knowing wink to the audience that indeed "the gloves are off" and the series will "go there" to compete in the marketplace. Certainly, Hammer Studios went there, early, and often, and by the time their Karnstein Trilogy was unveiled, exponentially more.[5] Yet this shift for Rialto didn't actually shrink the peculiar delta between Rialto Film and Hammer Film Productions. On the contrary, on the one hand, you have a German-made series that is set in London, with sex, sordidness, violence, mini-skirts, hip nightclubs, go-go boots, jazzy beats, and attempts at "British humor," while on the other you have an *actual* English production company whose productions eschew humor, tout horror and sex, and often set their diegesis in nineteenth-century Germany.

Yet, *Der Bucklige von Soho* was a substantial success, drawing in 2.2 million visitors. In fact, it was the most successful of the final twelve Rialto *Krimis*. What, then, accounts for the film's popularity and generally positive reception (apart from the newness of its color presentation)? Simply put, it was a perfectly auspicious example of Rialto's decision to renovate the series vis-à-vis the zeitgeist of the 1960s.

True, when measured against some European and American independent releases, *Der Bucklige von Soho* reads comparatively tame in its depictions of graphic violence, sexual explicitness, or cultural transgressions (although the white slave trade aspect here is more boldly on display than in previous productions like *Neues vom Hexer* and *Der Unheimliche Mönch*). Remember, the series had already created and maintained an iconic brand that spanned twenty films and nearly a decade. Excessive tampering with the basic formula bore too high a risk; rather, Rialto's present objective was to participate favorably in the larger intercontinental marketplace without alienating their core base while at the same time hopefully luring in new viewers.

Der Bucklige von Soho also proved a somewhat prescient motion picture, prefiguring films like Narciso Ibáñez Serrador's excellent *La Residencia* (1969) or Jess Franco's *99 Mujeres* (1969). The setting of an authoritarian boarding school had been a golden goose for Rialto in past productions, but *Der Bucklige von Soho* combined this with a prison/halfway house milieu and threw in the Church of England for good measure. The late 1960s and early 1970s would see an overabundance of these types of programmers flood screens in Europe and the United States (often double-billed at drive-ins).

Director Alfred Vohrer adeptly makes the switch to color, and his trademark moving camera silently glides from scene to scene in this enjoyable film. *Der Bucklige von Soho* marked the last Rialto *Krimi* performance for actress Gisela Uhlen. With her dynamic presence and commanding voice, the gifted actress continued to work for many decades, particularly on television and in the same genre. Carried largely by a first-rate cast (as was often the case), the allure of color, and a super-hip Peter Thomas score ("The Hump" is one of his best themes), *Der Bucklige von Soho* represents a solid start to the final evolutionary stage for the Edgar Wallace motion pictures.

DAS GEHEIMNIS DER WEISSEN NONNE / *THE TRYGON FACTOR* (1966)

Inspector Thompson (Allan Cuthbertson) of Scotland Yard visits the palatial Emberday estate which houses the Order of Vigilance Convent who are known for their ceramic artistry. Feigning identity as a tourist, he eventually meets with Sister Clare O'Connor (Diane Clare) to obtain information regarding recent crimes suspected to be connected to the Order, and, in exchange for this evidence, help O'Connor relocate. After briefly meeting with her, Thompson is suddenly attacked from behind by a leather-clad, masked figure and viciously drowned in a baptismal fount. Fearing for her life and sensing the danger surrounding her, O'Connor smartly uses a group of tourists as a shield to escape aboard a bus from what was certain to be her own murder.

Thompson's sudden disappearance triggers an investigation by Superintendent Cooper-Smith (Stewart Granger) under the command of Scotland Yard's Sir John (portrayed by James Robertson Justice in the English language release and by Siegfried Schürenberg in the German language dub). He proceeds to interview members of the Emberday family: poker-faced matriarch Lady Livia (Cathleen Nesbitt), her perpetually costumed man-child son Luke (James Culliford), and her flirty photographer daughter Trudy (Susan Hampshire). Cooper-Smith is unconvinced by their statements and insists on a search warrant, but Sir John refuses.

In the meantime, the Emberday family holds a bogus funeral of a supposed relative, Carlo, who is actually the renowned safe-cracker Emil Clossen (Eddi Arent). Under the supervision of ruthless Nun Superior (Brigitte Horney), Carlo engineers a bank vault robbery—a final heist of gold that will allow for lavish living abroad. Apparently, the Order conceals stolen gems and precious metals in the "Trygon" vases that are fired in the Emberday kilns. As Scotland Yard closes in on the criminal activities, the body count rises. As it turns out, however, the masked murderer is *not* the only killer.

Das Geheimnis der weissen Nonne was a loosely based (on certain motifs) adaptation of the Edgar Wallace novel *Kate Plus Ten* (1917). The novel was first adapted for the screen in 1938 as the British thriller *Kate Plus Ten*, directed by Reginald Denham for Richard Wainwright Production (released in the United States under the title *Queen of Crime*). There was no Goldmann *Taschen-Krimi* published in Germany for this Wallace title. *Das Geheimnis der weissen Nonne* was produced by Rialto Film (under their London subsidiary Film Preben Philipsen Ltd., formed in 1965) and shot in London between August 15 and October 7, 1966. It premiered on December 16, 1966, at the Passage cinema in Saarbrücken. Attendance dropped precipitously to 1.6 visitors.

Das Geheimnis der weissen Nonne is a beautifully shot production with careful and, at times, beautiful pictorial composition. The vivid color pallet found in the Emberday estate is awash in lush pinks, purples, blues, and reds, while the nearby Whiteheart Hotel boasts vibrant hues of green, orange, peach, and yellow. This approach in style anticipates the lush color photography utilized by Dario Argento in his seminal *Suspiria* (1977), which owes attribution to Mario Bava's *gialli* and Germany's *Krimis*. Unfortunately, however, one framing device in *Das Geheimnis der weissen Nonne* (the camera often positioned behind a series of foregrounded parallel bars or ornate iron work) conspicuously intrudes and is overused with no real symbolic or narrative significance. The film's other misfire, albeit an exciting one, is simply its cacophonous climax where bedlam ensues. To be clear, it's certainly not dull, but rather, incongruous with its first two acts.

Primarily a television director, Cyril Frankel confidently helms the production—an impressive feat considering the series deeply established tone, aesthetic, and fan base. Frankel keeps things moving at a brisk pace and makes worthy use of a fine international cast. Stewart Granger, fresh off a starring role in Rialto's adaptation of Karl May's *Old Surehand* (1965), segues comfortably into the role of Superintendent Cooper-Smith. In his early fifties, but still vibrant and charismatic, Granger fulfilled his contractual quota for Rialto on this production.

Also concluding contractual obligations with Rialto was the series' most symbolic actor, Eddi Arent. *Das Geheimnis der weissen Nonne* marked the end of an extraordinary twenty-one film run with the studio (this number merely reflects his Edgar Wallace work with the studio). This fact alone makes *Das Geheimnis der weissen Nonne* a notable entry in the *Krimi* canon. Indeed, Arent's departure was symbolically significant and a harbinger of the forthcoming challenges facing the survival of the series.

Other strong performances from the intercontinental cast distinguish the film. The much-loved, British national treasure Cathleen Nesbitt relishes the opportunity to play against type as a heartless villain, as does contemporary German actress Brigitte Horney. After her recent role in *Neues vom Hexer* (1965), Horney had expressed interest in playing a villain in future production and the veteran actress delivers as the ruthless Nun Superior. In like manner, the always delightful Robert Morley (although underused) adds a more authentic caricature of "Britishness" than what the series had proffered since its inception. Rounding out the cast are Sophie Hardy (her second and final Wallace outing) and English actress Susan Hampshire in a pivotal role.

Rialto's second color production would lamentably be its last coproduction with Great Britain. Rialto's prior coproductions with the United Kingdom, *Das Geheimnis der gelben Narzissen* (1961) and *Das Verrätertor* (1964) together with *Das Geheimnis der weissen Nonne* unequivocally resulted in some of the most distinctive entries in the *Krimi* canon. The blending of approaches and styles between the United Kingdom and West Germany made for lighthearted, fascinating, and harmonious cultural relations between the two nations and their unified love of a popular author, genre, and series.[6] Moreover, although shot in England with a largely English cast and crew, the cross-pollinating of dominant *Krimi* and *giallo* traits continued in *Das Geheimnis der weissen Nonne*. The film features bold primary and secondary color configurations that are reflected not only in the setting but also, impressively, in the costume design, an intrepid high key lighting scheme to underscore these elements, and iconography play with black leather, masks,

Figure 3.2 The Order of Vigilance Nuns Fence and Smuggle Stolen Gems through Their Renowned Trygon Ceramics Line in *Das Geheimnis der weissen Nonne* (*The Trygon Factor,* 1966). *Source: Stifung Deutsche Kinematek Berlin.*

and gloves. Crucially, the film also continues to accent the gender dynamics that were encouraged in early *gialli* and trumpeted in later productions.

One fact that is made manifestly and abundantly clear with *Das Geheimnis der weissen Nonne* is how much of a house style was emblazoned on Rialto's *Krimis*. Deviations from the firmly established tone and aesthetic were markedly noticed and, importantly, noted by spectators—accounting for different reception modes in West Germany, Great Britain, and Italy. As noted, however, this was not necessarily a detriment to the series as much as it was a potential opportunity for creators to use the canvas differently.

DIE BLAUE HAND / THE CREATURE WITH THE BLUE HAND (1967)

In the important backstory of *Die blaue Hand*, the Earl of Emerson fled to the United States when charged with embezzlement. In doing so, he abandoned his second wife, Lady Emerson (Ilse Steppat), and the four children from his first marriage. As the story opens in the present day, son Dave Emerson (Klaus Kinski in dual roles of Dave and his twin brother Richard) is on trial for the murder of the Emerson estate's gardener, Edward Amery. Dr.

Mangrove (Carl Lange), a psychiatrist and mental health authority, testifies that Dave is criminally insane, a danger to society, and must be incarcerated at the Mangrove asylum. Found guilty, Dave protests and screams repeatedly: "I'm innocent! I'm innocent! I'm innocent!" As with the teaser to *Der Bucklige von Soho*, *Die blaue Hand* similarly freezes frame on a gaping, screaming mouth. The trademark Wallace greeting (and successive bullet-holes) follows.

Sometime later, at Mangrove's asylum, a key is tossed into Dave's cell (by whom exactly is a mystery), allowing him to make a late-night escape via a rope ladder. Unsurprisingly, a pack of barking German Shepherds (that "pet" Rialto trope found in myriad Wallace adaptations) give chase to the fleeing Dave. With no place to go, he returns to his father's estate where the staff, his stepmother, and his three siblings—Robert (Peter Parten), Charles (Thomas Danneberg), and Myrna (Diana Körner)—still reside.

At the Emerson estate, Dave nearly reveals his presence to his brother Richard but somehow manages to avoid contact. Richard, however, mysteriously disappears that same evening—permitting Dave the perfect opportunity to now pose as his twin brother. After a quick change of clothes and a shave, no one is the wiser. Scotland Yard Inspectors Craig (Harald Leipnitz) and Sir John (Siegfried Schürenberg) arrive and begin interrogating the occupants about Dave's possible whereabouts. At the same time, however, a hooded, cloaked figure dons a knight's gauntlet with retractable metal claws (many years before Freddy Krueger) and begins slaying Emerson family members one by one.

Die blaue Hand is an "in name only" adaptation of the 1925 Edgar Wallace novel *the Blue Hand*. The film bears little resemblance to Wallace's book; in fact, the basic treatment for the story had passed through several hands. The first scenario was drafted by Herbert Reinecker in 1966 but then rejected. The second treatment was created by the team of Harald G. Petersson and Fred Denger in early 1967. However, in what had become a common occurrence, series producer Horst Wendlandt re-hired Herbert Reinecker to fashion a screenplay based on aspects of Petersson and Denger's treatment.

The film was shot entirely in West Berlin with CCC's Berlin-Haselhorst Film studio accommodating the interiors. Moabit prison, in particular, is highlighted as a location. Production began on February 9 and wrapped on March 22, 1967. *Die blaue Hand* enjoyed its premiere on April 28, 1967, at the Gloria-Palast in Berlin. In what had become a trend for the series (indeed the rationale behind the recent changes), ticket sales continued to decline, yet the film still managed a respectable 1.7 million visitors (outperforming such recent titles as *Die Gruft mit dem Rätselschloss*, *Das Verrätertor*, and *Das Geheimnis der weissen Nonne*).

Often cited as a fan favorite (despite its excessive narrative complexity), *Die blaue Hand* counterbalanced *Der Bucklige von Soho*'s overemphasis on humor, titillation, and featherlike frissons by incorporating genuine scares, though leavened somewhat by Vohrer's typical comedic statements. More importantly, however, Alfred Vohrer had ostensibly taken a visual cue from Mario Bava's *Sei donne per l'assassino* (*Blood and Black Lace*, 1964). Bava had neutrally appropriated Rialto's house style and fused it with his own unique artistic sensibility—with spectacular results. Respectively, Vohrer fashioned *Die blaue Hand* into an aesthetically more fully realized *Krimi* than his Wallace color debut, *Der Bucklige von Soho*. The finished film reads as more visually faithful to the spirit of its black and white progenitors. The boldness of the inventive setups (the lighting, blocking, and camera dynamics) of the earlier *Krimis* (primarily helmed by Reinl and Vohrer) are robustly integrated into *Die blaue Hand*'s color world.

Die blaue Hand is filled with many memorable scenes; Alfred Vohrer's stylistic sensibility was particularly well-suited to Reinecker's scenario. In one sequence, daughter Myrna is summoned to the Petit Maxim nightclub by her brother Dave (or so she believes). Upon arriving, she finds the club deserted and dimly lit. Moving gingerly through the space, she repeatedly calls out, "Dave?" Attempting to disguise his voice, Mangrove's lackey chauffeur Reynolds (Fred Haltiner) hides behind the bar and quietly beckons Myrna to come closer, slowly luring her to the Blue Hand who stands hidden behind a curtain—hidden, that is, save for his blue metal claws, which are perched high above and ready to strike. She rounds the corner and pauses, sensing a presence, then boldly pulls the fabric down to reveal the hooded assassin and provide a solid scare. But what makes the scene so memorable is Vohrer's unexpected and abrupt cuts to a very vocal and laughing bar parrot. Vohrer utilizing the squawking parrot as a suspense valve, to release the mounting pressure, prompts a smart and sharp pivot toward comedy that generates a true laugh-out-loud moment. Vohrer, more than any other director of the series (and perhaps even in the entire German film industry of the time), understood the axiom that horror and humor are ostensibly two sides of the same coin. Over time, this ethos undeniably and happily defined Vohrer's work in the series.

Another impressive (and surprising) scene is reminiscent of a well-known sequence from Clarence Brown's pre-code drama *Possessed* (1931), in which small-town girl Joan Crawford dreams of a better life as she gazes, awe-struck, through the lit windows of a slow-rolling train. Through each window frame is an illuminated vignette of life that conveys the magic and the metaphysics found at the very core of cinema itself.[7] Vohrer's magical movie carousel, conversely, offers lurid vignettes of penny dreadfuls. On the cellar floor of the asylum ward, Dr. Mangrove conducts a tour for Sir John and Inspector Hopkins. As he orates the history of each patient, the detectives gaze through the peephole of their cells. As Sir John brings his scrutinizing eye to the first aperture, he (and we, the audience) witnesses the tragic fate of a "chronic stripper" who feels compelled to don and then remove her clothes in perpetual performance. But performing for who? For herself, for Sir John or Inspector Gates, for Reinecker's script or Vohrer's camera, for an imagined audience, or for we the actual audience? Or, perhaps, for all of these reasons? The scene evocatively recalls the many erotic artifacts of cinema's antiquity, from Edison's *Anna Belle Serpentine Dance* (1895) to the novelty miniature peepshow spyglasses ubiquitous in the 1940s and 1950s (typically as keychains). In the second cell, an unnerving female doll fills the frame, followed by a distressed middle-aged woman pacing and relentlessly abusing the doll. We are told that the guilt of killing her baby fuels a compulsion to relive the trauma daily. Finally, in the third cell, we confront an apparent murderer who sits twitching on his cot, one milky eye gazed and fixed. Nothing is explicitly made of this moment or this character, but his appearance is a noteworthy lynchpin for the film's plot. This asylum scene is relatively short, but the signified effect of these pro-filmic "peepshows" lingers.

Die blaue Hand stylishly offers a vivid color potpourri of the *Krimi*'s most salient and successful tropes. Several issues, however, weaken the film's effectiveness. Foremost among them is Eddi Arent's palpable absence. No other actor became more synonymous with the series; consequently, there is a considerable emptiness left by his formidable wake. *Die blaue Hand* is also hindered by an overcomplicated plot that ransacks bits and pieces of previous films. True, the many elements from prior Rialto productions effectively combine in Reinecker's skillful hands, but *significant* portions from 1961's *Die Seltsame Gräfin* are blatantly recycled. In fact, the entire asylum scenario is surgically lifted and grafted into *Die blaue Hand*: the family madness, the kidnapping of the heroine, the evil psychiatrist, the cellar full of inmates, the drugging of the Inspector (by a "doctored" drink in both films) are just some of the many "borrowed" elements. Other old Wallace threads woven into this new *Krimi* tapestry include the heavy reliance on snakes from *Der Zinker* and the menacing animal motif from *Neues vom Hexer*.

Though *Die blaue Hand* lacks Arent's fastidious persona and unique brand of humor, Vohrer attempts to compensate by filling each act with many droll and brazen moments. It is, however, Carl Lange's Dr. Mangrove who truly shines, becoming an inspired yet outrageous indulgence. The sadistic, monocled doctor's actions enter into the comic realm of the Nazi super villain (which is odd, considering these are supposedly *English* characters). He commits perjury, kidnaps Myrna, orders multiple murders, inflicts insanity upon his nurse, separately drugs Inspector Craig and Myrna (one disturbing shot features his monocled visage raising a hypodermic syringe and then depressing it—in close up—into Myrna's veined arm), and tortures Myrna with rats and snakes, all the while gloating at his own wickedness. Later, during an interrogation scene (with a spotlight cast upon his face), Mangrove actually says, "What do you want from me, I only carried out my orders." These machinations are certainly over the top, but delightfully so. This trend would be further emphasized (with even *more* diabolic enthusiasm) in the series' next feature, *Der Mönch mit der Peitsche* (1967).

Composer Martin Böttcher's return was long overdue and provided a welcome contrast to the previous run of Peter Thomas scores. Although Peter Thomas' themes (particularly his title sequences) had undeniably come into their own, Böttcher worked with a more restrained ear and a better understanding of scene-to-scoring dynamics. On occasion, Thomas' cues were simply too heavy, too dominant, and too inconsonant for the scenes they were intended to highlight or underscore. Böttcher's playfulness and tight arrangements accentuate many of the film's most accomplished sequences.

By most measurable criteria, *Die blaue Hand* is the superior production compared to its two-color predecessors, *Der Bucklige von Soho* and *Das Geheimnis der weissen*. The film moves at a confident, brisk pace, with an unusually active Sir John and self-assured Inspector Craig. Alfred Vohrer keeps the material fresh with his inventive scene design, vivid imagination, and humorous asides.

DER MÖNCH MIT DER PEITSCHE / *THE COLLEGE GIRL MURDERS* (1967)

In an ominous cellar laboratory containing condensers, scales, bubbling beakers, funnels, flasks—all alive with brightly colored liquids and gasses—scientist Dr. Cabble (Wilhelm Vorwerg) toils away with the help of his assistant Winston Robson (Kurt Buecheler). The final phase of testing begins for his colorless and odorless poison gas: a tube pumps the vapor into a rat-filled enclosure where the rats immediately die. Cabble is overjoyed, commenting on the potential human possibilities. Cabble's assistant, however, voices his concerns and hence becomes the first victim of the weaponized aerosolized gas (by opening a poison-penned book to take notes). Later when Cabble delivers the deadly gas to his benefactor, his reward is not a pile of money but rather a broken neck—crushed by the snapping bullwhip of a hooded monk adorned all in red.

Meanwhile, in a London prison, inmate Cress Bartling (Narciss Raymond Sokatscheff) gains a new cellmate, petty thief Frank Keeney (Siegfried Rauch). Bartling immediately offers Keeney a huge sum of "no questions asked" money to do "a job." Smuggled out of the prison in a false-top garbage can, Keeney is then met by Greaves (Günter Meisner), a chauffeur in a silver Rolls-Royce, who transports Keeney to a mysterious hideaway filled with massive aquariums and crocodile pens. A shadowy bossman speaks exclusively through a loudspeaker (disguising his voice) and will only show his back to Keeney. The job? Visit the village's church and orchestrate an "accidental collision" with university student Pam Walsbury (Ewa Strömberg) that will result in the swapping of hymnals. Keeney agrees and manages the book switch. Moments later, when the organist begins the service's first hymn, Pam opens her hymnal and receives a stream of poisonous gas to the face. Keeney accepts another job, this time to murder college student Betty Falks (Grit Boettcher) after she boards an evening bus. Now, however, the poison is housed in a gun that shoots a web of sticky poisonous goo (Robert Stoker Jr., creator of the legendary cobweb gun, would be proud.) In a predictable fashion, more girls, faculty, and staff are murdered as doubts and suspicions grow among the cast of characters. Scotland Yard is especially perplexed as the various elements of a complex plot intersect and culminate in a farcical climax.

Continuing the trend of the last several productions, *Der Mönch mit der Peitsche* was not adapted from a Wallace novel, but instead was yet another retreading of plots, tropes, and sequences from within (and, importantly, from without) the franchise. The Berlin-bound production began on April 26 and wrapped on June 9, 1967. The CCC-Film studios in Berlin-Haselhorst provided interiors, while several series-iconic West Berlin locations are featured in the movie's exteriors. The picture was released on August 4, 1967, but held a formal gala premiere on August 11, at the Mathäser Filmpalast in Munich. *Der Mönch mit der Peitsche* enjoyed a modest improvement in sales (an increment of 100,000) over the last Rialto installment (*Die blaue Hand*) with 1.8 million visitors.

The first thing one notices about *Der Mönch mit der Peitsche* is that there is a great deal of cross-franchise influence occurring. Beyond mere influence, however, it is more accurate to assert that Baudrillard's precession of simulacra is the intellectual instrument responsible for forming and shaping this particular film and its parent franchises.

Author and screenwriter Norbert Jacques (Luxembourgian by birth, German by naturalization) created the fictional character of Dr. Mabuse for his novel *Dr. Mabuse der Spieler* (*Dr. Mabuse the Gambler*, 1921), which was realized as a silent motion picture just one year later in Erich Pommer's production of director Fritz Lang's epic *Dr. Mabuse der Spieler* (*Dr. Mabuse the Gambler*, 1922). The all-seeing, all-knowing, criminal mastermind proved so popular that sequels in both novel and film formats quickly followed. Lang would craft an entire trilogy from Jacques' iconic, fear-inspiring villain with *Das Testament des Dr. Mabuse* (*The Testament of Dr. Mabuse*, 1933) and the much later CCC-produced *Die 1000 Augen des Dr. Mabuse* (*The Thousand Eyes of Dr. Mabuse*, 1960).

While the Pommer and Lang adaptations were based on the original Jacques novels, the Artur Brauner CCC revitalization of the series in the 1960s was a reboot that attempted to fuse two popular and contemporaneous series together—Ian Fleming's James Bond 007 books and the Rialto Edgar Wallace movies. From his perch, Brauner kept a watchful eye on Rialto's newfound box-office success with its Wallace adaptations, and, indeed, CCC would enter into direct competition with Rialto by acquiring and adapting several Bryan Edgar Wallace titles beginning in 1962. In the interim, however, he took a "gamble" at resuscitating a beloved German villain who had mesmerized audiences forty years earlier.

No stranger to the genre, Brauner, who had a brief but spectacular run of crime films in the early 1950s, hired Mabuse series director Fritz Lang to give the public a "long-awaited" sequel to Lang's much-loved *The Testament of Dr. Mabuse* (1933) and complete, in grand German tradition, a Lang/Mabuse "trilogy." Lang was hesitant to delve into the past but reluctantly agreed.

Figure 3.3 Uschi Glas Worked Her Way Up from Minor to Lead Roles during Rialto's Color Era. *Der Mönch mit der Peitsche* (*The College Girl Murders*, 1967). Source: Stifung Deutsche Kinematek Berlin.

Brauner's intentions, however, were clear; this updating of the character would reflect both the look and feel of the Rialto Wallace adaptations but also the actions and methods of the literary character James Bond, who was all the rage in Germany (and numerous other countries). *Die 1000 Augen des Dr. Mabuse* became that film. As Brauner had predicted and hoped, Lang's return led to a revival of the Mabuse franchise that yielded a total of six films.[8]

By the time Rialto arrived at a film such as *Der Mönch mit der Peitsche* (following the sturdy success of *Die blaue Hand*), a "stew-like" writing approach had become de rigueur at the studio. What's more, the textural properties from the above franchises (Mabuse and Bond) were incorporated into this production, resulting in a film with a bit of an identity crisis. In short, an immense industry-wide feedback loop of influence began to control the direction of this, and other, analogous series. *Der Mönch mit der Peitsche* represents the epitome of this method, resulting in a pop-art composite of recently overused Wallace tropes (the all-girl school setting, hooded monks with whips, tiresome inheritances), Mabuse-esque flourishes (the villain's hideout, the perversion of science, communicating through a vox speaker, false identities), and James Bondian adventure (a supervillain, a moat of alligators, snakes, cages, etc.) all couched within the dated sexual politics of the 1960s. Or, as Kim Newman perfectly recaps,

> In a scene which could have come from a Monogram Lugosi, a Mabuse-haired mad scientist develops a new type of "undetectable" poison that can cause apparent heart attacks, then tests it out on assistant who queries his morality—forcing the sucker to open a book which contains a device that puffs the gas into his face. The scientist sells the gas to a chauffeur who works for a mystery villain whose Bond-style lair has a handy pit full of snapping crocodiles and runs the old Mabuse/Fantômas gambit of talking to minions over microphone through a figure at a desk who turns out to be a dummy [despite the lit cigarette in its fingers].[9]

With *Der Mönch mit der Peitsche*, Rialto was remaking its own recent remakes, with additional inspiration from similar franchises. This was primarily due to the insistence from series producer Horst Wendlandt that the films continue with proven formulae and templates during a time when Rialto was experiencing waning cultural relevance. At the same time, however, the film *is* fun, earning high marks in raw charm and camp value.

That being said, *Der Mönch mit der Peitsche* presents a difficult case within the *Krimi* spectrum. There are aspects of the film to admire, but there is also plenty to criticize. By recycling recent plots and imagery, the film devolves into cliché (albeit excellently executed cliché). Buttressing these clichés are uninspired performances (extremely rare in the series) and unimaginative direction. Fuchsberger plays his role so casually (constantly chewing gum, perhaps as a panacea for smoking) that he comes across as overly cool and withdrawn. Conversely, Schürenberg's Sir John haplessly overplays the comedic elements to provide the humor typically delivered by Eddi Arent. Alfred Vohrer, a director not known for "phoning it in" or resting on his laurels, appears to do just that with *Der Mönch mit der Peitsche*. The film certainly looks energetic and vivid—one of the most visually striking in the entire canon—but its core feels neglected and tired. Case in point: no attempt is made whatsoever to simulate England in this motion picture—not even with stock or recycled footage (what recycled footage is used, however, is of the snakes from *Die blaue Hand*, apparently to bestow further menace to the crocodile pit). Even Martin Böttcher's score, his fifth and final for the series, is lamentably a retreading of his own previous and similar cues from the franchise.

The Alfred Vohrer who directed *Die toten Augen von London* was unafraid, unapologetic, and openly experimented with film technique as well as genre expectations; this effort, however, feels just like that effort. *Der Mönch mit der Peitsche* is marked with fatigue by its studio and complacency by its producer, director, and cast. The film's saving grace is that it is unrestrained in its excesses. It is a beautifully photographed *Krimi* (considerable credit to cinematographer Karl Löb), replete with iconic images from the color era. The overly familiar plot nonetheless delivers high entertainment value simply because of its "over the top" execution. In the end, there's really not another *Krimi* just like it, which makes it important as well as divisive.

DER HUND VON BLACKWOOD CASTLE / *THE MONSTER OF BLACKWOOD CASTLE* (1968)

Mr. Tucker (Peter William Koch), on his way to Blackwood Castle, is purposely lured from the proper path onto treacherous moors. Along this trail, he is stalked by a dangerous hound with large fangs who presses him farther into the marshland where the dog finally attacks and kills him. A mysterious, cloaked figure stands atop the ravine to witness the murder. Meanwhile, Lady Agathy Beverton (Agnes Windeck), proprietor of the nearby Old Inn, voices her concern about Tucker's lateness and the howl of a nearby hound. Her brother, Lord Henry Beverton (Tilo von Berlepsch), and his friend Doc Adams (Alexander Engel) continue to play chess and ignore her concerns. Another guest, vacationing hunter Humphrey Connery (Heinz Drache), witnesses Tucker's body slowly being swallowed by the marshes but does nothing and later at the Inn says nothing—casting immediate suspicion upon his character.

The next day, Jane Wilson (Karin Baal) arrives at Blackwood Castle to settle the estate and claim the inheritance left to her by her estranged, late father, Captain Allan Thurnby (Otto Stern). The captain's faithful, eye-patched manservant Grimsby (Arthur Binder), and the family attorney Robert Jackson (Hans Söhnker), await Miss Wilson at the castle. Upon arriving, Wilson learns that her inheritance *is* Blackwood Castle. Jackson immediately suggests that she sell it for ten thousand pounds, she declines and decides to live in Blackwood Castle.

More bodies accumulate, Ms. Wilson is terrorized, and Scotland Yard is called in to solve the case. (Notably, *Der Hund von Blackwood Castle* unleashes the head of Scotland Yard, Sir John [Siegfried Schürenberg] himself, to lead the investigation). One sticking point that Sir John cannot yet fathom is the coroner's insistence that poison has been the cause of the (accumulating) deaths, despite large canine wounds upon the victim's necks. It's a traditional Wallace set-up for yet another tale of inheritance and murder, albeit with overtones of another famous mystery-crime author.

Refreshingly, *Der Hund von Blackwood Castle* reverses direction from its predecessor *Der Mönch mit der Peitsche. Blackwood Castle* heralded a return to the *Krimi* terra firma of yesteryear but with new faces and a comparatively fresh scenario. Originally, the Wallace novel *Der Engel des Schreckens* (*The Angel of Terror*) was planned as another German-UK coproduction to mark the release of Rialto's twenty-fifth title in the series. Alas, *Das Geheimnis der weissen Nonne* would become the final *Krimi* coproduction between Rialto and the United Kingdom. Instead, triple-threat director, producer, and screenwriter Franz Seitz Jr. was hired to write *Der Hund von Blackwood Castle* (under the pseudonym Georg Laforet). The idea was to use traditional Wallace elements but incorporate selected Sherlock Holmes flare, in particular from *The Hound of the Baskervilles* (1902). In other words, maintain the status quo but with a fresh coat of paint. As with numerous other recent productions, however, Herbert Reinecker was again commissioned (under the pseudonym Alex Berg) to rewrite Seitz's treatment in the summer of 1967.

Originally, Harald Reinl was considered for the project but was still shooting the German-Italian Jerry Cotton coproduction *Dynamite in Green Silk* (1968). Instead, Alfred Vohrer was offered and accepted the film—his eleventh in the series. Production began on October 16 and finished on November 27, 1967, in West Berlin. CCC's Berlin-Haselhorst provided studio services while various familiar locations in and around West Berlin were captured during a picturesque German autumn.

For Rialto's twenty-fifth *Krimi*, a jubilee gala was held at the Mathäser Filmpalast in Munich on December 27, 1967. For its national release, ticket sales took a dip but were still acceptable at 1.2 million. Despite its lukewarm first-run sales, *Der Hund von Blackwood Castle* developed a more devout

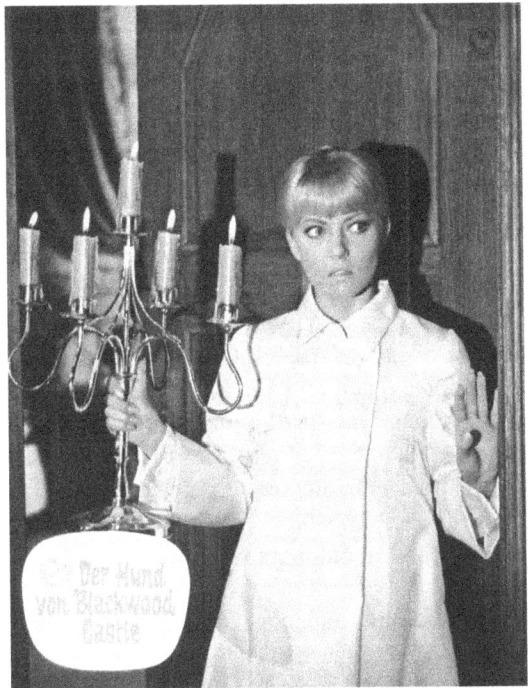

Figure 3.4 Gothic Touches Adorn the Arthur Conan Doyle-esque *Der Hund von Blackwood Castle* (*The Monster of Blackwood* Castle, 1968), Starring Karin Baal.
Source: Stifung Deutsche Kinematek Berlin.

following and earned a greater reputation through its frequent television screenings on ZDF1 (*Zweites Deutsches Fernsehen*), Germany's Public Broadcasting network, over the next two decades.

An additional commemorative ceremony was held at the Mathäser Filmpalast to honor series producer Horst Wendlandt. The *Hauptverband Deutscher Filmtheater*, or HDF (Association for Film Theater Owners), awarded its Golden Screen award to Wendlandt on January 18, 1968. An extravagant ball followed, which was attended by many of Rialto's personnel and stars from the series, including icons Karin Dor and Joachim Fuchsberger.

With *Der Hund von Blackwood Castle*, the series, unsurprisingly and perhaps inevitably, crossed over into Arthur Conan Doyle's territory. It's not an especially clandestine approach, given the title of the movie, and should not be immediately read as an appropriation but rather as a light homage to Doyle's *The Hound of the Baskervilles*. And, while the film's *Krimi* pedigree is keenly on display, it was perhaps preordained that Rialto would eventually embrace Doyle's Sherlock Holmes stories—given Wallace's literary kinship with them. As Kim Newman noted, "[The film] begins Baskerville Hall–style as someone poking around the misty environs of Blackwood Castle is menaced by a vampire-fanged hound and falls into a swamp."[10] Apart from the moor setting and the artificially fanged hound, however, any similarity to Doyle's novel fades and Rialto's house style carries the film. The other major narrative thread that runs through the movie's plot is inspired by Robert Louis Stevenson's *Treasure Island*, (1882) in which a sea captain's former crew conspires against him.

A harbinger of fading commitment, *Der Hund von Blackwood Castle* became the third consecutive Wallace production that chose not to incorporate London footage, recycled or otherwise. Instead, a panoply of familiar German locations, particularly Peacock Island's Pfaueninsel Castle, are rendered in a near sepia tonal quality, taking advantage of atmospheric European autumn. The interior locations, predominantly Blackwood Castle and the Old Inn, approximate the tone of earlier titles that had been successful stage plays. The sequences feel intimate and close, much in the same way as, for example, *Das Indische Tuch* was blocked for the camera. The result is a film that feels loose and expansive outdoors while maintaining an indoor coziness (particularly at the Inn).

One of the most welcome and novel aspects of *Blackwood Castle* lies in having Siegfried Schürenberg's Sir John, rather than leading men Fuchsberger, Drache, or, more recently, Leipnitz, take the sole lead of the investigation. For a Rialto *Krimi*, this is tantamount to having Watson head the investigation instead of Holmes. Still, it turned out to be a clever strategy that allowed the gifted Schürenberg to shine under an overdue spotlight. He is not *entirely* on his own, however, as his administrative assistant Miss Finley (Ilsa Pagé) becomes a trusty partner. The two make for a charismatic team, and their humorous chemistry really ignites in *Blackwood Castle*. Pagé began her *Krimi* career as a rebellious reform school girl (quickly placing her among the film's casualties) in *Der Bucklige von Soho* (1966). She graduated to the role of Sir John's executive assistant, Miss Mabel Finley, in *Die blaue Hand* (1967), and would portray Finley in an additional five more films. Plucky, patient, and stalwart, Pagé rightfully remains one of the series' beloved icons.

In addition to Schürenberg and Pagé, the entire cast is in excellent form—at least partly due, I would argue, to the absence of monks and whips (a recent trend that had been truly flogged to death). *Blackwood Castle* is dominated by strong female performances. Karin Baal, last seen in 1961's *Die toten Augen von London*, effectively channels the spirit of Karin Dor's many first-rate performances wherein Dor progressed from trusting and naive to assertive, self-confident, and brave. Veteran actress Mady Rahl, whose career was undergoing a 1960s revitalization (despite the Nazi regime's fetishization of her), had re-emerged as a seasoned and gifted actress. Still, it is Agnes Windeck who again proves to be the lethal scene-stealer, especially in this, her last Wallace *Krimi*. Her precise delivery, dry humor, kindly manner, and formidable presence prove awe-inspiring. Perhaps her greatest moment in all of her Rialto outings occurs when she exclaims that all of her boarders are dying before they can pay their bill! A grand dame of German theater and film, she continued to work in television and film nearly up until the time of her death in 1975.

Der Hund von Blackwood Castle also marked the Wallace debut for German actor Horst Tappert, who would become best known for his role of Chief Inspector Stephan Derrick on the TV crime series *Derrick*, which ran from 1974 to 1998. Tappert would go on to star in three more Rialto Wallace titles (as well as two Bryan Edgar Wallace entries for competitor CCC), effectively providing an audition reel for the series that would eventually make him a household name, earning him cult status in Germany and dozens of other international markets. Tappert would become a key asset to the series, especially in his next feature for Rialto, *Der Gorilla von Soho*, where he effortlessly graduated from villain to the role of the lead detective.

German news outlet *Der Spiegel* said of the actor:

> Tappert's affable portrayal of Inspector Derrick, an elegant, serious and empathetic official, embodied the character of an upstanding, postwar citizen in West Germany. It also helped to make the series popular abroad and Tappert one of the country's best-known actors internationally.

The German film industry in the 1950s and 1960s employed many men (in front of and behind the camera) who served in the German military during World War II. Every able man was conscripted, commissioned, or volunteered. By war's end, of course, the nation had wearily turned from able men to the Hitler Youth for defense. *Krimi* icon and leading man Joachim Fuchsberger, for example, entered the war at sixteen and trained as a *Fallschirmjäger* (paratrooper). He was later sent to the Eastern Front where he was wounded and captured.

Tappert, however, had said little of his war career over the years, but had commented in an interview that he "was a medic and was taken prisoner at the end of the war."[11] It was revealed posthumously, however, that Tappert was, in fact, under the command of Hitler's Waffen SS. "The report was based on the findings of sociologist Jörg Becker, who, while working on a biography of another academic, Elisabeth Noelle-Neumann, looked into the personal histories of members of a theatre company she founded."[12] It remains unclear under what circumstances Tappert joined the SS, but German military historian Jan Erik Schulte commented that "the pressure, particularly on young men, to become Waffen SS members in 1943 was indeed enormous," especially after the German High Command's defeat at Stalingrad. He went on to explain that "Tappert held the lowest rank in the SS, and although the corps as a whole had committed mass killings in the Soviet Union, it was not clear whether Tappert had been personally involved."

Series composer Peter Thomas' score is effective, memorable, and well-executed. The main theme for *Der Hund von Blackwood Castle* offers a trippy amalgamation of Thomas' own indelible signature, James Brown-esque staccato "Ooh's and ha's," and the well-known novelty song *They're Coming to Take Me Away* by Napoleon XIV. It ranks as one of Thomas' more unique efforts and is entirely befitting of a commemorative production.

By now, director Alfred Vohrer's embellishments were both expected and omnipresent. The usual accompaniment of "Vohrerisms" (a polar bear with a phone hidden in its chest, dangling skeletons, clever edits between locations, etc.) had now officially expanded over the last several productions to include compulsory snakes.

With a high body count (so much so that the film jokes self-reflexively that it's lost count) and an emphasis on the seasonal beauty of Berlin, *Der Hund von Blackwood Castle* and its energized cast provide a fast-moving thriller with many tropes endemic to the series and humor typical of its director. Is it the extravaganza one would expect in a twenty-fifth-anniversary film? Not entirely, but it is consistent with the series' history—embracing its rich traditions while acknowledging and adapting to new trends.

IM BANNE DES UNHEIMLICHEN / *THE ZOMBIE WALKS* (1968)

Having perished in a plane crash, Sir Oliver Ramsey's funeral services end on a rather odd note, quite literally. As pallbearers carry him away from the altar, a loud, maniacal, high-pitched laugh suddenly radiates from inside the coffin. The stunned pallbearers drop Ramsey's casket, and the cleverly animated but charmingly sinister credits roll.

Sir Oliver's brother, Sir Cecil (Wolfgang Kieling), however, is convinced that his brother seeks revenge from beyond the grave. Family lawyer Mr. Merryl's (Otto Stern) murder a short time later appears to confirm Cecil's doubts and concerns. Sir Cecil is also menaced by an uncanny skeleton-like figure that stalks the Ramsey estate. Scotland Yard's Inspector Higgins (Joachim Fuchsberger) arrives on the scene but quickly butts heads with photo-snapping journalist Peggy Ward (Siw Mattson), who is also investigating the case.

A slurry of characteristically confusing characters muddy this *Krimi*'s waters, including nurses, doctors, administrators, stewardesses, nightclub singers, reverends, caretakers (offering some new faces in Wolfgang Kieling,

Siv Mattson, and Peter Mosbacher), as well as a new head of Scotland Yard, Sir Arthur (Hubert von Meyerinck). The meandering and often confusing story ends, as it began, in the Ramsey family crypt.

Although some sources indicate that *Im Banne des Unheimlichen* is a loose adaptation of Edgar Wallace's novel *The Hand of Power* (1930), no similarities between that novel and this film exist; it's more likely this punchy alternative English language title was simply plucked from Wallace's oeuvre. *Im Banne des Unheimlichen* was shot from January 29 to March 13, 1968, in West Berlin and, after a conspicuous absence from recent films, the United Kingdom. London's Buckingham Street, New Scotland Yard, and Piccadilly Circus are prominently featured in the movie. These scenes, short though they may be, achieve considerable verisimilitude in terms of the story's setting. The most recent efforts from Rialto, shot exclusively in Berlin, suffer from a sense of dislocation when compared to the series as a whole, and were a sign of wavering logistical (and financial) commitment. The simple act of watching Joachim Fuchsberger buy a newspaper in London's Piccadilly Circus lends the film a spatial and temporal authenticity, allowing for a much more effective narrative suture to occur. The movie premiered on April 26, 1968, in three theaters simultaneously: Bremen's Ufa-Theater, Oberhausen's Europa-Palast, and Saarbrücken's Passage Kino. Ticket sales registered with

Figure 3.5 The Beautifully Rendered Entombment of Sir Oliver in *Im Banne des Unheimlichen* (*The Zombie Walks*, 1968). Source: Stifung Deutsche Kinematek Berlin.

a significant improvement over *Der Hund von Blackwood Castle*'s 1.2 million, drawing in 1.8 million loyal *Krimi* visitors.

Just as comedian Eddi Arent's departure from the series was intensely felt after *Das Geheimnis der weissen Nonne*, the most notable change from the twenty-fifth film to the twenty-sixth was the conspicuous absence of beloved series regular Siegfried Schürenberg in his recurring role of Scotland Yard Chief Sir John. Finding another actor to play the role of Sir John was as ill-advised as it was impossible, so Rialto pragmatically substituted Hubert von Meyerinck (who had a brief role in *Neues vom Hexer* [1965] and a more substantial one as General Perkins in *Der Bucklige von Soho* [1966]) as the *new* chief of Scotland Yard, Sir Arthur. Only a small handful of Rialto's once inexhaustible supply of actors appear in *Im Banne des Unheimlichen*. Returning were Joachim Fuchsberger, Ilse Pagé, and Pinkas Braun. In Braun's case, this would be his final *Krimi* outing. The Swiss actor had made his *Krimi* debut in 1962's *Das Rätsel der roten Orchidee* and quickly became an essential contributor to the series—usually as an outwardly cool but ruthless, steely eyed villain. Conversely, the movie showcases new faces for the series in Wolfgang Kieling, Siv Mattson, and Peter Mosbacher.

Im Banne des Unheimlichen is unquestionably one of the most atmospheric of Rialto's *Krimis*. It achieves a level of sinister ambiance present in only a handful of other titles. The picture accomplishes this impressive feat in several ways. First, the design of the villain, known as the "Laughing Corpse," is an inspired stroke of creepy genius. With strong visual echoes of "The Crimson Ghost" (the ghastly, cadaverous supervillain from the eponymous 1946 Republic serial and adopted mascot for the horror punk band The Misfits), the Laughing Corpse most assuredly is the "stuff of nightmares"—the classic bogeyman standing in the back-lit doorway, or hiding in your closet, or perhaps waiting under your bed. I can only imagine a generation of young viewers being traumatized by this particular villain. Much as *The Wizard Oz*'s "Wicked Witch of the West" or *Chitty Chitty Bang Bang*'s "Child Catcher" disturbed untold numbers of children for decades, the Laughing Corpse should also hold a place in the "kinder trauma" hall of fame.

The Laughing Corpse's method of murder is unique, oddly humorous, and unforgettable. Just before the kill, his jawbone languidly drops open to commit auditory assault from beyond the grave, inspiring in his victims a state of shocked, semi-paralysis. He then raises a hand, which bears a ring featuring a large scorpion whose poisonous tail suddenly pops up (with an audible "boing"), that he then slices across their necks. Death soon follows.

Director Alfred Vohrer and cinematographer Karl Löb created one of the series' more sophisticated and memorable lighting schemes; virtually any still from the film is striking. It is also possibly the foggiest *Krimi* ever made (even more so than *Der Hund von Blackwood Castle* or *Die toten Augen von*

London); night exteriors are bathed in a dense, almost south England fog (albeit artificially). And, in an effort to make the Laughing Corpse "pop" on the screen, Vohrer bathes his sunken visage in a green-gelled light (in both static and moving shots) that electrifies the visuals even more. Together, Vohrer and Löb create a beautiful world. The vivid and robust gelled interiors recall the striking work of another European partnership—that between director Terence Fisher and cinematographer Jack Asher. *Im Banne des Unheimlichen* also boasts densely dressed sets. Vohrer's obsessive mise-en-scène embellishments are dialed way up—which must've been particularly hard on the props department and/or taxidermy bills (there are a record number of mounted animals and, again, more squawking parrots). Still, all of this *mise-en-scène* extremism works beautifully and is in precise rhythm with Vohrer's baton. The film's narrative, on the other hand, remains substantially less successful.

By 1968, Rialto's production apparatus was perfectly tuned—capable of creating technically superior, professionally acted, and highly entertaining motion pictures. With twenty-six films in the series, this is self-evident. True, Edgar Wallace's novels held tremendous potential for cinematic adaptation, but by 1968 it was also true that this potential had been pretty thoroughly tapped. From a narrative standpoint, the series was not only remaking their earlier efforts but also engaging in a repetitive ritual that dangerously fatigues a franchise and can often lead to its exhaustion and burnout. Although *Im Banne des Unheimlichen* offers beautiful visuals, some genuinely eerie moments and comedy endemic to its director's cinematic ethos, it suffers from an acute case of narrative malaise, the same sickness that had, by now, overwhelmed the franchise. Nowhere is this more evident than in the film's resolution, which is a ridiculously long monologue that all too conveniently and briefly explains plot holes (or sweeps them under the rug), hidden information, and other annoying inconsistencies. For dedicated fans, this could only be read as a conspicuous cheat.

Peter Thomas' score, however, is a clear highlight. I've been critical of Thomas and justifiably so. His compositions for the series are, in a word, uneven. Thomas often wrote music that overpowered rather than supported the on-screen action. Yet, when he worked more creatively *with* the material, he was capable of delivering unique music (and some truly hip psychedelic songs). Thomas' work was in-step with the intercontinental pop film music of the 1960s, from Mark Murphy to John Barry, from Dusty Springfield to Julie Driscoll. A perfect case in point is *Im Banne des Unheimlichen*'s title track, "The Space of Today," sung by Finnish-Swedish entertainer Lill Lindfors (a finalist in the 1966 Eurovision Song Contest who also has a small role in the film). Thomas composed a knock-out cue that is ardently brought to life by Lindfors. "The Space of Today" is a track one could easily envision Shirley

Bassey, Fran Jeffries, or Eartha Kitt belting out. Prominently placed instruments in this Thomas score include bongos, a sitar, and an organ.

Overall, *Im Banne des Unheimlichen* remains an impressively shot late color era entry with a haunting villain, high body count (at one point, Sir Arthur reflexively quips "we'll soon have more corpses than in Hamlet!"), and an anemic resolution that strains credulity. Although not an outright remake, as the next film in the series unashamedly is, *Im Banne des Unheimlichen* "borrows" narrative elements from the black and white era, in particular *Die Bande des Schreckens* (revenge from the grave, suicide), and *Der Frosch mit der Maske* and *Der grüne Bogenschütze* (masked/costumed villains).

DER GORILLA VON SOHO / *GORILLA GANG* (1968)

International millionaires are being murdered, their floating bodies fished out of the Thames. Strangely, the corpses are found with little toy dolls that have faded and unfamiliar writing on them. Scotland Yard chief Sir Arthur (Hubert von Meyerinck) hires language specialist Susan McPherson (Uschi Glas) to aid Inspector Perkins (Horst Tappert) and his subordinate Sgt. Pepper (Uwe Friedrichsen) with the case and the odd writings. As McPherson deciphers traces of the language (in particular, the words crime, murder, and Gorilla) found on the dolls, Perkins begins to suspect that the "Gorilla Gang" has resurfaced and are behind the deaths. After some initial interviews, Perkins concludes that an array of wills, estates, inheritances, and suspicious beneficiaries provide more than sufficient motive for the multiple murders. If any of this seems familiar, that is because it is. *Der Gorilla von Soho* is a cinematic Xerox of 1961's *Die toten Augen von London*.

Der Gorilla von Soho was not intended to be a remake at all. It was, in fact, an "original" (inasmuch as the series was capable of originality at this stage) scenario submitted by Herbert Reinecker (again, under his pseudonym Alex Berg) that targeted the London Zoo as a narrative focal point. Series auteur Alfred Vohrer was to step down, allowing for Harald Philipp (fresh off of directing Rialto's *Winnetou und das Halbblut Apanatschi*, 1966) to assume creative control of the project. *Gorilla* was intended to follow *Der Hund von Blackwood Castle*, but distributor Constantin objected to two consecutive films that featured animals in their titles. Rialto agreed, halted work on *Gorilla*, and started preproduction on what would become *Im Banne des Unheimlichen*. In the interim, Philipp polished Reinecker's screenplay for *Gorilla*.

Production on *Der Gorilla von Soho* began on June 18 and wrapped on July 25, 1968. A fresh array of photogenic West Berlin locations were leveraged for the production, including the Gottlob Münsinger Oberschule (located on Eiswerder island) and Pfaueninsel Island's frigate shed (staged as a dock for the Gorilla Gang's hideout). Interiors were largely shot at the CCC Berlin Spandau studios. Stars Uschi Glas and Uwe Friedrichsen, along with a small second unit crew, traveled to London for exterior shots featured in the film. *Der Gorilla von Soho* brought in 1.7 million visitors—slightly less than its predecessor—continuing the downward trend in sales.

A palpable shift in tone makes itself felt in *Der Gorilla von Soho*, a change that began two years earlier with the release of *Der Bucklige von Soho*. By 1968, however, this shift had taken a more deliberate turn toward the prurient and exploitive. For the majority of *Krimi* devotees, *Der Gorilla von Soho* rates at or near the bottom of their list of favorite Wallace thrillers. Still, for others, given the film's many "trashy" elements (topless waitresses and models within the first few scenes), it's often name-checked as a guilty pleasure. My own attitude toward guilty pleasures echoes Robin Wood's classic assertion that they are "an entirely deplorable institution. If one feels guilt at pleasure, isn't one bound to renounce one or the other? Preferably, in most cases, the guilt."[13] The concept does beg the question of why anyone would willingly want to wear a cinematic cilice. Regardless, given the ubiquity of the phrase, *Der Gorilla von Soho* becomes a prime candidate for self-flagellating cinephiles, while for some others, myself included, it is simply "trashy fun" sans the guilt.

Figure 3.6 The German Title Card for *Der Gorilla von Soho* (*Gorilla Gang*, 1968) Reflects the Shift in the Series' Tone and Humor during Rialto's Color Era. *Source: Stifung Deutsche Kinematek Berlin.*

Placing emphasis on the "trashier" elements of a script was nothing new. Some of Rialto's earliest Wallace productions were brazenly risqué, but the mass media sexual ecosystem of 1959 differed vastly from that of 1968. Perhaps no decade in the twentieth century experienced as much turmoil, conflict, growth, sexual liberation, and hard-won advances in the arena of civil rights as the 1960s. *Der Gorilla von Soho* captures the dynamic, complex, often knotty, and occasionally sleazy "aura" of this era, stamping the film as modern—its temporal fingerprints intact. So, while *Gorilla* is considered to be "trash" by many, I would argue that it is (at a minimum) excellently made trash.

The sexual politics of the film (and the series) are also a product of this period. Heteronormative and often sexist, some of the films offer a rebuke to a loss of male-dominated power (whether imagined or real). One could argue, presumably, that the films depict a German parody of the "naughty" post-Profumo era sexual politics of the United Kingdom infused with the "dirty old man" antics popular at that time (e.g., *The Benny Hill Show*). But I stress that both scenarios can be, and likely are, true. While Sir John's wandering eyes and hands were played for "innocent" laughs, he was also frequently the target of such mockery. Sir Arthur, however, is wantonly lecherous and excessive in his lust, offputtingly so. His libidinous, id-driven police chief would be better situated in one of the countless contemporaneous "sex comedies" that flooded the European market from numerous participating countries (including West Germany). Accordingly, by the time notorious Spanish filmmaker Jesús (Jess) Franco was hired to shoot two Wallace *Krimis* for competitor CCC (the Edgar Wallace inspired *Der Teufel kam aus Akasava*, 1971, and Bryan Edgar Wallace's *Der Todesrächer von Soho*, 1972), the series was primed to enter its supernova stage by embracing the controversial director's more exploitive and freestyle narrative approach.[14]

As for Rialto's narrative ethos, Kim Newman suggests that

> From now on, the only thing on offer is recycling. There's a certain air of psychedelic sleaze that gets near Jess Franco territory: one of the main locations is a Soho club where pervs photograph posing naked women (and one muscleman) on pedestals.[15]

Newman articulates the tone of the film perfectly. The aura of the late 1950s entries shifted from a relatively tame nightclub naughtiness to a late 1960s seedy salaciousness. Indeed, in what is a tediously recurring gag, Sir Arthur "dates" one of the "models" at the Soho club.

To be clear, embracing, rather than rejecting, the film's excesses is definitely a wise viewing strategy, but where I am much less willing to forgive the film is in its conceptual design—its *raison d'être*. A color remake of

1961's *Die toten Augen von London* (arguably the most iconic title in the franchise) was risky and, moreover, superfluous. *Toten Augen* was a Rialto title that had acquired a privileged place after its initial release (and later pairing on a double bill in the United States as *Dead Eyes of London* with Ricardo Freda's *Lo spettro* [*The Ghost*, 1963]). *Die toten Augen von London* along with Rialto's premier *Krimi*, *Der Frosh mit der Maske* (1959), are perhaps the two most commonly signified titles in the iconography associated with the series. But rather than attempt an updating or homage of the material (successfully achieved with transformative remakes such as Werner Herzog's *Nosferatu the Vampyre* [1979], John Carpenter's *The Thing* [1981], and David Cronenberg's *The Fly* [1986], to name a few), *Gorilla* is unfortunately executed as a scene-for-scene (indeed, beat-for-beat) self-cannibalization of the celluloid created by its original director, Alfred Vohrer. Of course, diminishing profits had dictated that economics drive this current strategy, but I would argue that more creative thinking was called for. Unfortunately, Rialto's response (much like Hollywood had historically responded to genre fatigue) was to repeat their mistakes, hope for better results, and then "discover" the opposite to be true.

This is why, as a remake, *Der Gorilla von Soho* fails. It fails in the sense that it is non-transformative in any measurable way. Apart from location (Hamburg to Berlin) and motion picture stock (black and white to color), *Gorilla* is essentially, and unfortunately, an inferior copy-and-paste effort with stronger exploitation elements. *Die toten Augen von London* (released a mere seven years earlier) left far too indelible an imprint on the series and its fans to be cast away, forgotten, or superseded by a lesser color remake.

It is unclear precisely why a remake of *Die toten Augen von London* was sanctioned in the first place. But according to Joachim Kramp, for reasons still unknown, the original script—which centered on the London Zoo—was abandoned during preproduction.

> A possible explanation could be problems with the filming permit in the Berlin Zoo. Concerns about the cost and time required of the project are also suspected. In any case, Rialto Film was obliged to Constantin Film to complete an Edgar Wallace film by September 1968. Wendlandt and his preferred director Alfred Vohrer finally came up with the saving idea: A remake of the successful Edgar Wallace crime thriller *Die toten Augen von London*, which Vohrer had directed in 1961, adapted to the title *Der Gorilla von Soho*.[16]

Regardless of the circumstances that led to the film's creation, the result proved underwhelming. Disappointing box-office, negative reviews, and unenthusiastic word of mouth surrounded the film. Viewers found it so adverse as to make *Der Gorilla von Soho* the last theatrical experience for many long-time fans—prompting the *Darmstädter Echo* to proclaim "Wallace, oh Wallace and Scotland Yard, how you have changed."[17]

Notwithstanding its shortcomings, *Gorilla* offered some definite highlights. German chanteuse Beate Hasenau proved both striking and convincing as the blackmailing *fille de joie*, Cora Watson. Her performance vividly recalls Eva Pflug's portrayal of the seductive Lolita in Rialto's inaugural *Der Frosch mit der Maske* (1959), lending an affectionate sense of continuity and providing tidy closure to an archetypical character loop that began a full ten years earlier. And although the film is a lesser remake of earlier success, you would not know it from Peter Thomas' musical contribution. Thomas delivers a unique and memorable score that utilizes gongs and other southeast Asian voicings and instrumentation. Horst Tappert, in his second Wallace outing for Rialto, smoothly executes a transition from crook (in *Der Hund von Blackwood Castle*) to cop, while ceding romantic priveledges to his younger co-star (allowing Tappert to occupy the well-versed, authoritative figure more freely). Finally, there is ample humor in the film as well—a pronounced trademark during the series' more advanced years. Ultimately, *Der Gorilla von Soho* does not take itself seriously, suggesting that audiences should probably do the same.

DER MANN MIT DEM GLASAUGE / *THE MAN WITH THE GLASS EYE* (1969)

Leila (Heidrun Hankammer), a dancer with the "Las Vegas Girls" revue, meets her employer and lover Archibald Jefferson (Kurd Pieritz) in a hotel room where he offers her a new contract. Later, as the lovemaking begins, Jefferson's heart is pierced by a flying dagger—flung by a masked knife thrower. Leila is spared, but before her next performance, she is poisoned backstage while putting on her showgirl mask.

Meanwhile, Inspector Perkins (Horst Tappert) and Sir Arthur (Hubert von Meyerinck) of Scotland Yard have turned up an odd piece of evidence at the hotel crime scene—a glass eye. Perkins along with his youthful sidekick Sergeant Pepper (Stefan Behrens) begin their investigation, which leads them to a billiards club that serves as a front for drugs and sex trafficking. This in turn leads them back to the performers and showgirls of Jefferson's theater—of particular interest are shady "knife thrower" Rubiro (Jan Hendriks) and disgruntled ventriloquist Eric (Otto Czarski). One of the showgirls, Yvonne (Karin Huebner), is romantically involved with the aristocratic Bruce Sharringham (Fritz Wepper). Bruce's mother, Lady Sharringham (Friedel Schuster), ruthlessly repudiates her son's engagement. This stew of by now worn-out crime elements simmers, braises, and boils over, culminating in a wild western saloon-type fight and a bizarre climax aboard a cruise ship.

Despite the prior year's *Der Gorilla von Soho*'s disappointing reception and sagging box-office, it was decided to continue the series with another production for 1969. *Der Mann mit dem Glasauge* began production on November 4 and wrapped on December 18, 1968. The shooting locations included West Berlin (CCC-Film studios in Berlin-Haselhorst as well as the Berlin environs), the Port of Hamburg, and London. The film premiered on February 21, 1969, in the Mathäser Filmpalast in Munich. Continuing its downward trend in ticket sales, *Glasauge* registered 1.6 million visitors.

Der Mann mit dem Glasauge does not begin with the customary Wallace teaser, opting instead to dive right into its glitzy credits (over an excellent Peter Thomas composition). The Edgar Wallace rapid-fire bullets do, however, arrive after the film offers up its first thrown knife. *Glasauge*'s credit sequence reveals much about the status of the franchise and its contemporaneous relationship to pop culture at the conclusion of the 1960s. This title sequence, brightly lit and vividly rendered with marquees that flash prominent conventional counterculture avatars such as *The Graduate* (1967), *Easy Rider* (1969), and the Palace Theatre's run of *Mr. and Mrs.* (1968), acknowledge the series' most prescient and salient problem: relevancy.

With this film, and at this point, it is necessary to pause briefly and examine *Krimi*'s health and fragile vital signs at this stage of its life. The steady erosion and dilution of the series' more "authentic" relationship with Wallace's work were—in a very real sense—a direct result of evolving cultural norms and values, as well as the market's reply to this dynamism. Consequently, the production of *Der Mann mit dem Glasauge* is much more a product of the year 1969 than it is of Rialto film or Edgar Wallace. Rialto, like other major and minor studios—including those of Hollywood—was under increasing pressure to turn larger profits from their underperforming releases and franchises while trying to keep up with, or, indeed, merely catch up to, the runaway zeitgeist.

Simply put, Rialto had exhausted its resources. True, it was theatrically dishonest to attach Wallace's name to recent releases, and true, key actors and directors had departed the franchise, but the series' greatest loss—its most depleted resource—was not one of financial liquidity, but rather cultural liquidity; Rialto had expended all of its *cultural* capital. There was simply little appetite comparatively left in the movie-going public for these films. Moreover, the steady competition from German exploiter, Wolf C. Hartwig, had rendered the *Krimi* quaint by comparison. Hartwig, via his production company Rapid Film, had produced a series of *Sittenfilme* or vice films (sexualized low-budget efforts that frequently sensationalized violence and taboo subject matter) throughout the 1960s that successfully drew the disposable income away from *Krimi* fans.

Bearing all this in mind, and notwithstanding its faults, I actually find more to recommend in the much-maligned *Der Gorilla von Soho* (1968) than in 1969's *Der Mann mit dem Glasauge*. Granted, *Gorilla* is a poor remake of *Die toten Augen von London*, but it evinces certain pleasures that make it enjoyable, while *Glasauge* mostly fails to leverage its potential, such as it is. Naturally, the film has its defenders (then, and now), but for me, it represents the series' last gasp.

Like virtually every Rialto *Krimi*, *Der Mann mit dem Glasauge* is well-made, beautifully shot, and boasts some truly impressive set pieces. However, Edgar Wallace is so far removed from the milieu by now that it's beyond misleading to attach his name to the production. It *is* appropriate that this was to be Director Alfred Vohrer's last *Krimi* for Rialto. For, like Harald Reinl before him, although the material had denigrated considerably, Vohrer departs with his style and reputation intact. Such competence, however, cannot ameliorate the many flaws in *Der Mann mit dem Glasauge*.

Thus, although *Glasauge* was shot with the usual energy and technical merit that a Vohrer-helmed unit regularly delivered, it's difficult not to cast a nostalgic gaze back at the series' origins and measure just how far it had strayed. The absence of its defining icons, such as Eddi Arent, Joachim

Figure 3.7 These Wallace Henchmen Have Developed a Rather Simple but Effective Motivation Technique. *Der Mann mit dem Glasauge* (*The Man with the Glass Eye*, 1969). Source: *Stifung Deutsche Kinematek Berlin.*

Fuchsberger, Siegfried Schürenberg, Karin Dor, and Klaus Kinski, among others, compounded by the gradual disappearance of the *Krimiverse*'s exhilarating world of masked villains, cloaked monks, sadistic scientists, mute hunchbacks, blackmailing seductresses, croaking frogs, thieving sharks, barking hounds, diving gorillas, and bountiful snakes (among other interesting scoundrels, heavies, and dangerous animals), is lamentable. By 1969, these series-defining traits simply belonged to another world—a world that had inexorably moved on.

After the release of *Der Mann mit dem Glasauge* what little remained of the series' defining characteristics were abandoned, essentially displaced into a sort of *Krimi* purgatory. It was here that these tropes hung in suspension until the subsequent Italian coproductions attempted to make them semi-relevant again—but, as we will see, as much-transformed texts. One last German effort, however, *Die Tote aus der Themse*, was made in 1971 in hopes of reviving the series. And while *Die Tote aus der Themse* brought in slightly less money than *Glasauge*, it is the superior production and a suitable send-off for the West German productions.

Smartly, however, like some of its predecessors, *Glasauge* presciently leaned into these forthcoming Italian coproductions by slowly mixing ingredients from Italy's popular *gialli* into their batter—the very same *gialli* that drew inspiration from Germany's *Krimis*. *Glasauge*, in particular, contains several scenes that recall Mario Bava's *Krimi-giallo* hybrid *Sei donne per l'assassino* (1964), which in turn drew inspiration from Reinl and Vohrer's *Krimis*—especially in the highlighting of a silhouetted, hat-adorned, knife-wielding, leather-clad, murderer whose gender remains in question.

Eddi Arent's departure from the series in 1966 proved a significant loss to the franchise, particularly in his capacity for providing comedy relief to various leading men. The post-Arent movies are often overcompensated in this department, and *Glasauge* is the ne plus ultra example of this sort of grandstanding. Hubert von Meyerinck's unlikable Sir Arthur insinuates himself into too many scenes, usually spitting annoying orders or engaged in his unrestrained lechery. Moreover, it's unclear whether it was actor Stefan Behrens' or Director Alfred Vohrer's idea to have Sergeant Pepper provide one of the most annoying vocal performances in cinema history (he is not dubbed), but it grates mercilessly on the nerves. Yet, arguably the scariest, or at least the most unsettling, component in the film concerns Eric the ventriloquist and the creepy, child-like voice that projects from his oversized dummy. These and other contrivances indicate that the *Krimi* game had played itself out.

There are still some fine moments peppered throughout, however, with perhaps the high point being the superbly choreographed bar fight. It's well-staged and quite funny—which begs the question of why Vohrer didn't introduce one or two of these donnybrooks into his oeuvre sooner. Also, a top-shelf Peter Thomas score accompanies the film, especially the title credit music.

As a perceptive tombstone prophesied and eulogized simultaneously in *Der Hund von Blackwood Castle*, "*Jeder Anfang hat ein Ende*" (Every Beginning has an End) and *Glasauge* hastened this goodbye.

A DOPPIA FACCIA / DAS GESICHT IM DUNKELN / DOUBLE FACE (1969)

Helen Alexander (Margaret Lee), the primary shareholder of London's Brown & Brown Co., is enjoying a carefree sexual affair with her friend Liz (Annabella Incontrera) while ignoring her husband John (Klaus Kinski). Consequently, the emasculated John emotionally withdraws from the marriage. Humiliated but still wistful for the love they once shared, he confronts Helen about her infidelity but receives no real promise of reconciliation. Instead, Helen decides to simply go on vacation for a short period to presumably contemplate her future plans—alone. Before Helen's departure, however, an explosive device is planted near the gas tank of her E-Type Jaguar. On the way to Liverpool, her car explodes and she is (presumably) killed instantly.

Arriving at the scene are Scotland Yard Inspectors Steevens (Günther Stoll) and Gordon (Luciano Spadoni), who do not immediately suspect foul play, yet don't rule it out either. Suspicions arise, however, when they learn that John stands to inherit his late wife's controlling shares in Brown and Brown. Perhaps unwisely, the heartbroken John decides to take a posh vacation to try to recover from his grief. Upon his return, he finds the young "hippie" Christina (Christiane Krüger) squatting in his villa. The two become familiar enough that he agrees to accompany her to a psychedelic swingin' London party where she proudly exhibits the new adult film in which she appears. Christine's scene is shared with a woman who wears a wig and whose face remains covered. This mysterious woman also wears a one-of-a-kind ring belonging to John's late wife, and bears a tell-tale neck scar identical to Helen's. But when John later obtains the film and screens it for his father-in-law Mr. Brown (Sydney Chaplin), the ring and scar are missing from the footage. Consequently, John begins to question his sanity. Is this an actual case of revenge from beyond the grave or an explainable deadly conspiracy to wrest control of the company away from John Alexander?

Das Gesicht im Dunkeln is based loosely on motifs found in the 1924 Edgar Wallace novel *The Face in the Night*. Although, as was customary by now, little-to-no similarities existed between this novel and Rialto's coproduction. Entrusted to helm the film was well-known Italian director Riccardo Freda.

Principal photography occurred in Rome, London, and Liverpool between the dates of January 20 and March 15, 1969. *Das Gesicht im Dunkeln* premiered on July 4, 1969, at the Mathäser Filmpalast in Munich (in a significantly shortened version). It later opened (in an expanded running time) in Italian cinemas on July 26, 1969. Partnering with Colt Produzioni Cinematografich and Mega Film S.P.A., Rialto hoped that *Das Gesicht im Dunkeln* would deliver a wider audience, greater international viability, and consequently increased profits. Unfortunately for Rialto, it was the lowest performing film in the entire franchise, gathering a meager 600,000 visitors. Yet despite this misfire, Rialto remained undeterred and followed up this economic flop with three more productions.

Beginning with 1969's *Das Gesicht im Dunkeln*, the *Krimi*'s DNA altered dramatically. *Dunkeln* initiated the brief, final period where the *Polar Spaghetti* (Thriller Spaghettis) would constitute three of the final four Rialto productions. *Dunkeln* is not purely a *Krimi*, nor is it purely a *giallo*; rather it takes inspiration from both of these cinematic forms and then fuses them with elements from the *Poliziotteschi* (the Italian arm of the larger Euro-Crime sub-genre). When considered within the context of the rapidly growing number of *gialli* and the extensive catalog of *Krimis*, *Dunkeln* was not a success—certainly not financially. It was, however, successful enough to encourage more coproductions with Italy—based, in part, on some favorable reviews and a handful of impressive moments (including a clever climax). Far from exciting, though, *Dunkeln* remains a confusing, illogical, and, at times, boring film. Of course, these negative value judgments can be leveled at other entries in Rialto's library, just typically not all at once.

When he began work on *Das Gesicht im Dunkeln*, Italian director Riccardo Freda was an industry veteran as well as a genre pioneer who helped cement the popularity of the gothic horror film, the peplum, and the spy movie in Italy's post-neorealist motion picture industry. At this stage of his career, however, stark inconsistencies had manifested in Freda's work ethic and thus his work. As a result, *Das Gesicht im Dunkeln* failed to realize its potential.

Nevertheless, like every *Krimi* produced or coproduced by Rialto, *Das Gesicht im Dunkeln* is a polished production that boasts a few sequences of striking mood and atmosphere. One, in particular, would actually be far more at home in a film like Bernardo Bertolucci's *Il conformista* (*The Conformist*, 1970). It occurs shortly after John awakens from a drug-induced sleep (compliments of Christine) and then walks into the night to search for her, desperate to find more answers about his wife's death. Consumed by this obsession, he wanders through narrow, winding, rain-soaked, and amber-hued alleys, calmly pausing to light a cigarette and survey his surroundings (aware that he is indeed being followed). Sequences like this

Figure 3.8 Klaus Kinski Is Bathed in Buttery Streetlight in This Visually Stunning Set-up from *Das Gesicht im Dunkeln* **(*Double Face*, 1969).** *Source: Stifung Deutsche Kinematek Berlin.*

represent Freda at his very best. It's a pity there aren't many more scenes that approach this level of beauty. Indeed, poor process shots, substandard miniature sets, and unconvincing toy scale models damage the film's credibility. There is also the problem of the film's pace. Despite its clipped running time in the German version, *Dunkeln* still moves sluggishly, magnified by a dubbed (by frequent Kinski voice-over actor Gerd Martienzen) Kinski having to carry most of the narrative weight.

The cast, in the main, proves solid, but it's really Kinski in the spotlight for the duration. It's a heavy lift for an actor historically cast in supporting roles. Other characters, such as Günther Stoll's Inspector Steevens are given very little to do. Christiane Krüger, fresh off her *Krimi* debut in *Der Mann mit dem Glasauge*, makes for an alluring mischief-maker, but she cannot buoy this sinking film. An uneven script and uneven direction created a project of largely missed opportunities. Tellingly, Rialto's head of production, Horst Wendlandt, has no title card in the credits for *Das Gesicht im Dunkeln* (despite Rialto's participation)—a first since 1961.

DIE TOTE AUS DER THEMSE / ANGELS OF TERROR (1971)

At the seedy Hotel Portland, after a late-night drug deal has gone awry, expelled ballerina and Scotland Yard operative Myrna Fergusson (Lyvia Bauer) is shot by drug dealer and meatpacker Jim Donovan (Michael Miller). Sleeping with a call girl (Ingrid Steeger) in a nearby room, opportunistic (and cheapskate) photographer David Armstrong (Vadim Glowna) hears the gunshots and dashes to the crime scene to snap as many photographs as possible. Scotland Yard Inspector Craig (Hansjörg Felmy) promptly arrives to find that Fergusson's body has disappeared.

Meanwhile, Myrna's sister Danny (Uschi Glas) arrives from Australia and learns of her sibling's murder. Danny also learns from authorities that Myrna had left her ballet company in a state of disgrace and had been working with Scotland Yard to help bring down a powerful heroin smuggling ring. While meeting with Scotland Yard's Sir John (Siegfried Schürenberg), Danny encounters Armstrong, who informs her that his photographs tell a different story about his sister's death. Armstrong then produces the photographs, which indicate that Mryna's body had moved after the "murder," suggesting she is still alive. Danny steals the photos and departs. Shortly afterward, Armstrong is shot dead by a shadowy sniper.

Inspector Craig pays a visit to William Baxter's (Werner Peters) slaughterhouse where Donovan (fingered by the hotel clerk) works. But before the inspector can interview Donovan, he is also shot by the sniper. In fact, the usual suspects that pop up in typical *Krimi* fashion are sniped one by one, providing a high body count as the film builds toward its concluding act (which, if discussed further, would spoil several significant plot developments).

Die Tote aus der Thames is based loosely on motifs drawn from the Edgar Wallace novel *The Angel of Terror* (1922), which was adapted for the screen as *Ricochet* in 1963 (directed by John Llewellyn Moxey) as part of British Merton Park Studios' "Edgar Wallace Mysteries" series. London's Merton Park studios produced forty-nine popular hour-long second features from 1960 to 1965.[18] Rialto's *Die Tote aus der Thames*, however, bears no resemblance to *Ricochet*. *Die Tote aus der Thames* began production in London and West Berlin on January 11 and was completed on February 14, 1971. The premiere was held on March 30, 1971, in Mainz. The film brought in 1.4 million visitors—far better than the disappointing 600,000 tickets sold for *Das Gesicht im Dunkeln*.

Die Tote aus der Thames seemed to come out of nowhere, given that *Das Gesicht im Dunkeln*'s paltry earnings and poor reception appeared to be the final nail in Rialto's *Krimi* coffin; and no further efforts from series producer Horst Wendlandt were announced or expected. In the summer of 1970, however, an early *giallo* in the career of Italian director Dario Argento,

L'uccello dalle piume di cristallo (*The Bird with the Crystal Plumage*, 1970) was released. *L'uccello dalle piume di cristallo*, a coproduction between CCC and Seda Spettacoli S.p.A., was a superior production, a huge success, and marked a significant moment in the evolution of the genre. Constantin distributed the picture in West Germany with marketing ephemera that tenuously promoted the film as a Bryan Edgar Wallace adaptation.

In light of *Crystal Plumage*'s performance and its vague Wallace tie-in, Rialto decided to give its beloved series one final stab by having Wendlandt mobilize resources for another, possibly final, West German production to inaugurate the calendar year of 1971. Rialto was further encouraged by the warm and nostalgic reception of some recent theatrical re-releases from their Wallace catalog of titles (black and white, and color). The tea leaves read favorably, and the reasoning seemed sound. Predictably, however, the resultant movie prompted mixed reviews from critics and audiences (especially at this final stage). *Die Tote aus der Thames* is, however, not without charm and quite superior to its predecessor, *Das Gesicht im Dunkeln*.

Noticeably absent from *Die Tote aus der Thames* are the directorial flourishes of Reinl and Vohrer, yet Director Harald Philipp does a commendable job with the script and the cast. Filming extensively in London, the required core genre elements (which now included nudity) are present but orchestrated and deployed in a semi-unusual manner. It is often the outsider who can offer a new eye and a fresh perspective to an established franchise, and that's precisely what Philipp provides as he rises to meet the *Krimi* challenge. More of a metteur en scène than a specialist, the stalwart Philipp worked in a variety of genres—musicals, comedies, espionage, and war films—with competence, proficiency, and craftsmanship.

Case in point, *Die Tote aus der Thames* arguably delivers the most intense and visceral scenes found in the entire series. Ironically, these scenes do not occur at a castle, family estate, crypt, insane asylum, foggy London street, girl's boarding school, monastery, or seedy nightclub. Rather, they play out as sequences in Baxter's slaughterhouse and freezing works (shot in Berlin's Spandauer Schlachthof), a nice anticipation of 1974's *The Texas Chain Saw Massacre*.

The oldest known parietal art (or cave art) depicted interactions between humans and animals, usually bison, horses, aurochs, and deer (the most often hunted species by our ancestors). Depictions of slaughterhouses and stockyards have a long-standing tradition in the arts, too. From Bunuel's *Blood of the Beast* (1949) to Tornatore's *Cinema Paradiso* (1988), cinema has portrayed animal slaughter for a variety of affectual purposes throughout its history. Similarly, meat packing plants have seen their fair share of famous scenes, from *Rocky*'s (1976) Shamrock Meat Packing facility to the *Saw* franchise's (2004–present) deserted and trap-ridden Gideon Plant.

Setting a considerable amount of diegesis in Baxter's slaughterhouse (a site of brutality and death) truly separates *Die Tote aus der Thames* from the majority of titles in Rialto's Wallace library. A few films (e.g., *Die toten Augen von London*, *Das Gasthaus an der Themse*, and *Das Indische Tuch*) also leverage setting (both in their exterior locations and in soundstages) in clever and effective ways, but *Die Tote aus der Thames* is ingenious in unsettling the viewer.

The film compounds its slaughterhouse atmosphere of dread with the addition of humans pitted against humans. Early in the picture, Philipp smartly lingers on rote slaughterhouse devices and methods, making them difficult scenes to watch. The pig vats, scoops, conveyers, and traveling meat hooks loaded with freshly sawed pig halves surely prompt an abject response in many viewers. Later, the line between animal and human is blurred when Baxter imprisons his enemies in the deep freezer. The film's climax similarly and smartly transpires in the slaughterhouse, providing a congruent and brutal coda. Thus, the rising action and later (rather sweet and endearing) denouement for Rialto's final West German *Krimi* is, all things considered, quite satisfying.

Figure 3.9 This Candid Moment on the Set of *Die Tote aus der Themse* (*Angels of Terror*, 1971) Captures What Was to Be a Bittersweet Coda for the Beloved Siegfried Schürenberg (Pictured Here with Marlies Drager). This would be his last performance as Scotland Yard's Sir John. *Source:* Stifung Deutsche Kinematek Berlin.

The cast of *Die Tote aus der Thames* presents an enjoyable mix of new and old faces. Uschi Glas, now a veteran in her fourth Rialto *Krimi*, plays the part with just the right balance of determination and naiveté. Newcomer Hansjörg Felmy provides Inspector Craig with a noticeable physical presence, minimizing facial expression and thus limiting his emotional register. Far from charming, but at the same time cool and interesting (in the same vein as 1971's most famous detective Harry Callahan), Felmy, given time and opportunity, would have grown into the role as successfully as his predecessors. Indeed, he went on to play the much-admired investigator Heinz Haferkamp in Germany's crime series *Tatort* for seven years. As discussed in the conclusion, *Tatort* ultimately filled the void left by the *Krimi*'s theatrical exodus.

Die Tote aus der Thames bid a fond farewell to one of the series' most beloved icons, Siegfried Schürenberg, and his irascible Sir John. In typical Schürenberg fashion, he registers an appropriately hammy goodbye for both the studio and his fans. Had the series continued, it's unclear whether Schürenberg would have successfully adapted to the rapidly changing zeitgeist of the 1970s, but he did return for rival studio CCC in Jess Franco's marvelously messy *Der Todesrächer von Soho* (1972), a remake of CCC's *Das Geheimnis der schwarzen Koffer* (*Secret of the Black Trunk*, 1961).

Tragically, *Die Tote aus der Thames* turned out to be German actor Werner Peters' last movie. It was Peters' fourth *Krimi* for Rialto, but the always in-demand actor had appeared in over one hundred productions, including several for CCC's Dr. Mabuse and Bryan Edgar Wallace series. A productive and skilled actor with an intense presence, Peters fashioned a career out of playing loveable villains. Perhaps the most memorable of his Rialto roles was as Bertram Cody, the submissive husband of villainess Gisela Uhlen in *Die Tür mit den 7 Schlössern* (1962). The fifty-two-year-old Peters died on March 30, 1971 (ironically, the day of the film's premiere).

Finally, and fittingly, Peter Thomas' last *Krimi* score presents what I believe to be his strongest work in the series. His harp-driven, haunting score for *Die Tote aus der Thames* is the perfect melancholy coda to his extensive *Krimi* career. With *Die Tote aus der Thames*, Rialto's West German production team could walk away from the series unbowed.

DAS GEHEIMNIS DER GRÜNEN STECKNADEL / COSA AVETE FATTO A SOLANGE / WHAT HAVE YOU DONE TO SOLANGE? (1972)?

Henry Rossini (Fabio Testi), a married professor at St. Hilda's, a London Catholic academy for girls, is having an affair with student Elizabeth Seccles

(Christina Galbó). During an amorous, slow rowboat ride together down the Thames, Elizabeth sees (or imagines she sees) another girl being stabbed by a long knife. Unconvinced, Henry manages to persuade Elizabeth that she imagined the assault. The audience, however, is inclined to agree with her.

Shortly thereafter, Scotland Yard's Inspector Barth (Joachim Fuchsberger) arrives at what is indeed a crime scene only to discover that the murder was especially brutal and the fatal wounds exceptionally uncommon. Unfortunately, Barth only finds one small piece of physical evidence: a green pin. Later, when Henry hears about the Thames murder on the radio, and when another student is murdered in a similarly barbaric method, he urges Elizabeth to keep quiet or risk their affair becoming public knowledge. Regardless, Elizabeth comes forward and offers testimony to the academy. As a result of this ignominy, Henry's marriage to his wife Herta (Karin Baal) continues to crumble and professionally he is shunned. More students are murdered in grisly fashion and many plausible suspects are presented. Summarizing the plot any further, however, robs viewers of the pleasure of cracking this puzzling thriller and discovering the answer to the question posed in both its Italian and English titles, *What Have You Done to Solange?*

Ostensibly, *Das Geheimnis der grünen Stecknadel* was loosely based on motifs from the 1923 Edgar Wallace novel *The Clue of the New Pin*. More accurately, this Wallace connection was a marketing ploy to brand and sell the film to the German public as part of Rialto's ongoing series since there is little resemblance between this film and Wallace's novel. The movie was shot almost entirely in London from September 13 to November 1, 1971. The West German premiere was held on March 9, 1972, at the Passage Kino in Saarbrücken (significantly in a shortened version compared to the 107-minute Italian release, rendering the film incomprehensible in parts). The film brought in 1.1 million visitors, a respectable sum considering the film is not, in the slightest, a traditional *Krimi*. (Because the German theatrical release of the picture strips it of important sequences, and the Italian cut is the dominant market version, I will refer to it by its Italian title, *Cosa avete fatto a Solange?* throughout this entry.)

While *Das Gesicht im Dunkeln* (*Double Face*) was not strictly a *Krimi* or a *giallo*, *Cosa avete fatto a Solange?* unequivocally belongs to the *giallo* genus. It is in this light that the film can be best appreciated and read. In Rialto's Franco-German coproductions, *Die Tür mit den 7 Schlössern*, *Der Zinker*, *Der schwarze Abt*, and *Zimmer 13*, France was essentially a "silent partner." This enabled Rialto's house style to remain dominant, which disguised any perceptible coproduction fingerprints (other than financial). With *Cosa avete fatto a Solange*, however, the situation was now reversed: West Germany was the silent partner while Italy's distinct style and approach ascended to dominancy.

For *Krimi* purists, however, and in typical coproduction fashion, the film offered some attractions for its co-financer. Absent foggy London streets, treacherous moors, and diabolical villains, the film compensates with the inclusion of *Krimi* trouper Karin Baal (in her third outing) and the series' last remaining icon, Joachim Fuchsberger, who achieves an extraordinary orbit around the *Krimi* sun—commencing with the modest Danish production of *Der Frosch mit der Maske* (1959) and concluding with this German-Italian production, the penultimate in Rialto's catalog. Fuchsberger—older, more distinguished, and crankier in this role (perhaps because of those many years at irritable Sir John's side)—resolutely leads this baffling and disturbing investigation. Baal plays Herta Rossini icily, with attenuated make-up and frequent, sharp rebukes to her husband. After certain events occur, she later thaws as they both try to rekindle the embers of their nearly smothered marriage. Fans also rejoiced with the casting of Günther Stoll in an important role in his fourth outing for Rialto.

The strengths of *Cosa avete fatto a Solange* are many. The film's director, Massimo Dallamano, began his career as a cinematographer in the immediate aftermath of World War II. The results of his gifted eye can be seen in many exceptional films. Among his director of photography credits, for example, were Sergio Leone's *Per un pugno di dollari* (*A Fistful of Dollars*, 1964) and *Per qualche dollaro in più* (*For a Few Dollars More*, 1965). Like many cinematographers, Dallamano ultimately turned his viewfinder toward directing, and in 1972 he fashioned this remarkable film that improbably crossed multiple genre boundaries: thriller, police procedural, revenge film, *Krimi*, and, of course, *giallo*. *Solange* offers an elaborately staged and stunningly lensed murder puzzle. This incongruent juxtaposition of violence and beauty is at the heart of the *giallo*'s visual aesthetic. And, like the best the *giallo* can offer, newcomers and veterans of this fascinating genre alike will be kept guessing until the film's much-anticipated revelations.

Moreover, from a transgressive standpoint, *Cosa avete fatto a Solange?* crossed a red line that previous *Krimis* had avoided for a variety of reasons. Foremost among them were the financial curse of receiving an adult rating and/or incurring the axe of censorship from the FSK. Beyond that, the subject of the film's transgression was not really an established Anglo or West German theme of the franchise. Bearing this in mind, the following paragraph reveals crucial aspects of the film's transgressive nature and should be avoided if the reader has not seen it.

The topic of abortion was nothing new to motion pictures, particularly in pre-code era Hollywood. Films like *Corruption* (1917), *The Curse of Eve* (1917), and *The Road to Ruin* (1928), among many others, framed abortion as a scandalous and salacious attraction, and served as cautionary tales. The topic didn't abate in the decades following the implementation of the

Hays Code—even in major productions with A-list actors. For example, megastars Natalie Wood and Steve McQueen shined in Warner Brothers' *Love with the Proper Stranger* (1963), which dealt with abortion in a stark, frank, and visceral manner. *Solange*, however, raises the bar significantly and accomplishes this transgression in just the first five minutes of the film. A few years later, Spain would raise the bar even higher with releases like *Quién puede matar a un niño?* (*Who Can Kill a Child*, 1976) and *El Huerto del Frances* (*The Frenchman's Garden*, 1977), which continue these disturbing depictions of abortion. Moreover, the savagely cruel method of murder—a long, curved blade inserted into the victim's vagina—shattered previous ceilings of appropriateness. Nevertheless, a new transgression bar was established that would see the constant challenge through the 1970s, 1980s, and 1990s, culminating, for example, in a film like *Se7en* (1995), which featured several grisly murders committed in the name of the "Seven Deadly Sins." For the sin of lust, a man is forced to copulate with a prostitute while wearing a strap-on phallus fashioned from a massive metal blade.

As a *Krimi*, *Solange* would (and did) register as a disappointment among devoted fans. As a *giallo*, however, it ranks as one of the more important and superbly crafted entries. An excellent score by celebrated Italian composer Ennio Morricone also greatly enhances its effectiveness.

Despite Rialto's attempts to keep the *Krimi* alive in West Germany through coproductions with Italy, it was apparent that the *Krimi* was actually on life support. Regardless, Rialto would invest in one final effort.

DAS RÄTSEL DES SILBERNEN HALBMONDS / *SETTE ORCHIDEE MACCHIATE DI ROSSO* / *SEVEN BLOOD-STAINED ORCHIDS* (1972)

A knife-wielding, leather-gloved intruder breaks into a woman's home under the cover of night and murders her while she sleeps. A portrait of a young woman sits atop her nightstand. Shortly afterward, the same killer solicits a prostitute (Gabriella Giorgelli) in a dodgy section of Rome; she agrees to go with him. Upon entering a verdant woodland area, the killer suddenly bludgeons the streetwalker to death with a large wooden post. Before leaving, he places a half-moon crescent pendant in her hand, which later earns him the nickname the "Half-Moon Killer." Inspectors Vismara (Pier Paolo Capponi) and Lt. Palumbo (Aldo Barberito) arrive at the scene to investigate possible leads and gather physical evidence.

Meanwhile, for reasons yet unknown, bride-to-be Giulia Torresi (Uschi Glas) is made aware that she is now a target of the Half-Moon Killer.

Fearing that she may become victim number three, her fiancé, Mario Gerosa (Antonio Sabato), collaborates with the police to set a trap aboard their train while honeymooning. The plan works perfectly, but the killer manages to escape. Giulia is falsely reported dead and a funeral is held; however, there are no suspicious attendees, which only serves to baffle the investigators further. Under mounting pressure, Giulia suddenly remembers a disagreeable American tourist who left her hotel a few years prior who possessed the exact same half-moon pendant as a keychain. The man's identity is determined to be Frank Saunders, who was unfortunately killed in an auto accident, with his female companion in the accident apparently abandoning him to die alone. Things begin to coalesce and the body count rises in this bloody tale of revenge.

The German-Italian production of *Das Rätsel des silbernen Halbmonds* was the thirty-second and final entry in Rialto's Edgar Wallace *Krimi* series. The film was not based on any of Edgar Wallace's works but rather patterned after American author Cornell Woolrich's novel *Rendezvous in Black* (1948). Production began on September 6 and wrapped on October 23, 1971. Shot in Rome and Spoleto, Italy, the movie premiered in West Germany on June 30, 1972, at the Passage Kino in Saarbrücken. *Das Rätsel des silbernen Halbmonds* sold a depressing 600,000 tickets—second only to *Das Gesicht im Dunkel*'s record low of 300,000. This discouraging sum was the definitive proof Rialto needed to finally end its coproduction efforts.

A skilled tradesman, by 1972 Italian director Umberto Lenzi had amassed an impressive and diverse filmography that included several adventure movies, peplums, European spy films, *gialli*, *Poliziotteschi*, and an early entry in what would become his famous series of cannibal pictures. Among these, *Silbernen Halbmonds* ranks as a modest effort from the director. The elaborately staged death scenes (a non-negotiable prerequisite for *gialli*) are shot with vivid color, stylish lighting, inventive blocking, and creative camerawork. However, apart from the murders, much of the film suffers from an acute malaise of pace, generally unlikable characters, and an unnecessarily convoluted story. The plot in *Silbernen Halbmonds* is straightforward enough, but devolves into sluggishness via the careless arrangement of its simple revenge-based story elements. Unfortunately, this leads to scenes and sequences that feel loosely connected and uninteresting. Without a truly formidable aesthetic to bind it all together, the film stands as a middling entry in the *giallo* canon.

Among the entry's assets, however, are Italian composer Riz Ortolani's bass-driven, propulsively groovy score and the earlier mentioned staging of the murders. The most impressive of these deaths occur as American artist Kathy Adams (Marina Malfatti) arrives at her studio loft after an evening's art exhibit. She kicks off her heels and then attends to her meowing cats with a bowl of cold milk. Suspicious noises draw her out of the kitchen, but finding nothing unusual she continues to undress. The cats' meows, however, have now turned to cries. Back in the kitchen, horror registers on Kathy's face as she realizes that her cats have been poisoned. Tension rapidly mounts in this shadowy, densely dressed setting. Action moves very quickly via fast cuts and pans, yet time feels protracted. One of Kathy's works in progress, a female portrait, stares back at her, its eyes now vandalized with splattered and smeared bright red paint. In shock, she frantically reaches for the telephone. Suddenly, from behind, black gloves grasp her neck and cover her mouth. Her suffocated screams die in her throat as life slowly fades from her eyes and her body collapses. Upended cans trickle red and black paint onto Kathy's body, staining her naked torso with abstract patterns. Ironically, her head has come to lie within an empty frame, her own death creating a new "work of art" for her studio. In true *giallo* form, Lenzi makes death shockingly picturesque.

It should be noted that Riz Ortolani's score, while first-rate and appropriately spotted (the process of deciding where cues start and stop) unfortunately consists of recycled tracks from previous gialli, notably Lenzi's *So Sweet . . . So Perverse* (1969). To the film's credit, the music still works, but it also betrays an overall lack of craftsmanship and inattention to detail (in contrast

Figure 3.10 Life Will Shortly Imitate Art for Artist Kathy Adams (Marina Malfatti) in *Das Rätsel des silbernen Halbmonds* (*Seven Blood-Stained Orchids*, 1972). Source: Stifung Deutsche Kinematek Berlin.

to that found in the best offerings from the genre). As is, the film's death scenes and musical score remain its sole highlights.

With no connection to Edgar Wallace, England, Scotland Yard, Rialto's iconic actors, the general iconography of the series, or its tropes, it's accurate to say that *Silbernen Halbmonds* bears little-to-no resemblance to Rialto's Wallace films. Its link to the series is through its coproduction status and Rialto's misleading marketing strategies in West Germany. For West German audiences, the apparent and bare minimum attraction was the casting of Uschi Glas (and Marisa Mell in a minor role). Therefore, in fairness to the largely Italian casts and crews that worked on these films, and to put a fine point on the reception of the three German-Italian coproductions discussed in this chapter, they are best regarded and viewed as *gialli* and not as *Krimis*.

More to the point, it was obvious that the series should have hung up its trademark bowler a few films prior (ideally with *Die Tote aus der Themse*, which would have provided a respectable and appropriate finale). Of the last four films in the series, the middle two are praiseworthy endeavors. If Rialto had chosen to resolve the series with the releases of the West German *Die Tote aus der Themse* and the Italian-German *Das Geheimnis der grünen Stecknadel* (*Cosa avete fatto a Solange?*) the franchise would have ended on a more powerful, resonant, and much higher note.

Ultimately, there's not much to recommend in *Das Rätsel des silbernen Halbmonds*. It's a loosely held-together but stylish thriller with impressive death sequences and a hip (but recycled) score—which could be said of any number of Euro horror productions at that time. It's unlikely that this is how Rialto envisioned its beloved series bowing out, but such is the fate of a particular economic product produced in a particular economic system.

NOTES

1. "Soft focus, in fact, would prove fatal in the early 1950s. It put Technicolor on a collision course with another technical phenomenon of the decade—widescreen. There were, in fact, an assortment of widescreen processes—eight of them altogether. But they all shared the need for pinpoint sharpness. The anamorphic CinemaScope and double frame VistaVision lenses in particular had resolution and distortion problems of their own that left no tolerance for the soft focus limitation of the three-strip camera in the film negative." For more, please see "Crying in Color How Hollywood Coped when Technicolor Died," *Journal of the National Film and Sound Archive*.
2. Ibid.
3. Ibid.
4. Kim Newman, "Your Pocket Guide to *Krimis* 1959–1967," *Video Watchdog* no. 134 (Sept. 2007).

5. Hammer's highly sexualized "Karnstein Trilogy" consisted of *The Vampire Lovers* (1970), *Lust for a Vampire* (1971), and *Twins of Evil* (1971).
6. Tim Bergfelder, *International Adventures*.
7. Slavoj Žižek advanced this analysis of *Possession* (1931) in *The Pervert's Guide to Cinema* (2011).
8. Please see Selected Filmography for a list of these films.
9. Newman, *Video Watchdog*, 42.
10. Newman, *Video Watchdog*, 43.
11. https://www.spiegel.de/international/germany/report-reveals-derrick-actor-horst-tappert-was-an-ss-member-a-896765.html
12. https://www.thelocal.de/20130427/49399 retrieved August 10, 2020. For more on Elisabeth Noelle-Neumann please see her Spiral of Silence theory.
13. Robin Wood, *Film Comment*; New York 16, no. 2 (March/April 1980): 24–32.
14. For more on Jess Franco's *Krimis*, please see Nicholas G. Schlegel, "Hallo, hier spricht Jess Franco: How Franco Recoded the *Krimi*," in *The Films of Jess Franco*, eds. Antonio Lázaro-Reboll and Ian Olney (Detroit, MI: Wayne State University Press, 2018).
15. Newman, *Video Watchdog*, 44.
16. Translated from Joachim Kramp's entry for *Der Gorilla von Soho* in *Hallo—Hier spricht Edgar Wallace! Die Geschichte der deutschen Kriminalfilmserie 1959–1972* (Berlin, Germany: Schwarzkopf & Schwarzkopf, 2005), 203–4.
17. Review for *Der Gorilla von Soho*, *Darmstädter Echo*, 28. September 1968.
18. All forty-seven Merton Park productions are available in the Edgar Wallace Anthology box set from Network Studios.

Part III

CONCLUSION

Chapter 4

Krime Scene
The *Krimi* Autopsy

"What happened to the *Spanish Horror Film?*" This was the question that began the conclusion of my last book, *Sex, Sadism, Spain, and Cinema: The Spanish Horror Film* (2015). That book, much like this one, explored the history of a specific place (Spain), a specific time (the 1960s and 1970s), and a specific genre (horror). There are, in fact, some remarkable similarities and parallels between Germany's and Spain's post-World War II popular cinemas. Like its older *Krimi* cousins from Germany, Spanish horror emerged suddenly and with great success, skyrocketing into widespread popularity only to sputter out and vanish more than a decade later. Perhaps it reveals something about my scholarly ethos that I now find myself in the same research-oriented predicament, begging the same question, only now aimed at the mid-century Edgar Wallace German *Krimi*.

THE *KRIMI* AUTOPSY

Fortunately, we do know what happened to the German *Krimi*. As I have discussed throughout this book, many factors led to the waning popularity of Rialto's once-mighty and durable franchise. Among these attributable factors were the drastically altered zeitgeist (bridging a total of three decades, from the 1950s to the 1970s); the canonical counter-cinema that contemporaneously emerged from countries such as Italy, France, and Great Britain (and was later absorbed and assimilated by the United States in its own 1960s counterculture movement); additional 1960s competition from the growing German softcore exploitation industry; the outright legalization (and rapid proliferation) of pornography in West Germany in 1973; hindrances with distribution and exhibition; the box-office titans of the early "New Hollywood" blockbuster era (*The Godfather* [1972], *The Poseidon Adventure* [1972], *The Exorcist* [1973], *Jaws* [1975], among others); and, of course, the cyclical nature of genres which often simply advance into exhaustion, parody, or a state of a moratorium. However, genres rarely disappear altogether; more often than not, they are recycled—occasionally rising like phoenixes from their own ashes, revived and redefined by future generations of storytellers.

But first come the ashes, and, crucially, the German *Krimi* (and, more broadly, German popular cinema) found itself on the losing side of a *cultural war*. As Thomas Schatz has stressed, "The determining identifying feature of a film genre is its cultural context, its community of interrelated character types whose attitudes, values, and actions flesh out dramatic conflicts inherent within that community."[1] Indeed, a genre's cultural context is its heartbeat. When an arrhythmia occurs, the stirrings of a death rattle are usually not far behind. This proved to be the case with Rialto's franchise, which had neglected (despite late attempts at resuscitation) this genre's vital and mutable cultural cues.

At the same time, the NGC era had arrived, encouraged by the rebellion that "rolled through the streets of Germany in 1968 as students and other protestors set out to turn German society upside down through a strategy of 'continual revolt.'"[2] The Oberhausen Manifesto's declaration in 1962 had, over time, gathered significant momentum and become a dominant movement in its own right that would largely supplant GPC.

> For the angry young men and women associated with the New German Cinema, the prospect was clear: the cinema of their fathers and grandfathers was illegitimate. The films emanating from Goebbels' Ministry of Propaganda constituted an illusionist fantasy that either extolled or veiled racism and militarism; the conformist Adenauer films represented a continuation of this strategy. In response, young directors offered an auteurist counter-cinema and experimented with personal and autobiographical subjects, narrative intransitivity, estrangement effects, aperture, and unpleasure.[3]

Yet, despite this wholesale rejection of another generation's entertainment, genres are a fairly stubborn construct and, as stated earlier, rarely die outright. The *Krimi* simply cast too large a shadow over German culture to give up the ghost. What then happened to the Wallace *Krimi* after it reached the terminus of its long, lucrative ride? As the title of this book suggests, the success and popularity of the *Krimi* were a cultural phenomenon. The passionate and dedicated fanbase that animated these films for more than a decade couldn't be expected to suddenly go cold turkey, could they?

The answer was both yes and no. First, the Rialto *Krimi* found a vibrant second life in the homes of millions of German citizens. The televised syndication package of Rialto's large catalog of *Krimis* proved hugely popular in both East and West Germany. Indeed, audiences on the *other* side of the Oberhausen generation gap nostalgically relished the frequent airing of the previous decade's popular entertainment. Moreover, in the decades to come, generations of Germans were indoctrinated into Rialto's fascinating *Krimiverse* by devoted parents, grandparents, or simply by bored channel-flipping children and teens. Ironically, the rapid proliferation of televisions in German households (from 700,000 in 1956 to 7.2 million in 1962) was a major contributing factor to the *Krimi*'s diminishing profits—exponentially so by the end of the 1960s.[4] It is rather poetic that the *Krimi* should then be revived by the medium that helped "murder" its theatrical relevance. As of this writing, German television continues to program and run Edgar Wallace movie marathons on a regular basis, guaranteeing legions of new fans who are looking for something that is simultaneously new and old, fresh but familiar, ironic and self-aware. This was the prevailing attitude of the youthful consumers of the Wallace *Krimis* with whom I spoke while conducting research in Germany. They expressed interest in the series' refreshing humor, striking aesthetics, and silly scenarios—choosing to embrace, rather than reject, a previous generation's cultural pastime.

Second, although production ended at Rialto (and later CCC), the *Krimi* didn't disappear altogether. Instead, it underwent a modal transformation—a transformation from one medium (the big screen) to another (the small screen). Lost in this transitional milieu, however, was Edgar Wallace. Wallace's novels and themes were ultimately discarded from the formula in favor of a broad revival of the type of German TV crime series that was popular in the 1950s and 1960s, such as *Stahlnetz* (series one, 1958–1968), *Hafenpolizei* (1963–1966), *Polizeifunk ruft* (1966–1970), *Der Kommissar* (1969–1976), and *Hamburg Transit* (1970–1974), but with a new focus on realism and regional specificity (something the Wallace films sorely lacked) that would cross more German demographics and interests.

There was, however, conspicuous writing on the wall for this looming tonal shift in crime fiction and its engagement of domestic and regional authors. In the post-World War II era, crime as a genre

> was dominated by imports from England and the US, a situation that would not change again until the late 1960s. At this time, a new phenomenon began to register that first appeared under the label of the *Neuer Deutscher Kriminalroman* [New German Crime Novel] and was later called the *Soziokrimi*, from "*soziologischer Krimi*" [sociological crime novel].

Predictably, this shift in crime literature bled into cinema and television as well.

"New" German crime fiction made use of the positive connotations of newness in modern and modernizing societies. To be new meant to be up to date, to leave behind older patterns of mystery writing such as the "whodunit" and the cozy mystery of the English tradition.[5]

The flood gates opened, and opportunities for German writers to create and craft novels, television series, and motion pictures blossomed. It's not a mystery then that the casualty in this literary transition was, of course, Wallace himself.

Emerging from this era of "new," "up to date," and more sophisticated police procedurals were two series that would become historical markers for the genre. Making worthy use of their motto, *Wir sind deins* (We are yours), Germany's regional public-service broadcasters (ARD) launched the series *Tatort (Crime Scene)* in 1970. Whereas the dominant locus of the Rialto Wallace series was London (or, more generally, England), *Tatort* embraced regionalism by folding into the series the tropes of the emerging *Regionalkrimis* or *Regiokrimis*. The *Regionalkrimi* is a sub-genre of crime fiction popularized by regional German authors who set their thrillers in towns and villages which deeply connected with provincial and local readers. In adopting this narrative strategy (and employing these authors), *Tatort* boldly redefined the genre while also adapting to the progressively evolving climate of West Germany—through reunification in 1990 and beyond. As of this writing, the series is in its fiftieth season, with 1,150 episodes. *Tatort* is quite simply a *Krimi* juggernaut and Germany's third longest running series in the history of German broadcasting.

In like manner, geography played an important role in the second historic series, ZDF's (*Zweites Deutsches Fernsehen*) *Derrick*, which ran from 1974 to 1998. The immensely popular *Derrick* was an influential police procedural that focused on Chief Inspector Stephan Derrick of the *Polizeipräsidium München* (Munich Municipal Police Force) and its surrounding area. As an attractive bonus for Rialto fans, *Krimi* veteran Horst Tappert (*Der Hund von Blackwood Castle, Der Gorilla von Soho, Der Mann mit dem Glasauge*) starred as the eponymous Chief Inspector Stephan Derrick. *Derrick*'s 25 seasons and 281 60-minute episodes not only cemented a national affection for the show and Tappert, but was an international sensation, sold and broadcast in over 100 countries.

Rialto's immensely popular Edgar Wallace series (1959–1972) and its millions of fans were therefore not cast adrift, left to wander the *Krimi* desert, or forced to suddenly detox. On the contrary, Arent, Fuchsberger, Dor, Schürenberg, Kinski, et al. lived on in continuous TV syndication right up to the present day. Beyond this, German television took a shot at creating sociologically resonant police procedurals that showcased a new, exciting form of realism that proved hugely popular.

RIALTO'S WALLACE LEGACY

Beyond their marketplace value, the motion pictures discussed in this book achieved some unexpected but significant accomplishments. Among them, and most importantly, their very existence elevated the national mood in West Germany. After World War II, GPC gradually reconstituted Germany's once colossal motion picture industry. In doing so, they won the respect and loyalty of *new* audiences through a genuine commitment to entertain—and these films unequivocally entertained. The postwar question of guilt and ordinary citizens found some collective expression in the *Trümmerfilme* discussed in chapter 1. But a commercial film industry cannot subsist on a diet of rubble films alone. Conversely, the GPC cinema of the Adenauer era, with its heavy emphasis on escapism through the mass mobilization of popular genres, could be accused of dulling or deadening the German citizenry's senses to recent trauma. What is clear is that these two opposing approaches eventually found a sense of equilibrium in the decades that followed. Moreover, from a purely dialectical point of view, GPC provided the ambitious young auteurs of the NGC era (Wenders, Herzog, Fassbinder, etc.) the opportunity to earnestly and openly grapple with the existential detritus that Germany's postwar popular genres had actively avoided (which also speaks volumes).

Arriving at the end of its long, profitable run was not the business plan of Rialto (or broadly, German popular cinema, or any lucrative property), but in doing so, as Nietzsche would remind us, its "goal" was nevertheless realized. Furthermore, the Edgar Wallace *Krimi* would, like a character from one of Wallace's thrillers, return to haunt its fans for many decades to come. Apart from the immensely popular TV syndication of Rialto's movies (in both the classic and multichannel eras), Wallace *Krimi* found other popular outlets. Wallace's stage play roots were revived as live theatrical performances in "*Krimi*-Theaters." Based on Wallace's novels, as well as the Rialto adaptations of them, these stage plays continue to entertain audiences in Hamburg, Berlin, Bremen, Munich, Stuttgart, and other cities all year-round and to packed houses.

As Tim Bergfelder wrote in 2005,

> After two decades of suppression, the 1950s and 1960s have returned with a vengeance in the German media landscape and have all but elbowed out the remaining vestiges of the new German cinema. Whole German TV channels are nowadays devoted to the *Heimatfilm*, either in its 1950s variant or a new guises sitcoms and soap operas. The Edgar Wallace films have been continuously recycled on TV already since the 1970s.[6]

With the *Krimi*'s ubiquity so firmly established, Rialto was eventually honored with affectionate parodies of its Wallace franchise. The first arrived in 1994 with RTL's (Radio Television Luxembourg) *Otto-Die Serie*. This short-lived series consisted of black and white and color segments culled from the thirty-two Rialto Wallace *Krimis* which were then spliced into fresh comedic material. RTL's sketch-based comedy featured popular German comedian Otto Waalkes, but despite the *Krimis* widespread appreciation, *Otto-Die Serie* failed to capture sufficient audience and lasted only one season.[7] More successful was 2004's *Der Wixxer* (*The Wanker*). This affectionate parody premiered in Munich on May 10, 2004, and pulled in an enthusiastic 1.9 million visitors which ranked it fourth in German productions for the year. Older fans rejoiced and youthful audiences were charmed (and, as a corollary, sought out the original films to better understand the intertextual and self-referential humor).

In the tradition of Zucker, Abrahams, and Zucker's *Airplane* (1980), *Top Secret* (1984), and *The Naked Gun* (1988), *Der Wixxer* is indeed a clever and entertaining homage that succeeds in lovingly lampooning one of Germany's most popular film franchises. Set in England (like the original films), *Der Wixxer* aesthetically takes the scenario one step further by playing its pastiche "both ways." *Der Wixxer* cheekily alternates between *Krimi* eras by transitioning from color to black and white (and back again) whenever scenes occur at or near or even inside Blackwhite Castle (Blackwood Castle), the home of the Earl of Cockwood. It's a clever device in a film filled with successful gimmicks, word play, and sight gags.

The rogue's gallery of ersatz villains is especially amusing and no doubt sidesplitting for fans of the series. With a knowing wink, the villains (all members of The National Syndicate of Notorious Criminals) hold names such as *Der dicke Hai* (the Fat Shark), *Der Arsch mit den Ohren* (the Ass with Ears), and *der Fisch mit der Sense* (the Fish with the Scythe). Perhaps the true lily gilding moment occurs when the series' inaugural criminal mastermind *Der Frosch mit der Maske* (the Frog with the Mask) appears as a literal masked frog in the form of famous Muppet, Kermit the Frog (voiced by actor Andreas von der Meden: Kermit the Frog for German television's *Die Muppet Show*). *Der Wixxer*'s broad caricature of the series proved so popular that a sequel, *Neues vom Wixxer*, was released in 2007 to similarly enthusiastic reviews.

DAS ENDE

Throughout *German Popular Cinema and the Rialto Krimi Phenomenon: Dark Eyes of London*, I have endeavored to shine a light on the unfamiliar, often neglected, and frequently dismissed West German cinema of the post-World War II era: from *Trümmerfilm* to *Heimatfilme*, from Edgar Wallace to *Tatort*, from *Sittenfilme* to NGC, from Nazism to democratic republic. The case studies

Figure 4.1 "Cut!" Series Sleuths Joachim Fuchsberger and Heinz Drach Enjoy a Playful Moment on the Set of *Der Hexer* (*The Mysterious Magician*, 1964). Source: *Stifung Deutsche Kinematek Berlin*.

presented in the previous chapters reveal the profound importance of these films vis-à-vis the political, industrial, economic, social, and cultural changes experienced by the Federal Republic of Germany. In my view, these vital films made during these vital decades unequivocally assisted in communicating, cementing, and reconstructing a changed national identity.

With their Manichean worldview (where good triumphs over evil), the Wallace films carefully revived the Weimar era crime thrillers by grounding them in escapist fantasy and safely locating them in a former adversary's soil. Moreover, the series' progressive sense of irony, self-referentiality, intertextuality, and other endearing postmodern touches generated spectacular appeal, lasting box office, and a hyper-dedicated fan base. The cross-cultural and cross-industrial influence on the Italian (*giallo*) and Hollywood (slasher) motion picture industries cannot be overstated. Fortunately, the simple pleasures of the Rialto Wallace films live on today and hopefully these pleasures will continue to pass from generation to generation.

NOTES

1. Thomas Schatz, *The Genius of the System: Hollywood Filmmaking in the Studio Era* (New York: Pantheon Books, 1988), 21–22.

2. "'68 Movement Brought Lasting Changes to German Society," *Deutsche Welle*, Last modified April 11, 2008, https://www.dw.com/en/68-movement-brought-lasting-changes-to-german-society/a-3257581

3. Mattias Frey, *Postwall German Cinema: History, Film History and Cinephilia* (New York: Berghahn, 2015), 5.

4. Marco Abel and Christina Gerhardt, eds., *Celluloid Revolt: German Screen Cultures and the Long 1968* (Rochester, NY: Camden House, 2019), 89.

5. *Contemporary German Crime Fiction: A Companion* (Berlin, Germany: De Gruyter, 2019).

6. Bergfelder, *International Adventures*, 242.

7. In 1996, Radio Television Luxembourg again attempted to revive the Edgar Wallace series with three made-for-television films. A second season, consisting of five additional feature length titles, was shot in 1998 but not released until 2002 on subchannel Super RTL. The series featured actors from the classic Rialto era such as Eddi Arent (now as Sir John), Pinkas Braun, and Gisela Uhlen.

Selected Filmography

EDGAR WALLACE FILMS (PRE-WORLD WAR II)

Der grosse Unbekannte / Blackmail (1927)
The Ringer (1928)
The Terror (1928)
Der rote Kreis / The Crimson Circle (1929)
The Wrecker / Der Würger (1929)
Der Zinker / The Squeaker (1931)
Der Hexer / The Sorcerer (1932)
The Strangler (1932)
The Frightened Lady (1932)
Der Doppelgänger (1934)
The Mysterious Ship / Das mysteriöse Schiff (1934)
Return of the Terror (1934)
Sanders of the River (1935)
The Squeaker / Murder on Diamond Row (1937)
The Terror (1938)
Dangerous to Know / Gefährliche Mitwisser (1938)
The Dark Eyes of London / The Human Monster (1939)
The Chamber of Secrets / Chamber of Horrors (1940)
The Case of the Frightened Lady (1940)
The Ringer (1952)

EDGAR WALLACE FILMS—RIALTO FILM

Der Frosch mit der Maske / Face of the Frog (1959)

Der Rote Kreis / The Red Circle (1960)
Die Bande des Schreckens / The Terrible People (1960)
Der grüne Bogenschütze / The Green Archer (1961)
Die toten Augen von London / Dead Eyes of London (1961)
Das Geheimnis der gelben Narzissen / The Devil's Daffodil (1961)
Der Fälscher von London / The Forger of London (1961)
Die seltsame Gräfin / The Strange Countess (1961)
Das Rätsel der roten Orchidee / Secret of the Red Orchid (1962)
Die Tür mit den 7 Schlössern / La Porte aux sept serrures / The Door with Seven Locks (1962)
Das Gasthaus an der Themse / The Inn on the River (1962)
Der Zinker / L'Enigme du serpemnt noir / The Squeaker (1963)
Der schwarze Abt / The Black Abbot (1963)
Das indische Tuch / The Indian Scarf (1963)
Zimmer 13 / L'Attaque du fourgon postal / Room 13 (1964)
Der Hexer / The Mysterious Magician (1964)
Die Gruft mit dem Rätselschloss / The Curse of the Hidden Vault (1964)
Das Verrätertor / Traitor's Gate (1964)
Neues vom Hexer / Again the Ringer (1965)
Der unheimliche Mönch / The Sinister Monk (1965)
Der Bucklige von Soho / The Hunchback of Soho (1966)
Das Geheimnis der weissen Nonne / The Trygon Factor (1966)
Die blaue Hand / The Creature with the Blue Hand (1967)
Der Mönch mit der Peitsche / The College Girl Murders (1967)
Der Hund von Blackwood Castle / The Monster of Blackwood Castle (1968)
Im Banne des Unheimlichen / The Zombie Walks (1968)
Der Gorilla von Soho / Gorilla Gang (1968)
Der Mann mit dem Glasauge / The Man with the Glass Eye (1969)
Das Gesicht im Dunkeln / A doppia faccia / Double Face (1969)
Die Tote aus der Themse / The Body in the Thames / Angels of Terror (1971)
Das Geheimnis der grünen Stecknadel / Das Cosa avete fatto a Solange? / What Have You Done to Solange? (1972)
Das Rätsel des silbernen Halbmonds / Sette orchidee macchiate di rosso / Seven Blood-Stained Orchids (1972)

BRYAN EDGAR WALLACE FILMS—CCC (CENTRAL CINEMA COMPANY)

Das Geheimnis der schwarzen Koffer / The Secret of the Black Trunk (1962)
Der Würger von Schloss Blackmoor / The Strangler of Blackmoor Castle (1963)

Der Henker von London / The Mad Executioners (1963)
Das Phantom von Soho / The Phantom of Soho (1963)
Das Umgeheuer von London City / The Monster of London City (1964)
Das siebente Opfer / The Seventh Victim (1964)
Das Geheimnis der schwarzen Handschuhe / The Bird with the Crystal Plumage (1970)
Der Todesrächer von Soho / The Death Avenger of Soho (1972)
Das Geheimnis des gelben Grabes / The Dead Are Alive (1972)

DR. MABUSE FILMS

Dr. Mabuse, der Spieler / Dr. Mabuse the Gambler (1922)
Das Testament des Dr. Mabuse / The Testament of Dr. Mabuse (1933)
Die 1000 Augen des Dr. Mabuse / The Thousand Eyes of Dr. Mabuse (1960)
Im Stahlnetz des Dr. Mabuse / The Return of Doctor Mabuse (1961)
Das Testament des Dr. Mabuse / The Testament of Dr. Mabuse (1962)
Scotland Yard jagt Dr. Mabuse / Scotland Yard Hunts Dr. Mabuse (1963)
Die Todesstrahlen des Dr. Mabuse / The Secret of Dr. Mabuse (1964)
Club Extinction / Dr. M (1990)

Bibliography

Abel, Marco and Christina Gerhardt, eds. *Celluloid Revolt: German Screen Cultures and the Long 1968*. Rochester, NY: Camden House, 2019. Print.

Allmer, Patricia, Emily Brick, and David Huxley. "German and Northern European Horror." In *European Nightmares: Horror Cinema in Europe Since 1945*, edited by Patricia Allmer, Emily Brick, David Huxley. London: Wallflower Press, 2012. Print.

Angell, Joseph W. *Historical Analysis of the 14–15 February 1945 Bombings of Dresden*. USAF Historical Division Archives, 1950. https://media.defense.gov/2011/Feb/08/2001329907/-1/-1/0/Bombings%20of%20Dresden.pdf

Baschiera, Stefano and Francesco Di Chiara. "Exotic Landscapes and Italian Holidays in Lucio Fulci's Zombie and Sergio Martino's Torso." In *Cinema Inferno: Celluloid Explosions from the Cultural Margins*, edited by John Cline, Robert G. Weiner. Lanham, MD: Scarecrow Press, 2010. Print.

Baudrillard, Jean. *Simulacra and Simulation*. Ann Arbor: University of Michigan Press, 1994. Print.

The Beatles Anthology. Episode 1. Featuring George Harrison, John Lennon, Paul McCartney, Ringo Starr, and George Martin. Aired February 13, 1989, in broadcast syndication.

Bergfelder, Tim. *International Adventures: German Popular Cinema and European Co-Productions in the 1960s*. New York: Berghahn Books, 2005. Print.

Brockmann, Stephen. *A Critical History of German Film*, 2nd Edition. Melton, UK: Boydell & Brewer, Incorporated, 2020. 160. Print.

Clark, Neil. *Stranger than Fiction: The Life of Edgar Wallace, the Man Who Created King Kong*. Gloucestershire, UK: The History Press, 2014. Print.

Contemporary German Crime Fiction: A Companion. Berlin, Germany: De Gruyter, 2019. Print.

"Daß Publikum die Trümmer und auch die Schuldabtragungsfrage zu dieser Zeit nicht mehr wollte." Lichtspielträume. Kino in Hannover 1896–1991. Edited by Society for Film Studies e.V., Hanover 1991. A conversation with Hans Abich.

Darmstädter Echo, 28. September 1968.
Deighan, Samm. "Smooth Kriminal: The Dead Eyes of London (1961)." https://diaboliquemagazine.com/smooth-kriminal-the-dead-eyes-of-london-1961/
"Derrick und sein Schöpfer, der SS-Offizier." Hanns-Georg, Rodek. https://www.welt.de/kultur/article13604688/Derrick-und-sein-Schoepfer-der-SS-Offizier.html (accessed Aug. 10, 2020).
Deutsche Welle. "'68 Movement Brought Lasting Changes to German Society." April 11, 2008. https://www.dw.com/en/68-movement-brought-lasting-changes-to-german-society/a-3257581 (accessed June 25, 2019).
Dillman, Claudia and Olaf Möller, eds. *Beloved and Rejected: Cinema in the Young Federal Republic of Germany from 1949 to 1963*. Frankfurt, Germany: Deutsches Filminstitut - DIF e.V., 2016. Print.
Dixon, Wheeler Winston. "The Colonial Vision of Edgar Wallace." *Journal of Popular Culture* (1998). Print.
Elsaesser, Thomas. *New German Cinema: A History*. New Brunswick, NJ: Rutgers University Press, 1989. Print.
Fehrenbach, Heide. *Cinema in Democratizing Germany: Reconstructing National Identity after Hitler*. Chapel Hill: University of North Carolina Press, 1995. Print.
"Files Reveal Star Actor Horst Tappert's Nazi Past." https://www.thelocal.de/20130427/49399 (accessed Aug. 10, 2020).
Frankland, Noble; Webster, Charles. *The Strategic Air Offensive Against Germany, 1939–1945, Volume II*. HMSO, 1961. Print.
Frey, Mattias. *Postwall German Cinema: History, Film History and Cinephilia*. New York: Berghahn, 2015. Print.
Gemünden, G. "In the Ruins of Berlin: A Foreign Affair." In *German Postwar Films. Studies in European Culture and History*, edited by W. Wilms and W. Rasch. London: Palgrave Macmillan, 2008. Print.
Gerhards, Sascha. "Ironizing Identity: The German Crime Genre and the Edgar Wallace Production Trend of the 1960s." In *Generic Histories of German Cinema: Genre and Its Deviations*, edited by Jaimey Fisher. Woodbridge, UK: Boydell & Brewer, 2013. Print.
Hall, Katharina, ed. *Crime Fiction in German: Der Krimi*. Cardiff, UK: University of Wales Press, 2016. Print.
Hanke, Ken. "The 'Lost Horror Film Series: The Edgar Wallace Krimis." In *Fear Without Frontiers: Horror Cinema Across the Globe*, edited by Steven J. Schneider. Godalming, UK: FAB Press, 2003. Print.
Hantke, Steffen. "Postwar German Cinema and the Horror Film Thoughts on Historical Continuity and Genre Consolidation." In *Caligari's Heirs: The German Cinema of Fear after 1945*, edited by Steffen Hantke. Lanham, MD: Rowman and Littlefield, 2006. Print.
Hayes, Peter. *From Cooperation to Complicity: Degussa in the Third Reich*. Cambridge, UK: New Cambridge University Press, 2007. Print.
Heffernan, Kevin. *Ghouls, Gimmicks, and Gold: Horror Films and the American Movie Business, 1953–1968*. Durham, NC: Duke University Press, 2004. Print.

Heiduschke, Sebastian. *East German Cinema: DEFA and Film History*. London: Palgrave Macmillan, 2013. Print.
Kracauer, Siegfried. *From Caligari to Hitler: A Psychological History of the German Film*. New York: Noonday Press, 1959. Print.
Kramp, Joachim. *Hallo! Hier spricht Edgar Wallace*: die Geschichte der deutschen Kriminalfilmserie 1959–1972. Germany: Schwarzkopf & Schwarzkopf, 2001. Print.
Lucas, Tim. "Edgar Wallace and the Paternity of King Kong." *Video Watchdog*, July/ September 2006. Print.
Lucas, Tim. "Your Pocket Guide to Krimis 1959–1967." *Video Watchdog*, September 2007, Print.
Lyon, James K. "Bertolt Brecht's Hollywood Years: The Dramatist as Film Writer." *Oxford German Studies 6*. (1971), Print.
Merritt, Russell. "Crying in Color How Hollywood Coped when Technicolor Died." *Journal of the National Film and Sound Archive* 3, no. 2/3 (2008). Print.
Peary, Danny. *Cult Movie Stars*. New York: Simon & Schuster, 1991. Print.
Pitts, Michael R. *Famous Movie Detectives III*. Lanham, MD: Scarecrow Press, 2004. Print.
Phil, Nobile Jr. "A Genre Between Genres: The Shadow World of German Krimi Films." *Birth. Movies. Death.*, October 11, 2015. https://birthmoviesdeath.com /2015/10/11/a-genre-between-genres-the-shadow-world-of-german-krimi-films (accessed May 20, 2019).
Rentschler, Eric. "The Place of Rubble in the 'Trümmerfilm'." *New German Critique* no. 110 (2010): 12. http://www.jstor.org/stable/40926580 (accessed June 1, 2019).
Rentschler, Eric. *The Use and Abuse of Cinema: German Legacies from the Weimar Era to the Present*. New York: Columbia University Press, 2015. Print.
"Report Reveals 'Derrick' Actor Was SS Member." https://www.spiegel.de/international/germany/report-reveals-derrick-actor-horst-tappert-was-an-ss-member-a -896765.html (accessed Aug. 10, 2020).
Sandford, John, ed. *Encyclopedia of Contemporary German Culture*. Milton Park, UK: Taylor & Francis, 2013. Print.
Sanjek, David. "Foreign Detection: The West German Krimi and the Italian Giallo." *Spectator* 14, no. 2 (1994). Print.
Schatz, Thomas. *The Genius of the System: Hollywood Filmmaking in the Studio Era*. New York: Pantheon Books, 1988. Print.
Schivelbusch, Wolfgang. *In a Cold Crater: Cultural and Intellectual Life in Berlin, 1945–1948*. Berkeley: University of California Press, 2018. Print.
Schlegel, Nicholas G. "Hallo, hier spricht Jess Franco: How Franco Recoded the Krimi." In *The Films of Jess Franco*, eds. Antonio Lázaro-Rebol and Ian Olney (Detroit, MI: Wayne State University Press, 2018). Print.
Schlegel, Nicholas G. *Sex, Sadism, and Spain: The Spanish Horror Film*. Lanham, MD: Rowman and Littlefield, 2015. Print.
Shandley, Robert R. *Rubble Films: German Cinema in the Shadow of the Third Reich*. Philadelphia: Temple University Press, 2001. Print.
Screen Series: *Germany An Illustrated Guide and Index*, 1970. 146. Print.

Stuggarter Zeitung. Review of *Das Geheimnis der gelben Narzissen*, 1961.
"Supernatural Theater / Edgar Wallace Mystery "Krimi" Series." https://supernatural-theater.blogspot.com/2013/04/edgar-wallace-mystery-krimi-series.html (accessed April 10, 2019).
"They Won't Stay Dead." *The Dark Side: The Magazine of the Macabre and the Fantastic*, 2018. Print.
Wikipedia Contributors. "Die Edgar Wallace Filme." https://de.wikipedia.org/wiki/Edgar-Wallace-Filme (accessed April 10, 2019).
Wikipedia Contributors. "Great Train Robbery (1963)." *Wikipedia*, The Free Encyclopedia, https://en.wikipedia.org/wiki/Great_Train_Robbery_(1963) (accessed Aug July 20, 2019).
Wilms, Wilfried, and William Rasch, eds. *German Postwar Films: Life and Love in the Ruins*. New York: Macmillan, 2008. Print.
Wood, Robin. "Neglected Nightmares: In Defense of a Subverstienre and its Four Undersung Auteurs: Craven, Rothman, Clark, and Romero." *Film Comment* 16, no. 2 (1980): 24–32. http://www.jstor.org/stable/43452525

Index

Page references for figures are italicized

08/15 trilogy, 65
99 Mujeres, 38

Abbott and Costello, 53n74, 107
Abbott and Costello Meet Frankenstein, 116
Adenauer, Konrad, 11n2, 17, 25–26, 28, 32, 184, 187
Adorno, Theodor, 26, 46
Adventure in Berlin. See Die Spur führt nach Berlin
Again the Ringer (book), 124
Again the Ringer. See Neues vom Hexer
Aguilar, Carlos, 70
Airplane, 188
Alder, Thomas, 62
Allied Artists, 60
Allied Supreme Command, 19
American International Pictures (AIP), 29–30, 33, 60
Amicus Productions, 47
And the Heaven Above Us. See und über uns der Himmel
And Then There Were None, 147
The Angel of Terror (book), 169
Angels of Terror. See Die Tote aus der Themse

Angst, Richard, 42
Anthes, Eva, 59
Arent, Eddi, 35, 59, 61, 68, 70–71, 74, 76–77, 79, 80, 83, 85, 87–88, 91–92, 97, 99–102, *104*, 107–9, *111*, 113, 120, 123–24, 128, 130, 135, 139–40, 144, 149, 156, 164–65, 186
Argento, Dario, 12n19, 39, 50, 112, 139, 169
Armored Car Robbery, 121
Arnold & Richter, 99
Asher, Jack, 157
The Asphalt Jungle, 121
L'Attaque du fourgon postal. See Zimmer 13
Auschwitz, 78
Austria, 16, 41, *76*, 86, 88, 90, 100
auteur theory, 3

Baal, Karin, 74, *76*, 101, 150, *151*, 152, 173–74
Die Bande des Schreckens, 33, 58, 61, 62, 64, 66–71, 75, 80, 81, 98, 101, 158
Banks, Leslie, 81
Im Banne des Unheimlichen, 154–58
Barry, John, 157

Barthel, Waldfried, 29, 32
Bassey, Shirley, 157–58
Baudrillard, Jean, 46–48, 54n80, 146
Bava, Lamberto, 39
Becker, Jörg, 153
Behrens, Stefan, 162, 165
Belgium, 16
Benjamin, Walter, 26, 46
Bergfelder, Tim, 3, 9, 10, 11n5, 11n7, 12n23
The Berliner. See *Berliner Ballade*
Berliner Ballade, 23
Berlin Express, 23
Bertolucci, Bernardo, 167
Beswicke, Martine, 35
The Bird with the Crystal Plumage. See *L'uccello dalle piume di cristallo*
Bizonia, 24
The Black Abbot. See *Der Schwarze Abt*.
The Black Abbot (book), 102–5, 128, 131
Black Manta, 60
Die blaue Hand, 141–46, 148, 149, 152
Blood and Black Lace. See *Sei donne per l'assassino*
Blood Feast, 75
Blood of the Beast, 170
Blue Demon, (character), 30
The Blue Hand (book), 142
Bob le Flambeur, 121
The Body in the Thames. See *Die Tote aus der Themse*
The Body Snatcher, 69
Boettcher, Grit, 102, 146
Borchert, Ernst Wilhelm, 22
Borsche, Dieter, 74
Böttcher, Martin, 82–84, 87, 94, 98, 105, 145, 149
Braun, Pinkas, 38, 91–92, 99, 134, 156, 190n7
Brauner, Artur, 3, 12n11, 27, 31, 34, 41–42, 47, 99, 147–48
Breen, Joseph, 24
British Lion, 99, 106, 116

Die Büchse der Pandora, 5, 15
Der Bucklige von Soho, 10, 41, 113, 130, 133–38, 142–43, 145, 152, 156, 159
Buffalo Bill's Wild West Show, 47

Das Cabinet des Dr. Caligari, 5, 15, 34, 42–43, 86
The Cabinet of Dr. Caligari. See *Das Cabinet des Dr. Caligari*
Cahiers du Cinema, 3
Carpenter, John, 161
The Case of the Frightened Lady (film), 106
The Case of the Frightened Lady (stage play), 106
CCC (Berlin Studios), 58, 86, 99, 103, 113, 116, 124, 128, 135, 142, 146, 150, 159, 163
CCC (Central Cinema Company), 3, 10, 12n11, 12n16, 18, 27, 31–32, 34–35, 41–45, 47–48, 50, 58, 61, 71, 101, 105, 110, 112, 147, 153, 160, 170, 172, 185
Chamber of Horrors, 91
Christie, Agatha, 8, 50, 107
Cinema Paradiso, 170
CinemaScope, 99, 178n1
City in the Fog, 31
Clark, Neil, 36
Cleopatra, 41
The Clue of the New Pin (book), 173
The College Girl Murders. See *Der Mönch mit der Peitsche*
Cologne, 16
Colt Produzioni Cinematografich, 166
Columbia Studios, 29, 52n18, 71, 94
Il conformista, 167
Constantin Film, 3, 29–33, 44, 58, 64, 67, 69, 79, 92, 158, 161, 170
Cooper, James Fenimore, 19
Corman, Roger, 30
Corruption, 174
Das Cosa avete fatto a Solange?. See *Das Geheimnis der grünen Stecknade*

Cotton, Jerry, 27, 71, 150
Court, Hazel, 35
Cramer, Susanne, 65
Crawford, Joan, 143
Creature from the Black Lagoon, 68–69
The Creature with the Blue Hand. See *Die blaue Hand*
The Crimson Circle (book), 63
The Crimson Ghost, 156
Cronenberg, David, 161
Crosby, Bing, 73
The Curse of Eve, 174
The Curse of Frankenstein, 34, 121
The Curse of the Hidden Vault. See *Die Gruft mit dem Rätselschloss*
Cushing, Peter, 35, 47

The Daffodil Mystery (book), 78
Dagover, Lil, 85–87
Dallamano, Massimo, 174
The Dark Eyes of London (book), 74
The Dark Eyes of London (film), 74
Darth Vader, 60
Dawson, Basil, 79, 82
The Dead Eyes of London. See *Die toten Augen von London*
Decla Film, 5, 20
Deighan, Samm, 75
Delis, Daniela, 71
Denbeigh-Russel, Grace, 80, *81*
Denmark, 2, 109
Derrick, 153, 186
Deutsche Filmaktiengesellschaft (DEFA), 21–22, 43
Deutsche Filminstitut, 44
The Devil's Daffodil. See *Das Geheimnis der gelben Narzissen*
Diabolique (magazine), 75
Dickinson, Desmond, 80
Dixon, Wheeler Winston, 37–38, 75
Dr. Mabuse. See *Mabuse, Dr.* (film series)
Dr. No, 60
Dr. Terror's House of Horrors, 48

A doppia faccia. See *Das Gesicht im Dunkeln*
The Door with Seven Locks. See *Die Tür mit den sieben Schlössern*
Dor, Karin, 4, *8*, 35, 42, 48, 66, 70–71, 72, 73, 82–83, *84*, 85, 101, 109, 115, 119, 127, *129*, 130, 165
Double Face. See *Das Gesicht im Dunkeln*
Drach, Heinz, 91–92, 98, 106–7, 116, 118, 124, 149, *189*
Dracula. See *Horror of Dracula*
Dracula (film, 1931), 68, 86
Dracula (film, 1958). See *Horror of Dracula*
Dragnet, 71
Dresden, firebombing of, 78
Düsseldorf, 16
Dynamite in Green Silk, 150

Eastern German Democratic Republic (GDR), 17, 45
Eastmancolor, 133–34, 136–37
Easy Rider, 163
Ehe im Schatten, 22
Eichinger, Bernd, 28
Elbe River, 69
Ellenbruch, Peter, 28, 31–32
Elsaesser, Thomas, 23
L'Enigme du serpemnt noir. See *Der Zinker*
Eppler, Dieter, 69, 127
Esper, Dwain, 75
Evangelischer Filmbeobachter (Evangelical Film Observer), 26
Ewert, Renate, 62, *63*, 65
The Exorcist, 184
Expressionism, 5, 7

The Face in the Night (book), 166
Face of the Frog. See *Der Frosch mit der Maske*
Der Fall Rabanser, 31
Der Fälscher von London, 82–86, 103
Fangoria Magazine, 8, 43
Faust, 15

Fear Without Frontiers: Horror Cinema Across the Globe (book), 6
Fehrenbach, Heide, 16
The Fellowship of the Frog (book), 60
Felmy, Hansjörg, 169, 172
Filmdienst der Jugend (Film Service for the Youth), 26
Filmfax (magazine), 4, 11n9, 45
Film Noir, 31, 34, 40, 48, 51, 67, 69, 80, 88
Filmpause, 18
Les Films Jacques Willemetz, 92, 99
Finland, 45
Fisher, Terence, 157
Die Fledermaus, 100
Flickenschildt, Elisabeth, 42, 48, 66, 70, 82, 95, *96*, 98, 101, 107
The Fly, 161
A Foreign Affair, 23
The Forger (book), 83
The Forger of London. See *Der Fälscher von London*
Francis, Freddie, 35, 120–23
Frankenstein (film), 68–69
Frankfurt School, 26, 46
Franklin, Benjamin, 19
Frau Wirtin (film series), 27, 57
Freda, Riccardo, 49, 161, 166–67
Freiwillige Selbstkontrolle der Filmwirtschaft (FSK), 25–26, 61, 69–70, 114, 123, 174
The Frenchman's Garden. See *El Huerto del Frances*
French New Wave, 17, 50
Die freudlose Gasse, 42
Freund, Karl, 61
The Frightened Lady (book), 106
The Frightened Lady (film), 106
From Caligari to Hitler: A Psychological History of the German Film (book), 42
From Russia with Love, 41
Fröbe, Gert, 70, 73
Der Frosch mit der Maske, 2, 10, 33, 34, 39, 58–66, 68, 70, 71, 82, 83, 95, 98, 110, 112, 123, 128, 130, 158, 162, 174, 188
Fuchsberger, Joachim, 35, 48, 59, 64, 66, 74, 76, 78–79, 83, 85, 87, 92, 95, 97–99, 102, 105, 109, 113, 115, 118–19, 130, 131n7, 149, 151–56, 165, 173–74, 186, *189*
Fulci, Lucio, 12n20, 39
Fünf unter Verdacht, 31
Funk, Heinz, 82
Fürbringer, Ernst Fritz, 113, 115

Gainsborough Pictures, 106, 116
Gambit, 121
Gardner, Erle Stanley, 50
Das Gasthaus an der Themse, 39, 82, 94–*96*, 98, 99, 101, 171
The Gaunt Stranger (book), 116
The Gaunt Stranger (film). See *The Phantom Strikes*
Das Geheimnis der gelben Narzissen, 78–83, 93, 121, 140
Das Geheimnis der grünen Stecknadel, 50, 172–76, 178
Geheimnis der weissen Nonne, 127, 135, 138–42, 150, 156
Geheimnis Des Blauen Zimmers, 107
Gerhards, Sascha, 2, 9
Germania anno zero, 23
German Popular Cinema (GPC), 3, 5, 18, 26, 184, 187
Germany: Allied occupation of, 15–51; *besucher* (box office measurement) in, 58; bifurcation of, 17, 25, 185; censorship in, 24–25, 61, 69–70, 114, 123, 174; media consolidation in, 16–17; media reform in, 19–21; Weimar era and, 6, 15, 16, 27, 31, 34, 42–43, 48. See also World War II
Germany, Year Zero. See *Germania anno zero*
Das Gesicht im Dunkeln, 39, 49, 50, 166–70, 173
The Ghastly Ones, 75

The Ghost, 45, 74, 161. See also *Lo Spettro*
The Ghost and Mr. Chicken, 132n34
Giallo, 7, 10, 12n20, 39, 41, 44, 49–51, 110–12, 140, 165, 167, 169, 173–77, 189
Girls in Uniform. See *Mädchen in Uniform*
Glas, Uschi, 101, *147*, 158, 159, 169, 172, 175, 178
Gloria (film distributor), 29–30
The Godfather, 184
Goebbels, Joseph, 16–17, 184
Goldmanns Taschen-Krimi (Goldmanns' Pocket-Thrillers), 37, 49
Der Golem, 15
The Golem. See *Der Golem*
The Gorilla Gang. See *The Gorilla von Soho*
The Gorilla von Soho, 153, 158–64, 186
Gottlieb, Franz Joseph, 42, 105, 107
Gough, Michael, 35
The Graduate, 163
Graf, Robert, 82
Grand Slam, 121
Granger, Stewart, 139–40
The Great Escape, 82
Great Train Robbery of 1963, The, 110
The Green Archer (book), 71
The Green Archer (film). See *Der Grüne Bogenschutz*
The Green Archer (serial), 71
Grothum, Brigitte, 85, 95, 99, 101
Die Gruft mit dem Rätselschloss, 113–116, 124, 130, 142
Der Grüne Bogenschütze, 8, *33*, 62, 70–72, 80, 86, 104, 105, 130, 158
The Guest House on the Thames. See *Das Gasthaus an der Themse*

Hafenpolizei, 185
Hallo–Hier sprich Edgar Wallace! Die Geschichte der deutschen Kriminalfilmserie 1959–1972 (book), 7, 11, 39

Hamburg Transit, 185
Hammer Film Productions, 33–39, 41, 47, 54n83, 61, 119–122
The Hand of Power (book), 155
Hanke, Ken, 4, 9
Hantke, Steffen, 4
Hardy, Sophie, 115, 119, 140
Hartwig, Wolf C., 163
Hasenau, Beate, 162
Hasselhoff, David, 36
Hays, Wil, 24, 174
Heidi, 57
In der Heimat, 65
Heimatfilme, 1, 26–7, 32, 57, 71, 187–8
Herrmann, Bernard, 65, 167
Herzog, Werner, 161
Der Hexer, 39, *40*, 110, 114–19, 123, 124
Hill, Benny, 160
Hinds, Anthony, 34
Hitchcock, Alfred, 64–5, 97, 125, 131
Hold That Ghost, 107
Hong Kong, 6, 78
Hope, Bob, 73
Horkheimer, Max, 46
Horney, Brigitte, 124, 126–27, 139–40
Horror International (book), 6
Horror of Dracula, 34–35, 61, 121
The Hound of the Baskervilles (book), 150–51
House of Dracula, 116
House of Frankenstein, 116
House on Haunted Hill, 107
The House that Dripped Blood, 48
How to Steal a Million, 121
El Huerto del Frances, 175
The Human Monster, 74
Hummel, Gerhard F., 32
The Hunchback of Soho. See *Der Bucklige von Soho*
Der Hund von Baskerville (film), 100
Der Hund von Blackwood Castle, 149–54, 156, 158, 162, 166, 186, 188
Hungary, 35

Immoral Tales: European Sex & Horror Movies 1956–1984 (book), 6
The Indian Scarf. See Das indische Tuch
Das indische Tuch, 106–10, 114, 152, 171
Information Control Division (ICD), 19–21, 23–25
Irgendwo in Berlin, 22
The Italian Job, 121
Italy, 16, 18, 22, 30, 41, 49–50, 57, 110, 121, 134, 141, 165, 167, 173, 175–6, 183

James Bond (film series), 6, 27, 41, 45, 83, 117, *129*, 131, 136, 147–8
Japan, 6, 16, 51n2
Jary, Michael, 83
Jaws, 184
Jeffries, Fran, 158
The Joyless Street. See Die freudlose Gasse
Jugendschutzgesetz, 25
Junge Film-Union, 31

Kalinke, Ernst W., 42, 61, 113
Kammerspiel, 107
Kate Plus Ten (book), 139
Kate Plus Ten (film), 139
Kendall, Tony, 27
The Killing, 121
King Kong, 36
Kinski, Klaus, 4, *33*, 35, 75–79, 85–6, 88, 91–2, 95, 97–8, 100, 102, 107, 114, 120, 121, 123, *125*, 130, 141, 165, 166, *168*, 186
Kiss of Death, 80
Kitt, Eartha, 158
Knef, Hildegard, 22
Der Kommissar, 185
Kommissar X (film series), 1, 27, 57
Kracauer, Siegfried, 26, 42–3, 46
Kramp, Joachim, 7, 11, 38–9, 58, 104, 131n2, 161
Kriminalroman, 7

Krimi-Theaters, 187
Krimiverse, 49, 58, 67, 96, 118, 122, 126, 165, 185
Krueger, Freddy, 96, 142
Krüger, Christiane, 166, 168

The Ladykillers, 121
Lange, Carl, 59, 142, 144
Lange, Hellmut, 71, 82–83, *84*, 99
Lang ist der Weg, 23
The Last Laugh. See Der Letzte Mann
The Lavender Hill Mob, 121
Der Letzte Mann, 15
The League of Gentlemen, 121
Lee, Christopher, 35, 47, 78, 81, 88–89
Leipnitz, Harald, 113, 115, 128, 130, 142, 152
Lenzi, Umberto, 39, 110, 176–77
Lewis, H.G., 75
Lieven, Albert, 78, 120
Lindfords, Lill, 157
The Longest Day, 41
Love with the Proper Stranger, 175
Lowitz, Siegfried, 58, 82–83, 115, 118, 127, 130
Lucas, Tim, 6, 12n18, 36

M (film), 68
Mabuse, Dr. (film series), 5, 12n11, 15, 27, 34, 42–43, 57–58, 71, 85, 146–48, 172
Macdonald, Ross, 50
Mädchen in Uniform, 42
Mad Love, 61
Magna Pictures, 45
Majewski, Hans Martin, 83
Malfatti, Marina, 176, *177*
The Man Between, 23
Mancini, Henry, 101
Maniac, 75
The Man I Am Going to Kill. See Der Mann den ich töten werde
Der Mann den ich töten werde, 22
Der Mann mit dem Glasauge, 162–66, 168, 186

The Man with the Glass Eye. See *Der Mann mit dem Glasauge*
Marcuse, Herbert, 26, 46
The Mark of the Frog (book), 60
The Mark of the Frog (serial), 60
Marriage in the Shadows, 22–23. See also *Ehe im Schatten*
Marshall Plan, 24
Mattes, Willy, 62, 82
May, Karl, 1, 3, 27, 35, 57, 71, 100, 130, 133–34, 140
McQueen, Steve, 175
Mega Film S.P.A, 167
Mell, Marisa, 87, 90, 178
The Mephisto Waltz, 85
Merton Park Studios, 169, 179n18
Metropolis, 5, 15, 42, 86
Mexico, 6, 132n23
Meyen, Harry, 113, 115
MGM Studios, 20, 52n18
Milligan, Andy, 75
Mil Máscaras (character), 40
The Misfits, 156
The Missing Guest, 107
Mr. and Mrs., 163
Der Mönch mit der Peitsche, 44, 145–50
Mondadori, Arnoldo, 50
Mondadori Yellow Classics (*I Classici del Giallo Mondadori*), 49–50
Mondo Macabro, 6
The Monkees, 73
Monogram Studios, 74, 94, 148
The Monster of Blackwood Castle. See *Der Hund von Blackwood Castle*
Monty Python, 72
Die Mörder sind unter uns, 17, 22
Morricone, Ennio, 101, 175
Motion Picture Export Association of America (MPEA), 20–21, 24
Motion Picture Production Code, 20–21, 24
Moxey, John Llewellyn, 169
Murder By Death, 107
The Murderers are Among Us. See *Die Mörder sind unter uns*

Murder in the Blue Room, 107
Murder on Diamond Row. See *The Squeaker* (1937)
Murphy, Mark, 157
The Mysterious Magician. See *Der Hexer*
Mystery Science Theater 3000, 60, 131n3

Nachts im Nebel an der Themse, 60, 62, 82, 98
The Naked Gun, 188
Nesbitt, Cathleen, 139, 140
Neuer Deutscher Film (NGC), 10, 50, 184, 187, 188
Neues vom Hexer, 123–27, 135–36, 138, 140, 144, 156
Neues vom Wixxer, 188
Neuordnung (New Order), 15, 51n1
Newman, Kim, 36, 54n83, 61, 64, 70, 91, 112, 114, 128, 135, 148, 151, 160
Nibelungen, Die, 15
Nietzsche, Friedrich, 187
Nightmare, 121
Nobile Jr., Phil, 8, 43
Noelle-Neumann, Elisabeth, 153
North Atlantic Treaty Organization (NATO), 24
Nosferatu (1922), 5, 15, 68, 93, *137*
Nosferatu the Vampyre, 161
Nuotio, HT, 45

Oberhausen Manifesto, 3, 10, 17, 27–28, 50, 184–85
Ocean's 11, 121
The Old Dark House, 68
Old Shatterhand, 57
Old Surehand, 140
One Body Too Many, 107
On Her Majesty's Secret Service, 115
Ortolani, Riz, 167–67
Otto-Die Serie, 188

Pagé, Ilsa, 152, 156
Palmer, Lili, 91, 126

Pandora's Box. See Die Büchse der Pandora
Papworth, Keith, 82
Paramount Pictures, 20, 23, 52n18, 107
Paranoiac, 121
Pathé, 91
Pathé Exchange, 71
Peary, Danny, 73
Peters, Werner, 103, 169, 172
Petersen, Harald G., 116
Pflug, Eva, 60–62, 69, 82, 98, 162
The Phantom Strikes, 116
Philipp, Harald, 158, 170–1
Pieritz, Kurd, 102, 162
The Pink Panther, 121
The Police Report Reports. See Der Polizeibericht meldet
Der Polizeibericht meldet, 71
Polizeifunk ruft, 185
Poliziotteschi, 167, 176
Pommer, Erich, 20–21, 146–47
La Porte aux sept serrures. See Die Tür mit den sieben Schlössern
The Poseidon Adventure, 184
Possessed, 143
Postmodernism, 43, 46, 49, 70, 73, 106, 114, 126, 189
Preben Philipsen, 27, 29–34, 38, 41, 49, 64, 79, 139
precession of order, 46
Prisma Film, 29, 32, 63, 64, 74, 79
Producers Releasing Corporation (PRC), 94
Profumo, John, 160
Propagandakompanie (PK or Propaganda Company), 71
Protection of Young Persons Act. *See Jugendschutzgesetz*
Psycho, 64, 97, 125
Psychological Warfare Division (PWD). *See* Information Control Division (ICD)

Queen, Ellery, 50
Queen of Crime. See Kate Plus Ten

Rafelson, Bob, 73
Rahl, Mady, 152
Rasp, Fritz, 62, 85–87
Rathbone, Basil, 68
Ráthonyi, Ákos, 79, 80
Das Rätsel der roten Orchidee, 58, 87–90, 122, 156
Das Rätsel des silbernen Halbmonds, 90, 175–78
Raymond, Gary, 120
The Red Circle. See Der Rote Kreis
Reed, Oliver, 35
Regionalkrimi, 186
Reich Ministry of Popular Enlightenment and Propaganda, 16
Reinecker, Herbert, 116, 124, 136, 142–44, 150, 158
Reinl, Harald, 7, 42, 62, 64, 66, 68–71, 83, 85, 105, 109, 113, 123, 128, 130, 131, 143, 150, 164, 165, 170
Rendezvous in Black, 176
Rentschler, Eric, 18, 27–28
La Residencia, 138
Ricochet, 169
Riefenstahl, Leni, 71
Rififi, 121
Rilla, Walter, *84*, 109
The Ringer (stage play), 116
Ripper, Michael, 35
RKO, 23, 36, 52n18
The Road to Ruin, 174
Roberts and Barry Distributors, 45
Rocky, 170
Roland, Jürgen, 64–65, 71–73, 80
Roma, città aperta, 22
Rome, Open City. See Roma, città aperta
Room 13. See Zimmer 13
Room 13 (book), 109
Rosemary's Baby, 85
Rosenberg, Max J., 47
Die Rote Kreis, 2, 33, 34, 62–66, 70, 72, 80, 110
Rubble Film. *See Trümmerfilm*
Rütting, Barbara, 42, 99, 101, 124

Saebische, Karl Georg, 62, 71
Sangster, Jimmy, 35, 120, 121, *122*
Sanjek, David, 6–7
Santo (character), 40
Schatz, Thomas, 184
Schivelbusch, Wolfgang, 20
Schlagerfilm, 26, 32
Schneider, Bert, 73
Schneider, Romy, 28
Schneider, Stephen J., 6
schnitzel westerns, 1, 35, 57
Schoolgirl Report (film series). See *Schulmädchen-Report*
Schulmädchen-Report, 27, 57
Schürenberg, Siegfried, 35, 91, 92, 98, 101–2, 107, 109, 113–15, 124, 128, 136, 139, 142, 149, 150, 152, 156, *171*, 172, 186
Der Schwarze Abt., 101–8, 128, 129, 173
Scooby Doo, 41
The Secret of the Black Trunk, 3
The Secret of the Blue Room, 107
Secret of the Red Orchid. See *Das Rätsel der roten Orchidee*
Sei donne per l'assassino, 111, 143, 165
Die seltsame Gräfin, 85–87, 92, 94, 144
Sesselmann, Sabine, 79, 91
Sette orchidee macchiate di rosso. See *Das Rätsel des silbernen Halbmonds*
Se7en, 175
Seven Blood-Stained Orchids. See *Das Rätsel des silbernen Halbmonds*
Seven Thieves, 121
Sex, Sadism, Spain, and Cinema: The Spanish Horror Film, 6, 183
Shelley, Barbara, 35
Shelley, Mary, 34
Shepperton Studios, 47, 79
Sherlock Holmes (film series), 68
simulacra, the German *Krimi* and, 46–49
Simulacra and Simulation, 46
Singin' in the Rain, 45
Sinister Cinema, 4, 11n9, 46

The Sinister Monk. See *Der unheimliche Mönch*
Sissi, 28, 57
Sittenfilme, 163, 188
slasher film, the, 51, 189
Soave, Michele, 39
Société Nouvelle Cinématographie, 109
Somewhere in Berlin. See *Irgendwo in Berlin*
So Sweet... So Perverse, 177
The Sound of Music, 45
South Korea, 6
Soviet Union, The, 19, 24, 154
Soviet Zone, 21–23, 25
Spain, 6, 71, 175, 183
Lo Spettro, 45, 74, 161
Der Spiegel (newspaper), 123, 153
Springfield, Dusty, 157
Die Spur führt nach Berlin, 32
The Squeaker. See *Der Zinker*
The Squeaker (1927 book), 99
The Squeaker (1930 film), 99
The Squeaker (1937 film), 99
Stahlnetz (series one), 185
Staudte, Wolfgang, 21–22
Steeger, Ingrid, 169
Steppat, Ilse, 115, 127, 130, 141
Stoker, Bram, 34
Stoker Jr. Robert, 146
Stoll, Günther, 134, 136, 166, 168, 174
The Strange Countess. See *Die Seltsame Gräfin*
The Strangler of Blackmoor Castle. See *Der Würger von Schloss Blackmoor*
The Student of Prague. See *Der Student von Prag*
Der Student von Prag, 15
Stuggarter Zeitung (newspaper), 80
Stuttgarter Nachrichten (newspaper), 120
Subotsky, Milton, 47

Tappert, Horst, 153–54, 158, 162, 186
Taschenkrimi, 7
Tatort, 71, 172, 186, 188

Tausendjähriges (Thousand-Year Reich), 17
Technicolor, 133, 178n1
The Terrible People. See *Die Bande des Schreckens*
The Terrible People (book), 66
The Terrible People (serial), 66
The Terror (stage play), 103, 128
Der Teufel kam aus Akasava, 160
Thailand, 6
The Thing, 161
The Third Man, 59
Third Reich, the, 34, 42, 49
Thomas, Peter, 83–84, 87, 88, 90, 94, 101, 105, 107, 113, 115, 118, 123, 128, 138, 145, 154, 157, 162, 163, 166, 172
The Thomas Crown Affair, 121
Tiefland, 71
Der Todesrächer von Soho, 160
Topaz, 131
Top Secret, 188
Die Tote aus der Themse, 165, 169–72, 178
Die Toten Augen von London, 32, *33*, 45, 54n77, 62, 65, 72, 74–81, 92, 94, 95, 97, 100, 101, 117, 130, 149, 152, 156, 158, 161, 164, 171
The Traitor's Gate. See *Das Verrätertor*
The Traitor's Gate (book), 120
Transylvania, 35
The Treasure of Silver Lake, 134
Trooger, Margo, 115, 119, 120, 123, 124
Trümmerfilm, 17–23, 49
The Trygon Factor. See *Geheimnis der weissen Nonne*
Die Tür mit 7 Schlössern, 81, 91–94, 97, 104, 124, 172, 173
Turmpalast, 74

L'uccello dalle piume di cristallo, 170
Ultrascope, 99–100, 103, 106, 109, 114, 116, 124
Uncle Silas, 86

und über uns der Himmel, 22
Der unheimliche Mönch, 10, 103, 110, 127–31, 135, 138
United Artists, 29, 52n18

Variety, 45
V-E Day, 16
verisimilitude, *Krimis* and, 48, 54n84
Das Verrätertor, 39, 80, 110, 120–24, 140, 142
Video Watchdog (film digest), 6, 12n18, 53n59, 53n60, 54n83, 131n5
Vohrer, Alfred, 7, 38, 75, 76, 78, 80, 92–94, 95–97, 100, 105, 107, 111, 116–117, 119, 123, 126, 130, 138, 143–144, 145, 149, 150, 154, 156–157, 158, 161, 164–165, 170
Vorwerg, Wilhelm, 123, 127, 145

Wallace, Bryan Edgar, 3, 7, 12, 27, 33, 41–42, 47–48, 101, 147, 153, 160, 170, 172
Wallace, Edgar: biographical, 36–38; and the German *Krimi*, 38–45
Wallace, Penelope, 1, 38, 64
Weimar Republic, 6
Wendlandt, Horst, 27, 30, 34, 49, 76, 107, 126, 142, 148, 151, 161, 168–70
Western, the, 1, 3, 4, 27, 35, 57, 100, 130, 133
West Germany, 23–31, 43, 45, 71, 140–41
What Have You Done to Solange?. See *Das Geheimnis der grünen Stecknadel*
Whiplash, Snidely, 61
White Face (book), 112
Widmark, Richard, 80
Windeck, Agnes, 99, 102, 135, 149, 152
Winnetou, 57, 158
Winnetou und das Halbblut Apanatschi, 158
Wirtschaftswunder (economic miracle), 17, 23, 97
Der Wixxer, 188

The Wizard of Oz, 45, 156
Wood, Ed, 69
Wood, Natalie, 175
Wood, Robin, 159
Woolrich, Cornell, 50, 176
World War I, 23, 42–43
World War II, 1, 3, 5, 10, 15–23, 49, 67–8, 78, 81–82, 96, 99, 112, 127, 131n7, 153, 174, 183, 185, 187–88
Der Würger von Schloss Blackmoor, 42
Wussow, Klausjürgen, 62, *63*, 70
Wüstenhagen, Harry, 70

Yugoslavia, 1

Zelnik, Friedrich, 63
Zimmer 13, 109–15, 119, 130, 173
Zinker, Der (film, 1931), 99
Zinker, Der (film, 1937), 99
Zinker, Der (film, 1963), 98–104, 106, 119, 144, 173
The Zombie Walks. See Im Banne des Unheimlichen
Zyklon B, 78

About the Author

Nicholas G. Schlegel (PhD, Wayne State University) is an assistant professor of communication studies at Alfred University in New York and is the author of *Sex, Sadism, Spain, and Cinema: The Spanish Horror Film* (Rowman & Littlefield, 2015). Schlegel has also contributed chapters on director Jess Franco's *Krimi* output in *The Films of Jess Franco* (Wayne State University Press, 2018) and Japanese horror in *Draculas, Vampires, and Other Undead Forms: Essays on Gender, Race, and Culture* (Scarecrow Press, 2009). His research centers primarily on horror, cult, and exploitation cinema with a global emphasis. Nicholas enjoys history, travel, art, cooking, model building, and the ongoing project of framing his movie poster and autograph collection.

www.ingramcontent.com/pod-product-compliance
Lightning Source LLC
Chambersburg PA
CBHW061713300426
44115CB00014B/2673